RUSSIAN PHRASEBOOK
AND
DICTIONARY

Erika Haber

HIPPOCRENE BOOKS
New York

For my parents,
Karl and Olena Haber

RUSSIAN PHRASEBOOK
AND DICTIONARY

ACKNOWLEDGMENTS

I would like to thank my friends and colleagues for their advice and support on this project. I am particularly grateful to Stephen J. Fields for his concrete suggestions, continued encouragement and boundless friendship.

HOW TO USE THIS BOOK

In order to use this book most effectively, it is essential to read through the first chapter on the Russian language. This chapter provides charts for pronunciation of the English transcription, which allows you to "speak" Russian without knowing the Cyrillic alphabet. Once you are familiar with the pronunciation, look over chapter two, which lists everyday expressions. Each successive chapter covers basic words, phrases and concepts most often encountered by travellers to the Soviet Union in typical daily situations. Chapter fourteen helps you make sense of the Russian number system and provides you with frequently used time expressions. Finally, chapter fifteen gives reference information such as holidays and commonly encountered abbreviations.

A unique feature of this phrase book, the Russian-English, English-Russian Dictionary provides over 4,000 useful words, defined and listed with handy transliteration for easy, on-the-spot pronunciation.

A NOTE ON THE LAYOUT

A slash separates alternative Russian phrases for the same English word.

Russian nouns have gender: they can be masculine, feminine or neuter. Past tense verb forms in Russian also show gender and number. When both the masculine and feminine nominal and verbal forms are given, the masculine is presented first, usually followed by a slash and the feminine form.

TABLE OF CONTENTS

I. THE LANGUAGE

The Cyrillic Alphabet

The Russian language is written in Cyrillic, an alphabet developed from ancient Greek.

Russian letter	English sound	Russian letter	English sound
А/а	ah	Р/р	ehr
Б/б	beh	С/с	ehs
В/в	veh	Т/т	teh
Г/г	geh	У/у	oo
Д/д	deh	Ф/ф	ehf
Е/е	yeh	Х/х	kha
Ё/ё	yoh	Ц/ц	tseh
Ж/ж	zheh	Ч/ч	chah
З/з	zeh	Ш/ш	shah
И/и	ee	Щ/щ	shchah
Й/й	y	Ъ/ъ	hard sign
К/к	kah	ь/ь	soft sign
Л/л	ehl	Ы/ы	ih
М/м	ehm	Э/э	eh
Н/н	ehn	Ю/ю	yoo
О/о	oh	Я/я	yah
П/п	peh		

Pronunciation

Like English, Russian spelling is not strictly phonetic. One letter may have more than one sound value. That is why we use a system of transcription in which each symbol is assigned a constant value. The English transcription in this book will show you how to pronounce the Russian words even if you do not know the Cyrillic alphabet. The transcription only *approximates* the Russian sounds, however, since no sound is exactly like its Russian counterpart.

1

Vowels

Russian vowels are shorter and purer than the English vowel sounds they resemble. Depending on where the stress falls in a word, the sound value of some Russian vowels may change. The following chart provides the approximate sounds of stressed vowels.

Russian vowel	English approximation	English transcription
а	like the **a** in 'father'	ah
я	like **ya** in 'yard'	yah
э	like **e** in 'bet'	eh
е	like **ye** in 'yet'	yeh
о	like **o** in 'note'	oh
ё	like **yo** in 'yore'	yoh
и	like **ee** in 'beet'	ee
ы	like **i** in 'pit'	ih
у	like **oo** in 'shoot'	oo
ю	like **ew** in 'pew'	yoo

Consonants

Russian consonants can be pronounced as either 'soft' or 'hard', voiced or voiceless. 'Softening' (or palatalization) occurs when the letter is pronounced closer to the front of the mouth or hard palate. In Russian this occurs when consonants are followed by the vowels **я, е, ё, и, ю** or the 'soft sign' (ь). Sometimes the palatalization of a letter can change the meaning of a word. For instance, брат (braht) means 'brother', whereas брать (braht') means 'to take'. Voiced consonants, those that make the vocal cords vibrate, become voiceless when they occur at the end of a word or before a voiceless consonant. For instance, 'город' is phonetically represented as 'gohraht', not 'gohrahd' and 'вчера' becomes 'fchehrah', not 'vchehrah'. Likewise, voiceless consonants become voiced before voiced consonants. Fortunately, you do not have to learn the rules for this; all of these distinctions will be made for you in the English transcriptions provided.

2

Russian consonant	English approximation	English transcription
б	like the **b** in 'book'	b
в	like the **v** in 'vote'	v
г	like the **g** in 'goat'	g
д	like the **d** in 'dad'	d
ж	like the **s** in 'leisure'	z h
з	like the **z** in 'zebra'	z
к	like the **k** in 'cake'	k
л	like the **l** in 'lake'	l
м	like the **m** in 'mom'	m
н	like the **n** in 'nap'	n
п	like the **p** in 'pit'	p
р	like the **r** in 'red'	r
с	like the **s** in 'sail'	s
т	like the **t** in 'tail'	t
ф	like the **f** in 'fish'	f
х	like the **ch** in 'Bach'	k h
ц	like the **ts** in 'hats'	t s
ч	like the **ch** in 'chip'	c h
ш	like the **sh** in 'ship'	s h
щ	like **sh** followed by **ch**	shch

Diphthongs

When two vowels occur together in Russian, they are both pronounced. The only diphthongs in Russian are formed by a combination of a vowel and an ee-kratkoe (й).

Russian diphthong	English approximation	English transcription
ой	like the **oy** in 'toy'	o y
ей	like the **ey** in 'hey'	e y
ай	like **ye** in 'bye'	a y
яй	like the above sound with the y of 'yet' preceding it	y a y
ый	like the **i** in 'pit' followed by the y of 'yet'	i h y
ий	like the long **e** in 'maybe'	e e y
уй	like the **ooey** in 'phooey'	o o y
юй	like the above sound with the y of 'yet' preceding it	y o o y

3

Other Letters

separative signs	English transcription	explanation
ь	'	The 'soft sign' is not pronounced. It simply shows that the preceding consonant is soft.
ъ	"	The 'hard sign' is also not pronounced. It separates a prefix ending in a consonant from a stem beginning in a vowel.

semi-vowel		
й	y	The 'ee-kratkoe' is a semi-vowel and always occurs with a full vowel as in diphthongs.

Stress

Stress is very important in Russian. Only one syllable in each word is stressed. Secondary stresses, commonly found in English pronunciation, should be avoided. The location of the stress in a word determines the pronunciation of certain vowels. Unstressed vowels are less distinct and slightly shorter than their stressed counterparts.

unstressed vowel	pronounced like Russian vowel	example
o	a	окно́ – ahknoh, not ohknoh
e	и	еда́ – yeedah, not yehdah
я	и	язы́к – yeezihk, not yahzihk

Normally stress is not marked in Russian texts. In this book the stressed syllable will be printed in capital letters (ie: пустя́к – poostYAK).
Commonly, in phrases of several short words, only one word will be stressed in the phrase (ie: как вас зову́т?/kahk vahz zahVOOT?).

4

Declension

Unlike English, Russian expresses the relations between words in a sentence by inflection. Nouns and adjectives take different endings depending on their function in a sentence. In Russian these functions are grouped into six different categories called cases. Each case has its own endings. This explains why the same word may have different endings depending on its usage in a sentence.

II. ESSENTIAL EXPRESSIONS

The Basics

Yes./No.	Да./Нет.	dah/nyeht
Maybe.	Может быть.	MOHzheht biht'
Please.	Пожалуйста.	pahZHAHLstah
Thank you.	Спасибо.	spahSEEbah
Thank you very much.	Большое спасибо.	bahl'SHOHyeh spahSEEbah
Thank you for the help/infor-mation.	Спасибо за помощь/за информацию.	spahSEEbah zah POHmahshch/zah eenfahrMAHtsee-yoo
You're welcome.	Не за что./ Пожалуйста.	NYEHzahshtah/ pahZHAHLstah
Ok.	Ладно.	LAHDnah
I beg your pardon.	Простите.	prahsTEEtyeh
Excuse me.	Извините.	eezveeNEEtyeh
Why?	Почему?	pahcheeMOO
Because.	Потому что.	pahtahMOOshtah
That's the way it is.	Просто так.	PROHStah tahk
Good.	Хорошо.	khahrahSHOH
Bad.	Плохо.	PLOHkhah
Can you tell me, please..	Скажите, пожалуйста...	skahZHEEtyeh pahZHAHLstah
Help me.	Помогите мне.	pahmahGEEtyeh mnyeh
Is that right?	Правильно?	PRAHveel'nah
Be so kind...	Будьте добрый	BOOT'tyeh dahbRIHY
What?	Что?	shtoh
What's that?	Что это?	shtoh EHtah
What does that mean?	Что это значит?	shtoh EHtah ZNAHcheet
Where?	Где?	gdyeh
Where to?	Куда?	kooDAH
How?	Как?	kahk
How far?	Как далеко?	kahk dahleeKOH
How long?	Как долго?	kahk DOHLgah
When?	Когда?	kahgDAH
Who?	Кто?	ktoh

SKOLKA — How many

6

Who is that?	Кто э́то?	ktoh EHtah
I can't.	Я не могу́.	yah nee mahGOO
I want to	Я хочу́	yah khahCHOO
rest/	отдохну́ть/	ahddahkhNOOT'/
eat/	есть/	yehst'/
drink/	пить/	peet'/
sleep.	спать.	spaht'

(handwritten note next to "rest/": *Tired*)

Greetings

Hello.	Здра́вствуйте.	ZDRAHSTvooytyeh
Hi.	Приве́т.	preevYEHT
Good morning.	До́брое у́тро.	DOHbrahyeh OOtrah
Good afternoon.	До́брый день.	DOHbrihy dyehn'
Good evening.	До́брый ве́чер.	DOHbrihy VYEHchehr
Good night.	Споко́йний но́чи.	spahKOYnihy NOHchee
Goodbye.	До свида́ния.	dahsveeDAHneeyah
See you Later.	До ско́рой встре́чи.	dahSKOHray VSTRYEHchee
Bye.	До ско́рого./ Пока́.	dahSKOHrahvah/ pahKAH
All the best!	Всего́ до́брого.	vseeVOH DOHbrahvah

(handwritten annotations: "No" next to "Good night"; "Soon" next to "Later"; "offset")

Introductions

Forms of address equivalent to our Mr., Mrs. and Miss do not exist in Russian. Instead, people usually address one another by their first name and patronymic. To form the patronymic they add a suffix-- usually "-ovich" for men and "-ovna" for women-- to their father's first name. For example, if Ivan's father's name is Boris, he would be called "Ivan Borisovich". Likewise, if Anna's father's name is Mikhail, her patronymic would be "Anna Mikhailovna". If they know one another well or if they are talking to a child, Russians may use a diminutive form like Styopa or Svyeta.

Male foreigners are sometimes addressed as господи́н (gahspahDEEN) and women as госпожа́ (gahspahZHAH), but these are pre-revolutionary terms and are never used when addressing Soviet citizens.

What's your name?	Как вас зову́т?	kahk vahz zahVOOT
My name is...	Меня́ зову́т...	meenYAH zahVOOT
Pleased to meet you.	О́чень прия́тно.	OHcheen' preeYAHTnah
It's a pleasure to meet you.	О́чень рад с ва́ми познако́миться.	OHcheen' raht SVAHmee pahznahKOHmeetsah
May I introduce you to...	Разреши́те познако́мить вас...	rahzreeSHEEtyeh pahznahKOHmeet'vahs
my husband.	с мои́м му́жем.	smahEEM MOOzhehm
my wife.	с мое́й жено́й.	smahEY zhehNOY
How are you?	Как вы поживаете?	kahk vih pahzhehVAHeetyeh
I'm fine, thanks.	~~Прекра́сно.~~ спаси́бо, хорошо́	preeKRAHSnah spahSEEbah
And you?	А вы́?	ah VIH
~~I'm ok.~~ 50/50	Так себе́./ Ничего́.	tahk seeBYEH/ neecheeVOH
~~I'm not well.~~	~~Мне пло́хо.~~	mnyeh PLOHkhah
How're things?	Как дела́?	kahk deeLAH

Personal Information

Where are you from?	Отку́да вы?	ahtKOOdah vih
I am from...	Я из...	yah ees
America.	Аме́рики.	ahMYEHreekee
Canada.	Кана́ды.	kahNAHdih
England.	А́нглии.	AHNgleeee
What's your nationality?	Кто вы по-национа́льности?	ktoh vih pah nahtseeahNAHL'nahstee
I am...	Я...	yah

Й   ̆

8

Йа PLOHAH CIBIYA
ShVUS TJULU

English	Russian	Pronunciation
American. (m/f)	американец/ американка.*	ahmeereeKAHN- eets/ahmeeree- KAHNkah
Canadian. (m/f)	канадец/ канадка.	kahNAHdeets/ kahNAHTkah
British. (m/f)	англичанин/ англичанка.	ahngleeCHAHN- een/ahnglee- CHAHNkah
What are you doing here?	Что вы здесь делаете?	shtoh vih zdyehs' DYEHlaheetyeh
I am a tourist. (m/f)	Я турист/ туристка.	yah tyooREEST/ tyooREESTkah
I'm stuyding here.	Я учусь.	yah oochOOS'
I'm here on business.	Я здесь по делам.	yah zdyehs' pah deeLAHM
What's your profession?	Что вы по профессии?	shtoh vih pahprahf- YEHSseeee
I am a(n)...	Я...	yah
student. (m/f)	студент/ студентка.	stoodYEHNT/ stoodYEHNTkah
teacher. (m/f)	учитель/ учительница.	oocheetYEHL'/ -neetsah
professor.	профессор.**	prahfYEHSsahr
business- man. (m/f)	бизнесмен/ бизнесменка.	beezneesMYEHN/ -kah
journalist. (m/f)	журналист/ журналистка.	zhoornahlEEST/ -kah
nurse.	медсестра.	meedseesTRAH
housewife.	хозяйка.	khahzYAYkah
doctor.	врач.	vrahch
lawyer.	адвокат.	ahdvahKAHT

---

*Russian does not have articles (a, the), nor does it have a present tense form of the verb "to be".
When there is a different word used for the masculine and feminine forms, both forms will be given, with the masculine form first, followed by the feminine (f) form.
**Not all professions have a masculine and feminine form. Some, like professors, lawyers, and doctors, use one word for both male and female members of their professions.

9 STUDYING

English	Russian	Pronunciation
engineer.	инженéр.	eenzhehnYEHR
chemist.	хи́мик.	KHEEmeek
How long have you been here?	Скóлько врéмени вы ужé здесь?	SKOHL'kah VRYEHmeenee vih oozhEH zdyehs'
I have been here...	Я ужé здесь.	yah oozhEH zdyehs'
a day.	день.	dyehn'
a week.	недéлю.	neeDYEHlyoo
a month.	мéсяц.	MYEHseets
Do you like it here?	Вам тут нрáвится?	vahm toot NRAHveetsah
Yes, very much.	Да, мне óчень нрáвится.	dah mnyeh OHcheen' NRAHveetsah
No, not at all.	Нет, мне совсéм не нрáвится.	nyeht mnyeh sahfSYEHM nee NRAHveetsah
I'm having a wonderful time.	Я здесь прекрáсно провожý врéмя.	yah zdyehs' preeKRAHSnah prahvahZHOO VRYEHmyah
Where are you staying?	Где вы остановúлись?	gdyeh vih ahstahnahVEElees'
At the hotel...	В гостúнице...	vgahsTEEneetseh
Are you married? (m/f)	Вы женáты?/ Вы зáмужем?	vih zhehNAHtih/ vih ZAHmoozhehm
Yes, I am/No, I am not. (men)	Да, женáт./ Нет, не женáт.	dah zhehNAHT/ nyeht nee zhehNAHT
Yes, I am/No, I am not. (women)	Да, зáмужем./ Нет, не зáмужем.	dah ZAHmoozhehm/nyeht nee ZAHmoozhehm
Do you have children?	У вас есть дéти?	oo vahs yehst' DYEHtee

ribonik - child

Making Oneself Understood

English	Russian	Pronunciation
Do you speak... English?	Вы говорúте... по-англúйски?	vih gahvahREEtyeh pahahngLEEskee

Я ПРОВОЖД II cheteri COIN

у мне est chetvera
deytay

Russian?	по-русски?	pahROOSskee
German?	по-немецки?	pahneeMYEHtskee
French?	по-французски?	pahfrahnTSOOskee
Spanish?	по-испански?	paheesPAHNskee
Only a little.	Только немного.	TOHL'kah neemNOHgah
None at all.	Нет, совсем нет.	nyeht sahfSYEHM nyeht
I can understand Russian, but I don't speak it very well.	Я понимаю по-русски, но плохо говорю.	yah pahneeMAHyoo pahROOSskee noh PLOHkhah gahvahRYOO
Do you understand?	Вы понимаете?	vih pahnee-MAHeetyeh
I don't understand.	Нет, не понимаю.	nyeht nee pahneeMAHyoo
Please speak more slowly.	Пожалуйста, говорите медленее.	pahZHAHLstah gahvahREEtyeh MYEHdleenyehyeh
Please repeat that.	Пожалуйста, повторите.	pahZHAHLstah pahftahREEtyeh
Please write it down for me.	Пожалуйста, напишите это.	pahZHAHLstah nahpeeSHEEtyeh EHtah
Translate this for me, please.	Переведите, пожалуйста.	peereeveeDEEtyeh pahZHAHLstah
What does this/that mean?	Что это значит?	shtoh EHtah ZNAHcheet
What did he/she say?	Что он/она сказал(а)?*	shtoh ohn/ahNAH skahzAHL(ah)

---

*Past tense verb forms for women subjects end in the letter 'a'.

11

III. AT THE AIRPORT

Passport Control
When you arrive in the Soviet Union you will have
to go through "Passport control" (Паспортный
контроль/PAHSpahrtnihy kahnTROHL') where they
will check your passport and visa. Here they may
ask you several questions to verify your identity.
This is not the place to impress them with your
knowledge of Russian. The less you seem to know,
the sooner they will finish with you.

Your passport, please.	Ваш паспорт, пожалуйста.	vahsh PAHSpahrt pahZHAHLstah
Here it is.	Вот он.	voht ohn
How long are you staying?	На сколько времени вы здесь?	nah SKOHL'kah VRYEHmeenee vih zdyehs'
A few days.	Несколько дней.	NYEHskahl'kah dnyey
A week.	Неделю.	neeDYEHlyoo
Two weeks.	Две недели.	dvyeh neeDYEHlee
A month.	Месяц.	MYEHseets
Two months.	Два месяца.	dvah MYEHseetsah
I'm here...	Я здесь...	yah zdyehs'
on vacation.	в отпуске.	VOHTpooskyeh
on business.	по делам.	pahdeelAHM
to study.	учиться.	oochEET'sah
I don't under -stand.	Я не понимаю.	yah nee pahneeMAHyoo
I don't know.	Я не знаю.	yah nee ZNAHyoo

Customs
You will have to fill out customs declarations upon
entering and leaving the country. Be sure to declare
all jewelry, photographic equipment and other
valuables, so that you do not have to pay duty fees on
them when you leave. Selling your personal posses-
sions to Soviets (ie, dealing on the black market) is
illegal.

* СКОЛЬКО ВРЕМЕНИ ВЫ
(ПРО)БУДЕТЕ ЗДЕСЬ?
ТАМ

12

Customs.	Таможня.	tahMOHZHnyah
To pass through customs.	Проходить таможенный осмотр.	prahkhahDEET' tahMOHZHehnnihy ahsMOHTR
Customs Official.	Таможеник.	tahMOHZHehneek
Have you anything to declare?	Вы хотите что-нибудь объявить?	vih khahTEEtyeh shtohneeboot' ahb"yeeVEET'
Open this suitcase.	Откройте этот чемодан.	ahtKROYtyeh EHtaht chehmahDAHN
What is this?	Что это?	shtoh EHtah
You'll have to pay duty on this.	Вам надо заплатить за это пошлину.	vahm NAHdah zah-plahTEET' zah EH-tah POHSHleenoo
It's for my personal use.	Это для личного пользования.	EHtah dlyah LEESH-nahvah POHL'-zahvahneeyah
It's a gift.	Это подарок.	EHtah pahDAHrahk
May I bring this in?	Можно это провести?	MOHZHnah EHtah prahveesTEE
It's not new.	Это не новый.	EHtah nee NOHvihy
Do you have any more luggage?	Есть у вас ещё багаж?	yehst' oo vahs yeeSHCHOH bahgAHSH
Is that all?	Это всё?	EHtah vsyoh
I have...	У меня...	oo meenYAH
a carton of cigarettes.	блок сигарет.	blohk seegahrYEHT
a bottle of wine/ whiskey.	бутылка вина/ виски.	bootIHLkah veeNAH/ VEEskee
I don't under- stand.	Я не понимаю.	yah nee pahneeMAHyoo
Does anyone here speak English?	Говорит здесь кто-нибудь по-английски?	gahvahREET zdyehs' KTOHneeboot' pahahngLEEskee

Baggage

Luggage claim.	Выдача багажа.	VIHdahchah bahgahZHAH

13

English	Russian	Pronunciation
Porter.	Носильщик.	nahSEEL'shchehk
Are there any luggage carts?	Тележки есть?	teelYEHSHkee yehst'
Please carry this...	Пожалуйста, возьмите...	pahZHAHLstah vahz'MEEtyeh
luggage.	багаж.	bahgAHSH
suitcase.	чемодан.	chehmahDAHN
That's mine, (too).	Это моё, (тоже).	EHtah mahYOH (TOHzheh)
There's a suitcase missing.	Одного чемодана не хватает.	ahdnahVOH chehmahDAHnah nee khvahTAHeet
Take these things to the...	Отнесите эти вещи к...	ahtneeSEEtyeh EHtee VYEHshchee k
bus.	автобусу	ahfTOHboosoo
taxi.	такси.	tahkSEE
customs.	таможни.	tahMOHZHnee
baggage room.	камере хранения.	KAHmeeryeh khrahNYEHneeyah
How much do I owe you? (f)	Сколько я вам должен / должна?	SKOHL'kah yah vahm DOHLzhehn/ dahlzhNAH
My luggage is lost.	Багажа нет.	bahgahZHAH nyeht

Currency Exchange

It is best to change money at the airport or in your hotel. Hours of operation are often irregular, however, so you should plan ahead. Try not to exchange more than you need because the re-exchange rate is less than the exchange rate and you will lose money. You will have to present your passport and currency declaration form each time you change money. You may bring in as much foreign currency as you like, but Soviet money is not allowed out of the country.

English	Russian	Pronunciation
Currency exchange.	Обмен валюты.	ahbMYEHN vahLYOOtih

Where can I change some money?	Где можно обменять валюту?	gdyeh MOHZHnah ahbmeenYAHT' vahLYOOtoo
I'd like to change some dollars.	Я хотéл(а) бы обменять дóллары.	yah khahtYEHL(ah) bih ahbmeenYAHT' DOHLlahrih
Can you cash these traveler's checks?	Мóжете вы обменять эти дорóжные чéки?	MOHZHehtyeh vih ahbmeenYAHT' EHtee dahrOHZHnihyeh CHEHkee
Can you change this for rubles?	Мóжете вы обменять это на рýбли?	MOHZHehtyeh vih ahbmeenYAHT' EHtah nah ROOblee
What's the exchange rate?	Какóй валютный курс?	kahKOY vahLYOOtnihy koors
Can you give me smaller bills?	Мóжете вы дáть мне мéлкими купюрами?	MOHZHehtyeh vih daht' mnyeh MYEHLkeemee kooPYOOrahmee

Car Rental

Driving in the Soviet Union is only for the very brave at heart. Gas stations are scarce and gas is even scarcer. Road regulations are complex and strictly enforced, even on foreigners, who are subject to the full severity of Soviet law. You can rent cars at the airport or through some Intourist hotels, but you must have an international driver's license. Insurance premiums are usually included in the rental fee and gas is bought with coupons sold by Intourist, the Soviet tourism agency.

| Car rental. | Прокáт машин. | prahKAHT mahSHEEN |
| I'd like to rent a car. | Я хотéл(а) бы взять напрокáт машину. | yah khahtYEHL(ah) bih vzyaht' nahprahKAHT mahSHEEnoo |

15

English	Russian	Pronunciation
What's the rate...	Сколько это стоят...	SKOHL'kah EHtah STOHeet
per day?	в день?	vdyehn'
per week?	в неделю?	vneeDYEHlyoo
What's the charge per kilometer?	Сколько стоит километер?	SKOHL'kah STOHeet keelahMYEHteer
Are the price of gas and oil included?	Бензин и масло включены в цену?	beenZEEN ee MAHSlah vklyoochehNIH VTSEHnoo
I need it for...	Она мне нужна...	ahNAH mnyeh noozhNAH
a day.	на день.	nah dyehn'
3 days.	на три дня.	nah tree dnyah
a week.	на неделю.	nah neeDYEHlyoo
2 weeks.	на две недели.	nah dvyeh neeDYEHlee
Here's my (international driver's) license.	Вот мои (международные водительские) права.	voht mahEE (meezhdoonah-ROHDnihyeh vah-DEEteel'skeeyeh) prahVAH
Here's my credit card.	Вот моя кредитная карточка.	voht mahYAH kreeDEETnahyah KAHRtahchkah
I am not familiar with this car.	Я не знаком(а) с этой машиной.	yah nee znahKOHM-(ah) SEHtay mahSHEEnay
What is this?	Что это?	shtoh EHtah
Explain this to me.	Объясните это.	ahb"yeeSNEEtyeh EHtah
Show me how this mechanism works.	Покажите мне как этот механизм работает.	pahkahZHEEtyeh mnyeh kahk EHtaht meekhah-NEEzeem rahBOH-taheet
Where can I buy gas?	Где мне купить бензин?	gdyeh mnyeh kooPEET' beenZEEN

16

Where can I buy gas coupons?	Где можно купить талоны на бензин?	gdyeh MOHZHnah kooPEET' tah-LYOHnih nah beenZEEN
Gas pump.	Бензоколонка.	beenzahkahlOHNkah
Service station.	Автозаправочная станция.	ahftahzahPRAH-vahchnahyah STAHNtseeyah
Parking lot.	Стоянка (для автомобиля).	stahYAHNkah (dlyah ahftahmahBEE-lyah)

IV. AT THE HOTEL

Hotel arrangements must be made before you arrive in the Soviet Union and payment is expected in advance. Most Soviet hotels open to foreign tourists are run by Intourist. Although you may select an Intourist hotel you would like to stay in, the Intourist agency makes the final decision. A variety of services are usually available at your hotel, depending on its size. The larger ones will have a post office, currency exchange office, gift shop, restaurant, bar, dry cleaner, laundry, hair dresser and barbershop. Intourist hotels also usually have an information or service office (бюро́ обслу́ж-ива́ние/byooROH ahpSLOOzhehvahneeyeh), where the staff knows English and can answer your questions, give advice and book tours.

Check In

Upon checking in at your hotel, you will be given something resembling a temporary visa, called a про́пуск (PROHpoosk), which you will be expected to show at the door to gain entry to the hotel and again to the hall moniter to get your keys each time you return to your room.

Do you speak English?	Вы говори́те по-англи́йски?	vih gahvahREEtyeh pahahngLEEskee
My name is...	Моя́ фами́лия...	mahYAH fahMEEleeyah
I have a reservation.	Я заказа́л(а) зара́нее.	yah zahkahZAHL(ah) zahRAHNeeyeh
Here are my documents.	Вот мои́ докуме́нты.	voht mahEE dahkoomYEHNtih
I'd like a single/ double room.	Я хоте́л(а) бы но́мер на одного́/ на двои́х.	yah khahtYEHL(ah) bih NOHmeer nah ahdnahVOH/nah dvahEEKH

18

English	Russian	Pronunciation
I'd like a room with...	Я хотéл(а) бы нóмер с...	yah khahtYEHL(ah) bih NOHmeer s
a double bed.	двуспáльной кровáтью.	dvooSPAHL'nay krahVAHt'yoo
two twin beds.	двумя́ кровáтями.	dvoomYAH krahVAHteemee
a bath.	вáнной.	VAHNnay
a shower.	дýшем.	DOOSHehm
a private toilet.	туалéт./ уборная.	tooahlYEHT/ oobOHRnahyah
a telephone.	телефóном.	teeleeFOHnahm
a television.	телевизором.	teeleeVEEzahrahm
a balcony.	балкóном.	bahlKOHnahm
a view.	видом.	VEEDahm
Is there... room service?	Есть... обслýживание в нóмере?	yehst' ahpSLOOzheevahnee-yeh VNOHmeeryeh
a dining room?	столóвая?	stahLOHvahyah
a restaurant?	ресторáн?	reestahRAHN
air conditioning?	кондиционéр?	kahndeetsehah-NYEHR
heating?	отоплéние?	ahtahpLYEHneeyeh
hot water?	горя́чая водá?	gahRYAHcheeyah vahDAH
a garage?	гарáж?	gahrAHSH
May I see the room?	Мóжно посмотрéть нóмер?	MOHZHnah pahsmahtRYEHT' NOHmeer
Yes, I'll take it.	Да, э́то пойдёт.	dah EHtah pahydYOHT
No, I don't like it.	Нет, мне не нрáвится.	nyeht mnyeh nee NRAHveetsah
Do you have anything else?	Есть ли у вас другóй нóмер?	yehst' lee oo vas droogOY NOHmeer
I asked for a room with a bath.	Я просил(а) нóмер с вáнной.	yah prahSEEL(ah) NOHmeer SVAHNnay

19

Registration

Once your reservation has been confirmed, you will be asked to present your passport and fill out a registration form. Your passport may be kept over night for processing, but you should be able to pick it up the next day. If you plan to exchange money, be sure you do it before you register, since you'll need your passport to carry out the transaction.

English	Russian	Pronunciation
Registration.	Регистрация.	reegeeSTRAHtseeyah
Registration form.	Анкета для приезжающих.	ahnKYEHtah dlyah preeeeZHAH-yooshcheekh
Fill out this form.	Заполните анкету.	zahpahlNEEtyeh ahnKYEHtoo
Sign here.	Подпишитесь тут.	pahtpeeSHEEtyehs' toot
Your passport, please.	Ваш паспорт, пожалуйста.	vash PAHSpahrt, pahZHAHLstah
How long will you be here?	Как долго вы здесь пробудете?	kahk DOHLgah vih zdyehs' prah-BOOtyehtyeh
What does this mean?	Что это значит?	shtoh EHtah ZNAHcheet
What's my room number?	Какой у меня номер?	kahKOY oo meenYAH NOHmeer
My key, please.	Моя ключ, пожалуйста.	moy klyooch pahZHAHLstah
Take my luggage to my room, please.	Доставьте, пожалуйста, моя багаж в номер.	dahSTAHF'tyeh pahZHAHLstah moy bahgAHSH VNOHmeer
Is there an elevator?	Есть лифт?	yehst' leeft

The Staff

You will find that the most important person at your hotel will be the hall moniter. It is a good idea to be polite and friendly to her, because she can make your stay much more pleasant. If she likes you, she

20

will miraculously produce hard to find items like
lightbulbs and extra hangers.

Hall/Floor moniter.	Дежу́рная.	deeZHOORnahyah
Doorman.	Швейца́р.	shvayTSAHR
Porter.	Носи́льщик.	nahSEEL'shcheek
Maid.	Го́рничная.	GOHRneechnahyah
Receptionist.	Секрета́рша.	seekreeTAHRshah
Switchboard operator.	Телефони́стка.	teeleefahnEESTkah
Waiter.	Официа́нт.	ahfeetseeAHNT
Waitress.	Официа́нтка.	ahfeetseeAHNTkah
Manager.	Дире́ктор.	deeRYEHKtahr

Questions

The voltage in the USSR is 220 A.C.. The plugs and
sockets are like those used in Europe, so Americans
should bring electrical adaptors and converters for
their electrical appliances such as hair dryers and
electric razors.

Can you please bring me...	Прошу́ принеси́те мне...	prahSHOO preeneeSEEtyeh mnyeh
a towel.	полоте́нце.	pahlahTYEHNtseh
a blanket.	одея́ло.	ahdeeYAHlah
a pillow.	поду́шка.	pahDOOSHkah
a pillowcase.	на́волочку.	NAHvahlahchkoo
an ashtray.	пе́пельницу.	PYEHpeel'neetsoo
some hangers.	не́сколько ве́шалек.	NYEHskahl'kah VYEHshahleek
some soap.	мы́лу.	MIHloo
Where are the toilets?	Где убо́рная?	gdyeh oobOHRnahyah
Where is the...	Где...	gdyeh
restaurant?	рестора́н?	reestahRAHN
bar?	бар?	bahr
post office?	по́чта?	POHCHtah
information office?	бюро́ обслу́живание?	byooROH ahpSLOO-zhehvahneeyeh

21

hair dresser/ barber?	парихма́керская?	pahreekMAHKHeer-skahyah
currency exchange office?	мо́жно обменя́ть валю́ту?	MOHZHnah ahbmeenYAHT' vahLYOOtoo
light switch?	выключа́тель?	VIHklyoocheeteel'
electrical outlet?	розе́тка?	rahzYEHTkah

Problems

You should be aware that hot water is routinely shut off for several weeks at a time in the Soviet Union during the summer for annual repairs.

The ... doesn't work.	... не рабо́тает.	... nee rahBOHtaheet
shower.	душ.	doosh
faucet.	кран.	krahn
toilet.	туале́т.	tooahlYEHT
heating.	отопле́ние.	ahtahpLYEHneeyeh
air conditioning.	кондиционе́р.	kahndeetsehah-NYEHR
light.	свет.	svyeht
radio.	ра́дио.	RAHdeeoh
television.	телеви́зор.	teeleeVEEzahr
telephone.	телефо́н.	teeleeFOHN
electrical socket.	розе́тка.	rahzYEHTkah
There is no...	Нет...	nyeht
(hot) water.	(горя́чей) воды́.	(gahRYAHchey) vahDIH
lamp.	ла́мпы.	LAHMpih
light.	све́та.	SVYEHtah
fan.	вентиля́тора.	veenteeLYAH-tahrah
The sink is clogged.	Ра́ковина засорена́.	RAHkahveenah zahsahreeNAH
The door/ window is jammed.	Дверь/окно́ не закрыва́ется.	dvyehr'/ahkNOH nee zahkrihVAH-eetsah

| The door doesn't lock. | Замо́к в две́ри не рабо́тает. | zahmOHK vdveeREE nee rahBOHtaheet |
| Can it be repaired? | Мо́жно почини́ть э́то? | MOHZHnah pahchee-NEET' EHtah |

Check Out

I'm leaving today/ tomorrow morning.	Я уезжа́ю сего́дня/ за́втра у́тром.	yah ooyeeZHAHyoo seeVOHdnyah/ ZAHFtrah OOtrahm
Please prepare my bill.	Пригото́вьте мне счёт, пожа́луйста.	preegahTOHF'tyeh mnyeh shchoht pahZHAHLstah
Do you accept credit cards?	Мо́жно плати́ть креди́тной ка́рточкой?	MOHZHnah plahTEET' kreeDEETnay KAHRtahchkay
I think there's a mistake.	Мне ка́жется, что вы оши́блись.	mnyeh KAZHehtsah shtoh vih ahshEEBlees'
Could you please send someone to get my bags?	Пришли́те, пожа́луйста, кого́-нибудь вы́нести мои́ бага́ж.	preeSHLEEtyeh pahZHAHLstah kahVOHneeboot' VIHneestee moy bahgAHSH
Where can I get a cab?	Где мо́жно останови́ть такси́?	gdyeh MOHZHnah ahstahnahVEET' tahkSEE

If you feel really daring, ask your travel agent about the possibility of staying in a Soviet Bed and Breakfast--one of the latest results of glasnost'!

23

V. AT THE RESTAURANT

Eating out in the Soviet Union can be fun and interesting, but do not expect it to be like at home. Restaurants are generally inexpensive, but with the exception of some of the regional dining establishments, the food is mediocre at best. Soviet restaurant staff are not known for their eagerness to please and service can be quite slow. Do not be surprised to be seated at a table with people you don't know; it is a common practice in Eastern Europe, particularly in smaller restaurants. Dishes that don't have prices on the menu are not available. Your best bet is to ask your waiter for his suggestions and then choose accordingly.

Types of Establishments

Ресторáн (reestahRAHN)
Restaurants generally have a broad choice of dishes, as well as orchestras and dancing. Soviets usually go early and make a leisurely evening of it. Reservations are strongly recommended and can usually be made through your hotel. Restaurants typically close by 11pm.

Кафé (kahfYEH)
Cafe's can vary quite a bit, but in general the better ones resemble restaurants, except for a slightly more limited menu. They usually close between 9 and 10 pm.

Кооператúвное кафé
(kahahpeerahTEEVnahyeh kahfYEH)
Like its name suggests, cooperative cafes are privately run dining establishments. The quality of food and service should be higher due to the profit motive, but be prepared for higher prices, as well.

Столóвая (stahLOHvahyah)

As in the U.S., cafeteria's can be found in most institutions like universities, libraries and factories. They are self-serve and inexpensive. Alcohol is prohibited.

Закýсочная/Бюфéт (zahKOOsahchnahyah/boofYEHT)

Snack bars are found virtually everywhere in the Soviet Union from train stations to music conservatories. Here one can get a variety of light snacks such as open-faced sandwiches, fruit, cookies, bottled water and juices.

Пельмéнная (peel'MYEHNnahyah)

These are small cafes specializing in пельмéни (peel'MYEH-nee)--small, Siberian, meat-filled dumplings. Many of these specialty food places do not have seats; instead, customers eat side-by-side, standing up at counters.

Блúнная (BLEENnahyah)

Another type of specialty cafe, the блинная, offers paper-thin Russian pancakes filled with caviar or fruit, called блины (bleenIH). Блины are commonly ordered as hors d'oeuvres in larger restaurants, but can also be enjoyed as a meal onto themselves.

Пирожкóвая (peerahshKOHvahyah)

Similar to the Пельменная and Блинная, these small establishments specialize in пирожки (peerahzh-KEE)--large dumplings filled with meat, cheese or fruit and served with a dollop of sour cream.

Шашлы́чная (shahshLIHCHnahyah)

For those who want to try dishes from the Caucuses and Central Asia, this type of restaurant specializes in шашлы́к (shahshLIHK)--a shish kebob usually made with lamb and vegetables.

Кафе-кондитерская (kahfYEH-kahnDEEteer-skahyah)
Closer to what we normally think of as a cafe, this type of establishment serves tea, cookies, cake and other sweets.

Кафе-мороженое (kahfYEH-mahROHZH-ehnahyeh)
Similar to Western-style ice cream parlors, these cafes offer ice cream, cookies, and other sweets.

Чайная (CHAYnahyah)
This small tea shop offers a variety of teas, coffee, cookies and pastries.

Бар (bahr)
These days almost all existing bars are found in Intourist hotels. Patronage is usually limited to hotel guests and only foreign currency is accepted.

The Preliminaries

I'm hungry. (M/F)	Я голоден./ Я голодна.	yah GOHlahdeen/ yah gahlahdNAH
I'd like to eat/drink.	Мне хочется есть/пить.	mnyeh khahchEHTsah yehst'/peet'
Can you recommend a good restaurant?	Можете ли вы рекомендовать хороший ресторан?	MOZHehtyeh lee vih reekahMYEHNdahvaht' khahROHshee reestahRAHN?
Do you serve breakfast/ lunch/ dinner?	Подаёте ли вы завтрак/ обед/ ужин?	pahdahYOHtyeh lee vih ZAHFtrahk/ ahbYEHT/ OOZHeen
I'd like to make a reservation.	Я хотёл(а) бы заказать столик.	yah khahtYEHL(ah) bih zahkahZAHT' STOHleek
There are 2/3/4 of us.	Нас двое/ трое/ четверо.	nahs DVOHyeh/ TROHyeh/ CHEHtveerah

enough!   dastachna   ДОСТАТОЧНО   ХВАТИТ

We'll come at six.	Мы будем в шесть.	mih BOOdeem vshehst'
Where is the coat check?	Где гардероб/ раздевалка?	gdyeh gahrdeerOHP/ rahzdeevAHLkah
Coat check number.	Номерок.	nahmeerOHK
Where are the bathrooms?	Где уборная?	gdyeh oobOHRnahyah
Is this place taken/ reserved/ free?	Это место занято/ заказано/ свободно?	EHtah MYEHstah/ ZAHNeetah/ zahKAHZahnah/ svahBOHDnah
It's taken/ reserved/ free.	Оно занято/ заказано/ свободно.	ahNOH ZAHNeetah/ zahKAHZahnah/ svahBOHDnah
Have a seat!	Садитесь!	sahDEEtees'
We'd prefer a table...	Мы предпочитаем столик...	mih preedpahchee-TAHeem STOHleek
in the corner.	в углу.	voogLOO
by the window.	у окна.	oo ahkNAH
outside.	на открытом воздухе.	nah ahtKRIHTahm VOHZdookhyeh
May we have another table?	Дайте нам, пожалуйста, другой столик.	DAYtyeh nahm pahZHAHLstah droogOY STOHleek
Is smoking permitted here?	Можно здесь курить?	MOHZHnah zdyehs' kooREET'

Ordering

Waiter./ Waitress.	Официант./ Официантка.	ahfeetseeAHNT/ ahfeetseeAHNTkah
This way please.	Сюда, пожалуйста.	sooDAH pahZHAHLstah
May I have a menu, please.	Принесите, пожалуйста, меню.	preeneeSEEtyeh pahZHAHLstah meenYOO
Have you decided?	Вы уже выбрали?	vih oozhEH VIHbrahlee

(handwritten notes: "Bring me", "chosen?", "Richard dude")

27

English	Russian	Pronunciation
What do you recommend?	Что вы посовётуете?	shtoh vih pahsah-VYEHtooyehtyeh
I recommend...	Я совётую вам взять...	yah sahVYEHtooyoo vahm vzyaht'
Unfortunately, we don't have...	К сожалёнию, у нас нет...	ksahzhahLYEHneeyoo oo nahs nyeht
Why not take this instead.	Лучше возьмите вот это.	LOOCHsheh vahz'MEEtyeh voht EHtah
What would you like?	Что вы хотите?	shtoh vih khahTEEtyeh
Go ahead.	Слушаю вас.	SLOOshahyoo vahs
I'll have...	Я хочу...	yah khahCHOO
for appetizers...	на закуску...	nah zahKOOskoo
for the first course...	на пёрвое...	nah PYEHRvahyeh
for the second course...	на второе...	nah vtahROHyeh
for the third course/ desert...	на трётье/ на слáдкое...	nah TRYEHt'yeh/ nah SLAHTkahyeh
A small portion.	Мáленькую пóрцию.	MAHleen'kooyoo POHRtseeyoo
What would you like to drink?	Что вы бы хотёли выпить?	shtoh vih bih khahtYEHlee VIHpeet'
That's all, thank you.	Это всё, спасибо.	EHtah vsyoh spahSEEbah

The Meal

English	Russian	Pronunciation
Enjoy your meal!	Приятного аппетита!	preeYAHTnahvah ahppeeTEEtah
How is it?	Ну, как вам нрáвится?	noo kahk vahm NRAHveetsah
It's very tasty.	Очень вкýсно.	OHcheen' VKOOSnah

To take [handwritten annotation]

28

Please pass me...	Передайте, пожалуйста...	peereeDAYtyeh pahZHAHLstah
Please bring me...	Принесите мне, пожалуйста...	preeneeSEEtyeh mnyeh pah-ZHAHLstah
a cup.	чашку.	CHAHSHkoo
a glass.	стакан.	stahKAHN
a fork.	вилку.	VEELkoo
a knife.	нож.	nohsh
a spoon.	ложку.	LOHSHkoo
a plate.	тарелку.	tahRYEHLkoo
a napkin.	салфетку.	sahlFYEHTkoo
an ashtray.	пепельницу.	PYEHpeel'neetsoo
some salt.	соль.	sohl'
some pepper.	перец.	PYEHreets
sugar.	сахар.	SAHKHahr
water.	воду.	vahDOO
bread and butter.	хлеб и масло.	khlyehp ee MAHSlah
Can I have some more of this?	Принесите ещё немного этого.	preeneeSEEtyeh yeeSHCHOH neemNOHgah EHtahvah
Would you like anything else?	Вам ещё что?	vahm yeeSHCHOH shtoh

Complaints

I have a complaint.	У меня жалоба.	oo meenYAH zhahlahBAH
This is...	Это...	EHtah
cold.	холодное.	KHOHlahdnahyeh
hot.	горячее.	gahRYAHchee
too spicy.	слишком острое.	SLEESHkahm OHStrahyeh
too sweet/ salty.	слишком сладкое/ пересоленое.	SLEESHkahm SLAHTkahyeh/pee-reeSOHleenahyeh
sour.	кислое.	KEESlahyeh
stale.	не свежее.	nee SVYEHzhee
tough.	жёсткое.	ZHOHSTkahyeh
overdone.	пережарено.	peereeZHAHreenah

underdone.	недожа́рено.	needahZHAHreenah
This is dirty.	Это гря́зное.	EHtah GRYAHZnahyeh
I don't like this.	Это мне не нра́вится.	EHtah mnyeh nee NRAHveetsah
You can take this away.	Мо́жно э́то убра́ть.	MOHZHnah EHtah oobRAHT'
There's been a mistake.	Вы не ошиби́лись?	vih nee ahshEEBlees'
This isn't what I ordered.	Я э́того не зака́зывал(а).	yah EHtahvah nee zahKAHzihvahl-(ah)
I ordered...	Я заказа́л(а)...	yah zahkahZAHL(ah)
I don't want it.	Я э́того не хочу́.	yah EHtahvah nee khahCHOO

The Check

Although tipping is officially discouraged, it is still appreciated and often expected when serving foreigners. Between five and ten percent is about average for waiters. More than extra rubles, Soviets welcome small gifts such as a pack of cigarettes or chewing gum, perfume, cigarette lighters or key chains.

We're finished.	Мы зако́нчены.	mih zahKOHN-chehnih
I have had enough.	Мне хва́тит.	mnyeh KHVAHteet
Bring me the check, please.	Принеси́те мне счёт, пожа́луйста.	preeneeSEEtyeh mnyeh shchoht pahZHAHLstah
There's been a mistake.	Вы не ошиби́лись?	vih nee ahshEEBlees'
How did you get this total?	Что вхо́дит в э́ту су́мму?	shtoh FKHOHdeet VEHtoo SOOMmoo
Is a tip included?	Чаевы́е включены́ в счёт?	chaheeVIHyeh fklyoochehNIH fshchoht
Pay the cashier.	Плати́те в ка́ссу.	plahTEEtyeh FKAHSsoo

We'd like to pay separately.	Мы хотéли бы платúть отдéльно.	mih khahtYEHLee bih plahTEET' ahdDYEHL'nah
Do you accept...	Вы берёте...	vih beerYOHtyeh
traveler's checks?	дорóжные чéки?	dahrOHZHnihyeh CHEHkee
credit cards?	крепúтные кáрточки?	kreeDEETnihyeh KAHRtahchkee
Intourist food vouchers?	обéденные талóны Интюрúста?	ahbYEHDeennihyeh tahLOHnih eentyooREESTah
Thank you, this is for you.	Спасúбо, это для вас.	spahSEEbah EHtah dlyah vahs

Snack Bars and Cafeterias

At Soviet snack bars, just like in the U.S., you usually pick up what you want yourself or else ask someone behind the counter for it. Soviet Cafeteria's are a bit more complex. First, you decide what you want from a printed menu at the cashier's window. Then, you tell the cashier what you want, pay her and receive food coupons for the desired items. Next, you either take the coupons to the serving line and pick up your meal, or you take a seat and someone collects your coupons and brings you your food. Be sure to carry small bills with you because the cashiers very often will not accept anything larger than a three-ruble note. Since people tend to hang on to their one- and two-kopeck pieces to use on public phones, do not be surprised to receive candy as small change.

What's this?	Что это такóе?	shtoh EHtah tahKOHyeh
Please give me one of those.	Дáйте, пожáлуйста, одúн такóй.	DAYtyeh pahZHAHLstah ahDEEN tahKOY
I'd like (that), please.	Я хотéл(а) бы (это), пожáлуйста.	yah khatYEHL(ah) bih (EHtah) pahZHAHLstah

31

Please give me a piece of that.	Да́йте, пожа́луйста, кусо́к э́того.	DAYtyeh pahZHAHLstah koosOHK EHtahvah
May I help myself?	Я могу́ взять сам(а́)?	yah mahGOO vzyaht' sahm(AH)
Just a little.	То́лько немно́го.	TOHL'kah neemNOHgah
A little more, please.	Побо́льше, пожа́луйста.	pahBOHL'sheh pahZHAHLstah
Enough?	Доста́точно?	dahsTAHTahchnah
Anything else?	Еще́ что?	yeeSHCHOH shtoh
That's all, thank you.	Э́то всё, спаси́бо.	EHtah vsyoh spahSEEbah
How much is it?	Ско́лько сто́ит?	SKOHL'kah STOHeet
Is that to go?	С собо́й?	sahBOY

VI. FOOD AND DRINK

The main thing to keep in mind with regards to the various foods and drinks listed in this chapter is their limited availability. Not everything will be available everywhere you go, so be prepared to experience new foods and methods of preparation.

Breakfast

Where can I have breakfast?	Где можно завтракать?	gdyeh MOHZHnah ZAHFtrahkat'
What time is breakfast served?	Во сколько завтрак?	vahSKOHL'kah ZAHFtrahk
How late is breakfast served?	До которого часа можно завтракать?	dahkahTOHrahvah cheeSAH MOHZHnah ZAHFtrahkat'
I'd like...	Я хотел(а) бы...	yah khahtYEHL(ah) bih
(black) coffee.	(чёрный) кофе.	(CHOHRnihy) KOHfyeh
with milk.	с молоком.	smahlahKOHM
with sugar.	со сахаром.	sahSAHkhahrahm
without sugar.	без сахара.	byehs SAHkhahrah
tea.	чай.	chay
with lemon.	с лимоном.	sleeMOHnahm
with milk.	с молоком.	smahlahKOHM
with honey.	с мёдом.	SMYOHdahm
with sugar.	со сахаром.	sahSAHkhahrahm
cocoa.	какао.	kahKAHoh
milk.	молоко.	mahlahKOH
juice.	сок.	sohk
orange.	апельсиновый.	ahpeel'SEEnahvihy
grapefruit.	грейпфрутовый.	greypFROOtahvihy
tomato.	томатный.	tahMAHTnihy
kefir (a yogurt drink).	кефир.	keeFEER

33

bread.	хлеб	khlyehp
toast.	поджа́ренный хлеб.	pahdZHAHreennihy khlyehp
a roll.	бу́лочку.	BOOlahchkoo
butter.	ма́сло.	MAHSlah
cheese.	сыр.	sihr
pot cheese.	творо́г.	tvahrOHK
jam.	варе́нье.	vahRYEHN'yeh
honey.	мёд.	myoht
hot cereal.	ка́шу.	KAHshoo
hot buck-wheat cereal.	гре́чневую ка́шу.	GRYEHCHneevooyoo KAHshoo
hot rice cereal.	ри́совую ка́шу.	REEsahvooyoo KAHshoo
farina.	ма́нную ка́шу.	MAHNnooyoo KAHshoo
oat meal.	овся́ную ка́шу.	ahfSYAHnooyoo KAHshoo
eggs.	я́йца.	YAYtsah
scrambled eggs.	я́ичницу-болту́нью.	yahEECHneetsoo-bahlTOON'yoo
a fried egg.	я́ичницу.	yahEECHneetsoo
a boiled egg.	варёное яйцо́.	vahrYOHnahyeh yayTSOH
a hard-boiled egg.	круто́е яйцо́.	krooTOHyeh yayTSOH
salt./pepper.	соль./пе́рец.	sohl'/PYEHreets

Appetizers

Served in several courses beginning with a variety of hot and cold appetizers, a Russian meal can last an entire evening. Russian appetizers are quite hearty and may often seem like an entire meal onto themselves.

Appetizers.	Заку́ски.	zahKOOSkee
For an appetizer I want...	На заку́ску я хочу́...	nah zahKOOSkoo yah khahCHOO

English	Russian	Pronunciation
(black/red) caviar.	(зернистую/ кетовую) икру.	zeerNEESTooyoo/ keeTOHvooyoo eekROO
cold, boiled pork with vegetables.	буженину с гарниром.	boozhehNEEnoo zgahrNEERahm
cold roast beef with vegetables.	ростбиф с гарниром.	ROHSTbeef zgahrNEERahm
assorted meat/fish plate.	ассорти мясное/ рыбное.	ahssahrTEE meesNOHyeh/ RIHBnahyeh
smoked/ pickled herring.	копчёную/ маринованную селёдку.	kahpCHOHnooyoo/ mahreeNOHvahn- nooyoo seelYOHT- koo
meat/fish in aspic.	мясное/рыбное заливное or студень.	meesNOHyeh/RIHB- nahyeh zahleev- NOHyeh or STOOdeen'
sausage.	колбасу.	kahlbahSOO
sturgeon.	осетрину.	ahseetREEnoo
lox.	сёмгу.	SYOHMgoo
pancakes with...	блины...	bleenIH
caviar.	с икрой.	seekROY
herring.	с сельдем.	SSYEHL'deem
sour cream.	со сметаной.	sahsmeeTAHnay
jam.	с вареньем.	zvahrYEHN'yehm
small pies filled with...	пирожки...	peerahshKEE
meat.	с мясом.	SMYAHsahm
cabbage.	с капустой.	skahPOOstay
rice.	с рисом.	SREEsahm
potatoes.	с картошкой.	skahrtOHSHkay
meat-filled dumplings.	пельмени.	peel'MYEHnee
marinated/ salted mushrooms	маринованные/ солёные грибы.	mahreeNOHvahn- nihyeh/sahlYOH- nihyeh greebIH

mushrooms baked in a sour cream sauce.	жульéн из грибы́.	zhool'YEHN ees greebIH
chicken baked in a sour cream sauce.	жульéн из ку́рицы.	zhool'YEHN ees KOOreetsih
Russian vegetable salad.	винегрéт.	veeneegRYEHT
cucumber salad.	салáт из огурцóв.	sahLAHT ees ahgoorTSOF
tomato salad.	салáт из помидóров.	sahLAHT ees pahmeeDOHrahf
cabbage salad.	салáт из капу́сты.	sahLAHT ees kahPOOstih
radish salad.	салáт из редйски.	sahLAHT ees reeDEESkee
potato salad.	картóфельный салáт.	kahrTOHfeel'nihy sahLAHT
meat salad.	столи́чный салáт.	stahlEECHnihy sahLAHT
saurkraut.	ки́слую капу́сту.	KEESlooyoo kahPOOstoo
liver pate.	паштéт из печёнки.	pashTYEHT ees peechOHNkee
olives.	маслины.	mahsLEEnih
radishes.	редйски.	reeDEESkee

Soups

For the first course I want...	На пéрвое я хочу́...	nah PYEHRvahyeh yah khahCHOO
Please bring me some...	Принеси́те мне, пожáлуйста...	preeneeSEEtyeh mnyeh pahZHAHLstah
borsch.	бóрщ.	bohrshch
boullion.	бульóн.	bool'OHN
cabbage soup.	щи.	shchee

36

chicken soup...	курйный суп...	kooREEnihy soop
with noodles.	с лапшóй.	slahpSHOY
with rice.	с рйсом.	SREEsahm
cold kvas soup.	окрóшку.	ahkROHSHkoo
cold vegetable soup.	свекóльник.	sveeKOHL'neek
fish soup.	ухá.	ooKHAH
mushroom soup.	грибнóй суп.	greebNOY soop
pea soup.	горóховый суп.	gahROHKHahvihy soop
pickled cucumber soup.	рассóльник.	rahsSOHL'neek
potato soup.	картóфельный суп.	kahrTOHfeel'nihy soop
spicy Georgian beef soup.	харчó.	khahrCHOH
tart meat/ fish soup.	мяснýю/ рыбную солянку.	meesNOOyoo/ RIHBnooyoo sahlYAHNkoo
vegetable soup.	овощнóй суп.	ahvahshchNOY soop

Grains and Cereals

I'd like...	Я хотéл(а) бы...	yah khahtYEHL(ah) bih
rice.	рис.	rees
pilaf.	плов.	plohf
pasta.	макарóны.	mahkahROHnih
potatoes.	картóфель.	kahrTOHfeel'
fried.	жáреный.	ZHAHreenihy
boiled.	отварнóй.	ahtvahrNOY
mashed.	пюрé.	pyoorYEH
baked.	печёный.	peechOHNihy
buckwheat.	грéчневую кáшу.	GRYEHCHneevooyoo KAHshoo

37

Vegetables

English	Russian	Pronunciation
What kind of vegetables are available?	Какие у вас óвощи?	kahKEEyeh oo vahs OHvahshchee
Cabbage.	Капýсту.	kahPOOstoo
Red cabbage.	Крáсную капýсту.	KRAHSnooyoo kahPOOstoo
Beets.	Свёклы.	SVYOHKlih
Tomatoes.	Помидóры.	pahmeeDOHrih
Potatoes.	Картóфель.	kahrTOHfeel'
Radishes.	Редíски.	reeDEESkee
Cucumbers.	Огурцы́.	ahgoorTSIH
Egg plant.	Баклажáн.	bahklahzhAHN
Mushrooms.	Грибы́.	greeblH
Peas.	Горóхы.	gahROHKHih
Green beans.	Фасóли.	fahSOHlee
Wax beans.	Жёлтые фасóли.	ZHOHLtihyeh fahSOHlee
Carrots.	Мóркви.	MOHRkvee
Onions.	Лук.	look
Leeks.	Зелёный лук.	zeelYOHnihy look
Corn.	Кукурýза.	kookooROOzah
Green peppers.	Слáдкие пéрцы.	SLAHTkeeyeh PYEHRtsih
Red peppers.	Крáсные пéрцы.	KRAHSnihyeh PYEHRtsih
Parsley.	Петрýшку.	peeTROOSHkoo
Turnips.	Рéпы.	RYEHpih
Garlic.	Чеснóк.	cheesNOHK
Cauliflower.	Цветнýю капýсту.	tsveetNOOyoo kahPOOstoo
Horseradish.	Хрен.	khryehn

Preparation

English	Russian	Pronunciation
How is this dish prepared?	Как приготовля́ют э́то блю́до?	kahk preegahtahvLYAHyoot EHtah BLYOOdah
It's...	Онó...	ahNOH
baked.	печёное.	peechOHNahyeh
boiled.	варёное.	vahrYOHNahyeh
braised.	тушёное.	tooshOHNnahyeh

breaded.	панированое.	pahneeROHvah-nahyeh
chopped.	рубленное.	ROObleennahyeh
fried.	поджаренное.	pahdZHAHreen-nahyeh
ground.	молотое.	MOHlahtahyeh
marinated.	маринованное.	mahreeNOHvahn-nahyeh
poached.	отварное.	ahtvahrNOHyeh
raw.	сырое.	sihrOHyeh
roasted.	жареное.	ZHAHreenahyeh
smoked.	копчёное.	kahpCHOHNahyeh
steamed.	паровое.	pahrahVOHyeh
stuffed.	фаршированное.	fahrsheeROHvahn-nahyeh

Meat and Meat Dishes

For the second course I want...	На второе я хочу...	nah ftahROHyeh yah khahCHOO
What kind of meat do you have?	Какое у вас мясо?	kahKOHyeh oo vahs MYAHsah
What kind of meat dishes do you have?	Какие у вас мясные блюда?	kahKEEyeh oo vahs meesNIHyeh BLYOOdah
Mutton.	Баранину.	bahRAHNeenoo
Lamb.	Молодую баранину.	mahlahDOOyoo bahRAHNeenoo
Lamb chop.	Баранья отбивную.	bahRAHN'yah ahtbeevNOOyoo
Beef.	Говядину.	gahvYAHDeenoo
Pork.	Свинину.	sveeNEEnoo
Pork chop.	Свиная отбивную.	sveeNAHyah ahtbeevNOOyoo
Veal.	Телятину.	teelYAHTeenoo
Veal cutlet.	Телячья отбивную.	teelYAHCH'yah ahtbeevNOOyoo
Ham.	Ветчину.	veetcheeNOO
Roast beef.	Ростбиф.	ROHSTbeef

39

Pot roast.	Тушёную говя́дину.	tooshOHNooyoo gahvYAHDeenoo
Meat patties.	Биточки.	beetOHCHkee
Beefsteak.	Бифште́кс.	beefSHTYEHKS
Bacon.	Беко́н.	beekOHN
Meat loaf.	Руле́т мясно́й.	roolYEHT meesNOY
Meat balls.	Тефте́ли.	teefTYEHlee
Sausages.	Соси́ски.	sahSEEskee
Shnitzel.	Шни́пель.	SHNEEtsehl'
Meat stew.	Рагу́.	rahGOO
Liver.	Печёнку.	peechOHNkoo
Kidneys.	По́чки.	POHCHkee
Cutlet.	Котле́ту отбивну́ю.	kahtLYEHtoo ahtbeevNOOyoo
Tongue.	Язы́к.	yeezIHK
Shish kebob.	Шашлы́к.	shahshLIHK
Ground lamb kebob.	Люля́-кеба́б.	lyoolYAH-keeBAHP
Goulash.	Гуля́ш.	goolYAHSH
Beef casserole.	Жа́ркое.	ZHAHRkahyeh
Lamb stew.	Ушно́е.	ooshNOHyeh
Chopped meat in a sauce.	Азу́.	ahZOO
Beef Stroganoff.	Бефстро́ганов.	beefSTROHgahnahf
Cabbage rolls with meat.	Голубцы́.	gahloopTSIH

Poultry and Game

What kind of poultry/ wild game dishes do you have?	Каки́е у вас блю́да с пти́цой/ ди́чей?	kahKEEyeh oo vahs BLOOdah spteeTSOY/ DEEchey
Chicken.	Ку́рицу.	KOOreetsoo
Duck.	У́тку.	OOTkah
Goose.	Гусь.	goos'
Turkey.	Инде́йку.	eenDEYkoo
Woodcock.	Ва́льшнеп.	VAHL'Tshneep
Pigeon.	Го́лубь.	GOHloop'

Hazel grouse.	Рябчик.	RYAHPcheek
Rabbit.	Кролик.	KROHleek
Hare.	Заяц.	ZAHeets
Venison.	Оленину.	ahLYEHneenoo
Chicken Kiev.	Котлеты по-киевски.	kahtLYEHtih pah-KEEeefskee
Georgian fried chicken.	Цыплёнок табака.	tsihpLYOHnahk tahbahKAH
Chicken cutlets.	Пожарские котлеты.	pahZHAHRskeeyeh kahtLYEHtih

Fish and Seafood

What kind of fish do you have?	Какие у вас рыбы?	kahKEEyeh oo vahs RIHBih
I'll take...	Я возьму...	yah vahz'MOO
sturgeon.	осетрину.	ahseetREEnoo
pike-perch.	судак.	soodAHK
trout.	форель.	fahrYEHL'
pike.	щуку.	SHCHOOkoo
flounder.	камбалу.	KAHMbahloo
carp.	карп.	kahrp
halibut.	палтус.	PAHLtoos
cod.	треску.	treesKOO
salmon.	лососину.	lahsahSEEnoo
tuna.	тунец.	toonYEHTS
herring.	сельдь.	syehl't'
sea food.	дары моря.	DAHrih MOHRyah
prawns.	креветки.	kreeVYEHTkee
crayfish.	раки.	RAHkee
oysters.	устрицы.	OOStreetsih

Fruit

Most restaurants do not offer fresh fruit on their menus, but you may be able to buy it at public markets, snack bars and kiosks.

What kind of fruit do you have?	Какие у вас фрукты?	kahKEEyeh oo vahs FROOKtih

41

Is it fresh?	Они свежие?	ahNEE SVYEHzhehyeh
Apples.	Яблоки.	YAHBlahkee
Oranges.	Апельсины.	ahpeel'SEEnih
Tangerines.	Мандарины.	mahndahREEnih
Pears.	Груши.	GROOshee
Peaches.	Персики.	peerSEEkee
Plums.	Сливы.	SLEEvih
Melon.	Дыня.	DIHNyah
Watermelon.	Арбуз.	ahrBOOS
Bananas.	Банан.	bahNAHN
Apricots.	Абрикосы.	abreeKOHsih
Pineapple.	Ананас.	ahnahnAHS
Grapes.	Виноград.	veenahgRAHT
Raisins.	Изюмы.	eezYOOmih
Figs.	Инжиры.	eenZHEErih
Dates.	Финики.	FEEneekee
Lemon.	Лимон.	leemOHN
Grapefruit.	Грейпфрут.	GREYPfroot
Prunes.	Чернославы.	cheernahSLEEvih
Currants.	Смородина.	smahROHdeenah
Strawberries.	Клюбника.	klyoobNEEkah
Wild strawberries.	Земляника.	zeemleeNEEkah
Cherries.	Черешня.	cheerYEHSHnyah
Blackberries.	Ежевика.	yeezhehVEEkah
Cranberries.	Клюква.	KLYOOKvah
Raspberries.	Малина.	mahLEEnah
Blueberries.	Черника.	chehrNEEkah

Dessert

Soviets claim that their ice cream, sold at kiosks year-round, is the best in the world. Whether you agree or not, it is certainly worth a taste.

What do you have for dessert?	Что у вас на десерт?	shtoh oo vas nah deesYEHRT
I'd like...	Я хотел(а) бы...	yah khatYEHL(ah) bih
ice cream.	мороженое.	mahROHZHehnahyeh
a cookie.	печенье.	peechEHN'yeh

pie.	пиро́г.	peerOHK
pastry.	пиро́жное.	peerOHZHnahyeh
honey	медо́вый	meedOHvihy
cake.	пря́ник.	PRYAHneek
cake.	торт.	tohrt
stewed fruit.	компо́т.	kahmPOHT
thin pancakes with jam.	блинчики́.	bleencheeKEE
thin fruit jelly.	кисе́ль.	keesYEHL'
marzipan pastry.	карто́шку.	kahrtOHSHkoo
filled doughnuts.	по́нчики.	POHNcheekee
an eclair.	эклер.	ehkLYEHR
chocolate.	шокола́д.	shahkahLAHT
baked pudding.	запека́нку.	zahpeeKAHNkoo

Drinks

Russians are a tea-drinking people. Tea is usually served pre-sweetened with honey, jam or sugar. Although coffee has gained in popularity, it is still much more expensive and harder to find than tea. Bottled fruit juices and waters are also very popular, but ice and cold drinks are not. Drinking tap water, especially in Leningrad, is not a good idea.

What do you have to drink?	Каки́е напи́тки у вас?	kahKEEyeh nahPEETkee oo vas?
Please bring me...	Пожа́луйста, принеси́те мне...	pahZHAHLstah preeneeSEEtyeh mnyeh
(black) coffee.	(че́рный) ко́фе.	(CHOHRnihy) KOHfyeh
with milk.	с молоко́м.	smahlahKOHM
with sugar.	со са́харом.	sahSAHkhahrahm
without sugar.	без са́хара.	byehs SAHkhahrah
tea.	чай.	chay

with lemon.	с лимо́ном.	sleeMOHnahm
with milk.	с молоко́м.	smahlahKOHM
with honey.	с мёдом.	SMYOHdahm
with jam.	с варе́ньем	svahrYEHN'ehm
a soft drink.	пе́пси.	PYEHPsee
I'd like a	Я хоте́л(а)	yah khahtYEHL(ah)
glass of...	бы стака́н...	bih stahKAHN
milk.	молока́.	mahlahKAH
lemonade.	лимона́да.	leemahNAHdah
I'd like a	Я хоте́л(а) бы	yah khahtYEHL(ah)
bottle of...	буты́лку...	bih bootIHLkoo
mineral	минера́льной	meeneeRAHL'nay
water.	воды́.	vahDIH
I'd like a	Я хоте́л(а) бы	yah khahtYEHL(ah)
bottle of ...	буты́лку ...	bih bootIHLkoo
juice.	со́ка.	SOHkah
apple.	я́блочного.	YAHBlahchnahvah
cherry.	вишнёвого.	veeshNYOHvahvah
grape.	виногра́дного.	veenahgRAHDnahvah
grapefruit.	гре́йпфрутого.	GREYPfrootahvah
orange.	апельси́ного.	ahpeel'SEEnahvah
plum.	сливо́вого.	sleeVOHvahvah
tangerine.	мандари́ного.	mahndahREEnahvah

Alcoholic Drinks

In an attempt to curb alcoholism, a law was passed in 1985 prohibiting restaurants from serving alcohol before 2 pm. The most popular Russian wines come from Georgia and the Crimea. Sweet, and similar to a sparkling wine, Soviet champagne is a good choice with dessert. Vodka comes in a variety of flavors and is most often served chilled in 50 gram shot glasses. It is the custom to drink the shot all at once and chase it with bread or raw vegetables.

Do you serve	У вас есть	oo vahs yehst'
alcohol?	алкого́личные	ahlkahGOHleech-
	напи́тки?	nihyeh nahPEET-
		kee

44

English	Russian	Pronunciation
Which wine would you recommend?	Какóе вѝно вы рекоменду́ете?	kahKOHyeh VEEnah vih reekahmeen-DOOeetyeh
How much is a bottle of...	Скóлько стóит бутъ́шку...	SKOHL'kah STOHeet bootIHLkoo
I'd like a glass/ bottle of...	Я хотéл(а) бы стакáн/ бутъ́шку...	yah khatYEHL(ah) bih stahKAHN/ bootIHLkoo
wine.	винá.	veenAH
red wine.	крáсного винá.	KRAHSnahvah veenAH
white wine.	бéлого винá.	BYEHlahvah veenAH
dry wine.	сухóго винá.	sookhOHvah veenAH
sweet wine.	слáдкого винá.	SLAHTkahvah veenAH
Georgian wine.	грузи́нского винá	groozEENskahvah veenAH
Soviet champagne (sparkling wine).	совéтского шампáнского.	sahvYEHTskahvah shahmPAHN-skahvah
beer.	пи́во.	PEEvah
kvas.	квáса.	KVAHsah
vodka.	вóдки.	VOHTkee
pepper-flavored vodka.	перцóвки.	peertsOHFkee
lemon-flavored vodka.	лимóнки.	leemOHNkee
cherry-flavored vodka.	вишнёвки.	veeshNYOHFkee
dark, smooth, old vodka.	стáрки.	STAHRkee
whiskey.	ви́ски.	VEESkee
straight up.	натурáльное.	nahtoorAHLnahyeh
with ice.	со льдóм	sahl'dOHM
with soda.	с сóдовой.	sahSOHdahvay

45

Azerbaijani/ Armenian brandy.	азербайджáнский/ армя́нский конья́к.	ahzeerbaydzhAHN- skeey/ahrmYAHN- skeey kahn'YAHK
a gin (and tonic).	джин (с тóником).	dzheen (STOHneekahm)
a scotch.	шотля́ндское.	shahtLAHNTskahyeh

Toasts

To your health!	За вáше здорóвье!	zah VAHsheh zdahROHV'yeh
To peace and friendship!	За мир и дрýжбу!	zah meer ee DROOSHboo
I wish you happiness/ health/ success!	Желáю вáм счáстья/ здорóвья/ успéха!	ZHEHlahyoo vahm SHAHST'yah/ zdahROHV'yah/ oosPYEHkhah
Congrat- ulations!	Поздравля́ю вас!	pahzDRAHVlyahyoo vahs

46

VII. SERVICES

Currency Exchange

If you do not exchange your money upon arrival at the airport or in your hotel, you may also exchange it at a foreign-trade bank. Be forewarned, however, that they are less common than in the States and often keep strange hours. Remember that you will need your passport and currency exchange declaration to carry out the transaction. The ruble is the equivalent of 100 kopecks. Trading or exchanging money with individual Soviets is illegal.

Currency exchange.	Обмéн валю́ты.	ahbMYEHN vahLYOOtih
Where can I exchange money?	Где мóжно обменя́ть валю́ту?	gdyeh MOHZHnah ahbmeenYAHT' vahLYOOtoo
Where can I find the nearest foreign-trade bank?	Где нахóдится ближáйший внéшторг банк?	gdyeh nahKHOH-deetsah blee-ZHAYsheey VNYEHSHtahrg bahnk
When does the bank open?	Во скóлько открывáется банк?	vahSKOHL'kah aht-krihVAHeetsah bahnk
How late is the bank open?	Во скóлько закрывáется банк?	vahSKOHL'kah zahkrihVAHeet-sah bahnk
The bank is open from 9:30 am to 1 pm.	Банк рабóтает с 9.30 до 1.	bahnk rahBOHtaheet spahlahVEEnah deesYAHtahvah dah cheesAH
What is the exchange rate for dollars today?	Какóй сегóдня обмéнный курс дóллара?	kahKOY seeVOH-dnyah ahbMYEH-nihy koors DOHL-lahrah?

47

English	Russian	Pronunciation
I'd like to change some dollars.	Я хотéл(а) бы обменя́ть до́ллары.	yah khahtYEHL(ah) bih ahbmeen-YAHT' DOHLlahrih
I'd like to cash some traveler's checks.	Я хотéл(а) бы разменя́ть доро́жные чéки.	yah khahtYEHL(ah) bih rahzmeen-YAHT' dahROHZH-nihyeh CHEHkee
Can I purchase an international money order here?	Мо́жно здесь достáть междунаро́дный почто́вый перево́д?	MOHZHnah zdyehs' dahsTAHT' meezh-doonahROHDnihy pahchTOHvihy peereeVOHT
What's the charge?	Ско́лько сто́ит?	SKOHL'kah STOHeet
I'm expecting money from America.	Для меня́ должны́ быть дéньги из Амéрики.	dlyah meenYAH dahlzhNIH biht' DYEHNgee ees ahMYEHreekee
Has it arrived?	Они́ ужé пришли́?	ahNEE oozhEH preeshLEE
Go to the cashier's office.	Иди́те в кáссу.	eeDEEtyeh FKAHSsoo
Where is the cashier's office?	Где кáсса?	gdyeh KAHSsah
When is the cashier open?	Когдá кáсса откры́та?	kahgDAH KAHSsah ahtKRIHtah
Are you the cashier?(f)	Вы касси́р(ша)?	vih kahsSEER(shah)
Here's my identification.	Вот моё удостоверéние ли́чности.	voht mahYOH oodah-stahveerYEHNee-yeh LEECHnahstee
Here's my passport.	Вот моя́ пáспорт.	voht moy PAHSpahrt
Where do I sign?	Где мне подписáть?	gdyeh mnyeh pahtpeeSAHT'

May I please have large bills?	Да́йте мне, пожа́луйста, кру́пными купю́рами.	DAYtyeh mnyeh pahZHAHLstah KROOPnihmee koopYOORahmee
May I please have small bills?	Да́йте мне, пожа́луйста, ме́лкими купю́рами.	DAYtyeh mnyeh pahZHAHLstah MYEHLkeemee koopYOORahmee
Can you give me small change?	Да́йте мне, пожа́луйста, ме́лкими моне́тами.	DAYtyeh mnyeh pahZHAHLstah MYEHLkeemee mahNYEHtahmee
I think you've made a mistake.	Мне ка́жется, что вы ошиблись.	mnyeh KAHZHeht-sah shtoh vih ahshEEBlees'

Mail

In addition to the regular postal services, the main branch post office provides international telegram and telephone services, as well. In Moscow and Leningrad, the main post offices are open twenty-four hours. Packages to be sent out of the USSR must be brought to a post office unwrapped. There they will be weighed, inspected, wrapped and stamped.

Post office.	По́чта.	POHCHtah
Letter./	Письмо́./	pees'MOH/
Letters.	Пи́сьма.	PEEs'mah
Where's the nearest post office?	Где ближа́йшая по́чта?	gdyeh bleeZHAYshahyah POHCHtah
Where's the main post office?	Где почта́мт?	gdyeh pahchtAHMT
When does the post office open /close?	Во ско́лько открыва́ется/ закрыва́ется по́чта?	vahSKOHL'kah ahtkrihVAHeetsah /zahkrihVAHeet-sah POHCHtah

49

English	Russian	Pronunciation
The post office is open from 9 to 6.	Почта работает с 9. до 6.	POHCHtah rahBOHtaheet sdeevyahTEE dah shehsTEE
Where can I find a mailbox?	Где можно найти почтовый ящик.	gdyeh MOHZHnah nayTEE pahchTOH-vihy YAHshcheek
Can I buy ... here?	Можно здесь купить...	MOHZHnah zdyehs' kooPEET'
envelopes.	конверты.	kahnVYEHRtih
post cards.	открытки.	ahtKRIHTkee
stamps.	марки.	MAHRkee.
Please give me ten airmail stamps for letters/ post cards to the USA.	Дайте мне, пожалуйста, десять марок для авиаписем/ авиаоткрыток в США.	DAYtyeh mnyeh pahZHALstah DYEHseet' MAH-rahk dlyah AHvee-ahPEEseem/ AHveeahahtKRIHT-ahk vsshah
I'd like to send this letter/post card by...	Я хотёл(а) бы послать это письмо/ открытку...	yah khahtYEHL(ah) bih pahsLAHT' EHtah pees'MOH/ ahtKRIHTkoo
surface mail.	простой почтой.	prahsTOY POHCHtay
airmail.	авиапочтой.	ahveeahPOHCHtay
registered mail.	заказной почтой.	zahkahzNOY POHCHtay
special delivery.	спешной почтой.	SPYEHSHnay POHCHtay
Will this go out today?	Это отправится сегодня?	EHtah ahtPRAHveet-sah seeVOHdnyah
I'd like to send this to...	Я хотёл(а) бы послать это в...	yah khahtYEHL(ah) bih pahsLAHT' EHtah f
America.	Америку.	ahMYEHReekoo
Canada.	Канаду.	kahNAHdoo
England.	Англию.	AHNgleeyoo
Germany.	Германию.	geerMAHneeyoo
France.	Францию.	FRAHNtseeyoo
I'd like to send this parcel.	Я хотёл(а) бы послать эту посылку.	yah khatYEHL(ah) bih pahsLAHT' EHtoo pahsIHLkoo

It contains books/ souvenirs/ fragile material.	Она́ содержит кни́ги/ сувени́ры/ хру́пкий материа́л.	ahNAH sahdYEHR- zheet kneeGEE/ sooveeNEErih/ KHROOPkee mahteereeAHL
Wrap it up, please.	Заверни́те, пожа́луйста.	zahveerNEEtyeh pahZHAHLstah
Write the address here.	Напиши́те а́дрес вот здесь.	nahpeeSHEEtyeh AHdrees voht zdyehs'
Return address.	Обра́тный а́дрес.	ahbRAHTnihy AHdrees
Have I received any mail?	Есть ли для меня́ пи́сьма?	yehst' lee dlyah meenYAH PEEs'mah
My name is...	Моя́ фами́лия...	mahYAH fahMEEleeyah
Here's my passport.	Вот моя́ па́спорт.	voht moy PAHSpahrt

Telegrams

Most larger post offices have a telegraph department.

I'd like to send a telegram.	Я хочу́ посла́ть телегра́мму.	yah khahCHOO pahsLAHT' teeleeGRAHMmoo
Where can I send a telegram?	Отку́да мо́жно посла́ть телегра́мму?	ahtKOOdah MOHZH- nah pahsLAHT' teeleeGRAHMmoo
May I have an inter- national telegram form?	Да́йте мне, пожа́луйста, междунаро́дный бланк.	DAYtyeh mnyeh pahZHAHLstah meezhdoonahROHD -nihy blahnk
What is the rate per word?	Ско́лько сто́ит сло́во?	SKOHL'kah STOHeet SLOHvah
What will the total cost be?	Ско́лько бу́дет сто́ить телегра́мму?	SKOHL'kah BOOdeet STOHeet' teelee- GRAHMmoo

51

How long will it take to reach the USA/England?	Скóлько врéмени идёт телегрáмма в США/Áнглию?	SKOHL'kah VRYEH-meenee eedYOHT teeleeGRAHMmah vsshah/VAHNglee-yoo

Telephones

Phone books do not exist in the Soviet Union. Local calls can be made at any time from any phone. International calls, however, can only be made by reservation at the telephone office of the main post office or through your hotel. They must be booked in advance. To make a local call from a phone booth you first drop in two kopecks, pick up the phone, wait for a long, continuous buzz, then dial. Long signals mean the phone is ringing; shorter ones mean the line is busy.

Public phone.	Телефóн-автомáт.	teeleeFOHN-ahftahMAHT
Where's the nearest telephone?	Где ближáйший телефóн?	gdyeh bleeZHAY-sheey teeleeFOHN
May I use your phone?	Мóжно от вас позвонúть?	MOHZHnah aht vahs pahzvahNEET'
Hello (on the phone).	Аллó./ Слýшаю.	ahlLOH/ SLOOshahyoo
Who is this?	Кто говорúт?	ktoh gahvahREET
This is...	Это говорúт...	EHtah gahvahREET
My name is...	Меня зовýт...	meenYAH zahvOOT
I'd like to speak to...	Я хотéл(а) бы говорúт с...	yah khahtYEHL(ah) bih gahvahREET s
He/She isn't in.	Егó/Её нет.	yeeVOH/yeeYOH nyeht
When will he/she return?	Когдá он/онá вернётся?	kahgDAH ohn/ahNAH veerNYOHtsah
Tell him/her that I called.	Передáйте, что я позвонúл(а).	peereeDAYtyeh shtoh yah pahzvahNEEL(ah)

English	Russian	Pronunciation
Take a message, please.	Передайте, пожалуйста, что...	peereeDAYtyeh pahZHAHLstah shtoh
My number is...	Моя номер телефона...	moy NOHmeer teeleeFOHNah
Ask him/her to call me back.	Попросите его/её позвонить мне.	pahprahSEEtyeh yeeVOH/yeeYOH pahzvahNEET' mnyeh
I don't understand.	Я не понимаю.	yah nyeh pahneeMAHyoo
Do you speak English?	Вы говорите по-английски?	vih gahvahREEtyeh pahahngLEEskee
I can't hear you.	Не слышно.	nee SLIHSHnah
Can you speak slowly/louder?	Говорите медленнее/громче, пожалуйста.	gahvahREEtyeh MYEHdleennyeh-yeh/GROHMcheh pahZHAHLstah
With whom do you want to speak?	С кем вы хотите говорят?	skyehm vih khahTEEtyeh gahvahREET
You've got the wrong number.	У вас неправильный номер.	oo vahs neePRAHveel'nihy NOHmeer
Dial again.	Наберите ещё раз.	nahbeeREEtyeh yeeSHCHOH rahs
The number has been changed.	Номер телефона поменялся.	NOHmeer teeleeFOHNah pahmeenYAHLsah
The phone is broken.	Телефон не работает.	teeleeFOHN nee rahBOHtaheet
Long-distance phone call.	Междугородный разговор.	meezhdoogahROHD-nihy rahzgahv-OHR
International phone call.	Международный разговор.	meezhdoonahROHD-nihy rahzgahv-OHR
Can I dial direct?	Могу ли я сам(а) набрать?	mahGOO lee yah sahm(AH) nahbRAHT'

English	Russian	Pronunciation
Operator, please get me this number.	Телефонистка, пожалуйста, соедините меня с этим номером.	teeleefahnEESTkah pahZHAHLstah saheedeeNEEtyeh meenYAH SEHteem NOHmeerahm
I'd like to order a phone call to the USA.	Я хотёл(а) бы заказать разговор с США.	yah khahtYEHL(ah) bih zahkahzAHT' rahzgahvOHR ssshah
How much does a call to New York cost?	Сколько стоит телефонный разговор с Нью-Йорком?	SKOHL'kah STOHeet teeleeFOHNnihy rahzgahvOHR sn'yooYOHRkahm
I want to reverse the charges.	Я хочу, чтобы разговор был за счёт вызываемого.	yah khaCHOO SHTOHbih rahzgahvOHR bihl zah shchoht vihzih-VAHeemahvah
What number are you calling?	Какой номер?	kahKOY NOHmeer
Do I have to wait long?	Мне долго ждать?	mnyeh DOHLgah zhdaht'
How long do you want to speak?	Сколько минут вы хотите говорит?	SKOHL'kah meenOOT vih khahTEEtyeh gahvahrEET
Wait a minute!	Подождите!/ Минуточку!	pahdahzhDEEtyeh/ meeNOOtahchkoo
Your call is in booth #2.	Ваш разговор в кабине номер два.	vahsh rahzgahvOHR fkahBEEnyeh NOHmeer dvah
Your time is up.	Время кончилось.	VRYEHmyah KOHNcheelahs'
How much did the call cost?	Сколько стоил разговор?	SKOHL'kah STOHeel rahzgahvOHR
There's a call for you.	Вас вызывает по телефону.	vahs vihzihVAHeet pah teeleeFOHNoo
Hold on, please.	Не вешайте трубку.	nee veeSHAYtyeh TROOPkoo
It's busy.	Линия занята.	LEEneeyah zahneeTAH

There's no answer.	Не отвечают.	nee ahtveeCHAYyoot
I can't get through.	Я не могу дозвонится.	yah nee mahGOO dahzvahNEEtsah
We've been cut off.	Нас разъединили.	nahs rahz"eedee-NEElee

Dry Cleaning and Laundry

Laundry and dry cleaning services are often available in your Intourist hotel. Ask your floor monitor (дежурная) for details and assistance.

Where can I get my laundry washed?	Куда отдать бельё в стирку?	kooDAH ahdDAHT' beel'YOH FSTEERkoo
Where is the nearest dry cleaner?	Где ближайшая химчистка?	gdyeh bleeZHAYshahyah kheemCHEESTkah
I need these things...	Эти вещи надо...	EHtee VYEHshchee NAHdah
dry cleaned.	почистить.	pahCHEESTeet'
washed.	выстирать.	VIHsteeraht'
ironed.	погладить.	pahgLAHdeet'
No starch, please.	Не крамалите, пожалуйста.	nee krahmahLEEtyeh pahZHAHLstah
Can you get this stain out?	Можно вывести это пятно?	MOHZHnah VIHveestee EHtah peetNOH
Can you mend/sew this?	Вы это можете заштопать/зашить?	vih EHtah MOHZHehtyeh zahSHTOHpaht'/zahSHEET'
Sew on this button, please.	Пришейте, пожалуйста, эту пуговицу.	preeSHEYtyeh pahZHAHLstah EHtoo POOgahveetsoo
When will it be ready?	Когда оно будет готово?	kahgDAH ahNOH BOOdeet gahTOHvah
Is my laundry ready?	Бельё готово?	beel'YOH gahTOHvah

How much do I owe you? (f)	Сколько я вам должен (должна)?	SKOHL'kah yah vahm DOHLzhehn (dahlzhNAH)
This isn't mine.	Это не моё.	EHtah nee mahYOH
I'm missing something.	Чего-то не хватает.	cheeVOHtah nee khvahTAHeet
This is torn.	Это порвано.	EHtah POHRvahnah
Can I borrow...	Можно попросить на минуту...	MOHZHnah pahprahSEET' nah meeNOOtoo
a needle and thread?	иголку и нитку?	eegOHLkoo ee NEETkoo
scissors?	ножницы?	NOHZHneetsih

Optician

Optician.	Оптика.	OHPteekah
Where can I find an optician?	Где мне найти оптику?	gdyeh mnyeh nayTEE OHPteekoo
I have broken my glasses.	У меня разбились очки.	oo meenYAH rahsBEElees' ahchKEE
The frame is broken.	Оправа сломана.	ahpRAHvah SLOHmahnah
The lenses are broken.	Стёкла разбита.	STYOHKlah rahzBEEtah
Can you fix them?	Можно их починить?	MOHZHnah eekh pahcheenEET'
How long will it take?	Когда они будут готовы?	kahgDAH ahNEE BOOdoot gahTOHvih
Here's my prescription.	Вот мой рецепт.	voht moy reetsEHPT
I've lost/ ripped a contact lense.	Я потерял(а)/ рвал(а) мою контактную линзу.	yah pahteerYAHL-(ah)/rvahl(ah) mahYOO kahnTAHKTnooyoo LEENzoo

Can you replace it?	Есть ли у вас такие линзы?	yehst' lee oo vahs tahKEEyeh LEENzih
I have hard/soft lenses.	У меня твёрдые/мягкие линзы.	oo meenYAH TVYOHRdihyeh/ MYAHKHkeeyeh LEENzih
Do you sell contact lens fluid?	Есть ли у вас жидкость для контактных линз?	yehst' lee oo vahs ZHEETkahst' dlyah kahnTAHKTnihkh leenz

Shoe Repair

Shoe repair.	Ремонт обуви.	reemOHNT OHboovee
Shine my shoes, please.	Почистите туфли, пожалуйста.	pahcheesTEEtyeh TOOflee pahZHAHLstah
Can these shoes be repaired?	Можно починить эти туфли?	MOHZHnah pahcheenEET' EHtee TOOflee
I need new soles/ heels.	Мне нужны новые подмётки/ каблуки.	mnyeh noozhNIH NOHvihyeh pahd-MYOHTkee/ kahbLOOkee
The heel/ strap broke.	Каблук/ ремешок сломан.	kahbLOOK/ reemeeshOHK SLOHmahn
Can this be sewn up?	Можно это зашить?	MOHZHnah EHtah zahSHEET'
How much will it cost?	Сколько мне будет стоить?	SKOHL'kah mnyeh BOOdeet STOHeet'
When will they be ready?	Когда они будут готовы?	kahgDAH ahNEE BOOdoot gahTOHvih

Barber/Hairdresser

| Barber./Hair -dresser. | Парикмахерская. | pahreekMAHKHeer-skahyah |
| Where is the nearest barber? | Где ближайшая парикмахерская? | gdyeh bleeZHAY-shahyah pahreek-MAHKHeerskahyah |

57

English	Russian	Pronunciation
Is there a hair-dresser in the hotel?	Есть парик-ма́херская в э́той гости́нице?	yehst' pahreek-MAHKHeerskahyah VEHtay gahsTEE-neetseh
Can I make an appoint-ment for Monday?	Мо́жно записа́ться на понеде́льник?	MOHZHnah zahpee-SAHTsah nah pahneedYEHL'neek
Have a seat.	Сади́тесь.	sahDEEtees'
Hair cut.	Стри́жка.	STREESHkah
Hair style.	Причёска.	preeCHOHSkah
Part (hair).	Пробо́р.	prahBOHR
Dye.	Окра́ска.	ahKRAHSkah
A hair cut, please.	Постриги́те меня́, пожа́луйста.	pahstreeGEEtyeh meenYAH pah-ZHAHLstah
Just a trim.	То́лько подстриги́те меня́.	TOHL'kah paht-streeGEEtyeh meenYAH
Take a little off the sides, please.	Подстриги́те немно́жко с боко́в, пожа́луйста.	pahtstreeGEEtyeh neemNOHSHkah sbahkOHF pahZHAHLstah
Not too short.	Не сли́шком ко́ротко.	nee SLEESHkahm KOHrahtkah
Just a little more, please.	Чуть побо́льше, пожа́луйста.	choot' pahBOHL'-sheh pahZHAHL-stah
Shampoo and set, please.	Вы́мойте и уложи́те во́лосы, пожа́луйста.	VIHmaytyeh ee oolahZHEEtyeh VOHlahsih pahZHAHLstah
Blow-dry my hair.	Уложи́те мне во́лосы фе́ном.	oolahZHEEtyeh mnyeh VOHlahsih FYEHNahm
A shave, please.	Побре́йте меня́, пожа́луйста.	pahBREYtyeh meenYAH pahZHAHLstah
Trim my beard/ mustache/ sideburns.	Подстриги́те мою́ бо́роду/ мои́ усы́/ мои́ бакенба́рды.	pahtstreeGEEtyeh mahYOO BOHrah-doo/mahEE ooSIH/ mahEE bahkeen-BAHRdih

Dye my hair in this color.	Покрáсьте вóлосы в э́тот цвет.	pahKRAHS'tyeh VOHlahsih VEHtaht tsvyeht
I would like a facial/ manicure/ permanent.	Я хотéла бы очищéние массáж лицá/ маникю́р/ перманéнт.	yah khahtYEHlah bih ahcheeSHCHEH-neeyeh mahs-SAHSH leeTSAH/ mahneekYOOR/ peermahnYEHNT
Thank you. How much do I owe you? (f).	Спасúбо. Скóлько я вам дóлжен (должнá)?	spahSEEbah SKOHL'kah yah vahm DOHLzhehn (dahlzhNAH)

Film Development

It is best to bring enough film and photography supplies from home. If you do purchase Soviet film, be sure to have it developed at a "photo-laboratory" (фотолаборатóрия) before you leave, as their processing procedure differs from ours. The list of things which are off-limits to photographers in the Soviet Union includes train stations, airports, military installations and much more. It is impolite to photograph people without their permission.

Photography.	Фотогрáфия.	fahtahGRAHfeeyah
Camera.	Фотоаппарáт.	fahtahahppahRAHT
Film.	Плёнка.	PLYOHNkah
Black and white film.	Чёрно-бéлая плёнка.	CHOHRnah-BYEHlahyah PLYOHNkah
Color film.	Цветнáя плёнка.	tsveetNAHyah PLYOHNkah
Thirty-six exposure.	Трúдцать шесть кáдров.	TREEtsaht' shehst' KAHDrahv
How much does processing cost?	Скóлько стóит проявúть плёнку?	SKOHL'kah STOHeet praheeVEET' PLYOHNkoo
I'd like this enlarged.	Я хотéл(а) бы увелúчить э́то.	yah khahtYEHL(ah) bih ooveelEECHeet' EHtah

59

| I'd like another copy of this print. | Я хотéл(а) бы ещё однý кóпию. | yah khahtYEHL(ah) bih yeeSHCHOH ahdNOO KOHpee-yoo |
| When will they be ready? | Когдá фотогрáфии бýдут готóвы? | kahgDAH fahtah-GRAHfeee BOO-doot gahTOHvih |

VIII. TRANSPORTATION

Public transportation in the Soviet Union is cheap, clean and efficient. Buses, street cars and trolleys all cost five kopecks per ride and run from 6 am till 1 am. Tickets are usually purchased on board by dropping a five-kopeck coin into a cash box and tearing off a paper ticket. If the bus or trolley is crowded, it is common practice to merely pass the coin towards the direction of the box and a ticket will be passed back to you. Spot checks are done occasionally and passengers without tickets are fined. Stops are marked with an 'A' for buses, 'T' for trolleys and a different capital 'T' for street cars. These signs also carry the name of the stop, the name of the terminal stop, and time table or interval between buses. The routes are denoted by numbers. If a passenger asks you if you are getting off and you are not, it is expected that you will move out of the way for him to get by.

Buses, Street Cars and Trolleys

Bus.	Автобус.	ahfTOHboos
Street car.	Трамвай.	trahmVAY
Trolley.	Троллейбус.	trahlLEYboos
Where is the bus/street car/trolley stop?	Где остановка автобуса/ трамвая/ троллейбуса?	gdyeh ahstahnOHF-kah ahfTOHboosah /trahmVAHyah /trahlLEYboosah
How often does the bus/street car/trolley run?	Как часто останавливается автобус/ трамвай/ троллейбус?	kahk CHAHstah ahstahnNAHVlee-vaheetsah ahf-TOHboos/trahm-VAY/trahlLEYboos
When's the next bus?	Когда идёт следующий автобус?	kahgDAH eedYOHT SLYEHdooyooshch-eey ahfTOHboos
Bus driver.	Водитель.	vahDEEteel'
Fare.	Проезд.	prahYEHST
Monthly pass.	Ежемесячный билет.	yeezhehMYEHseech-nihy beelYEHT

61

Five-kopeck piece.	Пятикопеечная монета.	peeteekahPYEHeechnahyah mahNYEHtah
Cash box.	Касса.	KAHSsah
Pass me a ticket, please.	Передайте мне, пожалуйста, билет.	peereeDAYtyeh mnyeh pahZHAHLstah beelYEHT
What bus do I take to get to Red Square?	Какой автобус идёт до Красной площади?	kahKOY ahfTOHboos eedYOHT dah KRAHSnay PLOHshchahdee
Do I have to transfer?	Мне надо пересесть?	mnyeh NAHdah peereeSYEHST'
Does this bus go near Moscow State University?	Пройдёт ли этот автобус мимо МГУ?	prahyDYOHT lee EHtaht ahfTOHboos MEEmah emgahoo
How many stops until we reach the center of town?	Сколько остановок до центра города?	SKOHL'kah ahstahNOHVahk dah TSEHNtrah GOHrahdah
You've gotten on the wrong bus.	Вы сели не на тот автобус.	vih SYEHlee nee nah toht ahfTOHboos
Can you tell me where to get off.	Вы не скажете, на какой остановке мне надо выйти.	vih nee SKAHzhehteh nah kahKOY ahstahNOHFkyeh mnyeh NAHdah VIHytee
You've missed your stop.	Вы проехали свою остановку.	vih prahYEHkhahlee svahYOO ahstahNOHFkoo
Are you getting off?	Вы сейчас выходите?	vih seeCHAHS vihKHOHdeetyeh
I want to get off here/at the next stop.	Я хочу сойти здесь/на следующей остановке.	yah khahCHOO sahyTEE zdyehs/nah SLYEHdooyooshchey ahstahNOHFkyeh

Excuse me, can I get through?	Извините, можно пройти?	eezveeNEEtyeh MOHZHnah prahyTEE
Excuse me, I'm getting off at the next stop.	Извините, я выхожу на следующей.	eezveeNEEtyeh yah VIHkhahzhoo nah SLYEHdooyoo-shchey
Just a minute!	Минуточку!	meeNOOtahchkoo
I'm getting off now.	Я скожу.	yah skahZHOO

Subway

Soviet subways are clean, quick and efficient. The stations are marked by a large red 'M', which is illuminated at night. The Moscow system is a tourist attraction in itself, since each station is built from a different architectural design. In order to get to the trains, you must drop a five-kopeck piece into a turnstile. In case you do not have exact change, most stations have change machines or cashiers. Trains run from 6 am till 1 am. Smoking is prohibited.

Subway.	Метро.	meetROH
Entrance.	Вход.	fkhoht
Exit.	Выход.	VIHkhaht
No entrance.	Нет входа.	nyeht FKHOHdah
No exit.	Нет выхода.	nyeht VIHkhahdah
Way out.	Выход в город.	VIHkaht VGOHraht
To the trains.	К поездам.	kpaheezDAHM
Transfer.	Переход.	peereeKHOHT
Keep to the left/right.	Держитесь левой/правой стороны.	deerZHEEtyehs' LYEHvay/PRAHvay STOHrahnih
Change machines.	Кассы-автоматы.	KAHSsih-ahftahMAHtih
May I have change, please.	Разменяйте, пожалуйста.	rahzmeeNEEtyeh pahZHAHLstah

Where's the nearest subway stop?	Где ближа́йшая ста́нция метро́?	gdyeh bleeZHAY-shahyah STAHN-tseeyah meetROH
Does this line go to...	Эта ли́ния идёт до...	EHtah LEEneeyah eedYOHT dah
What line should I take to...	По како́й ли́нии мне пое́хать до...	pah kahKOY LEEneeee mnyeh dahYEHkhaht' dah
Do I have to transfer?	На́до пересе́сть?	NAHdah peereeSYEHST'
Can you tell me what the next station is?	Скажи́те, пожа́луйста, кака́я сле́дующая ста́нция?	skahZHEEtyeh pah-ZHAHLstah kah-KAHyah SLYEH-dooyooshchahyah STAHNtseeyah
The next station is...	Сле́дующая ста́нция...	SLYEHdooyooshchah-yah STAHNtseeyah
Can you tell me where to get off?	Вы мне ска́жете когда́ на́до сходи́ть?	vih mnyeh SKAHzhehtyeh kahgDAH NAHdah skhahDEET'
Careful, the doors are closing.	Осторо́жно, две́ри закрыва́ются.	ahstahROHZHnah DVYEHree zah-krihVAHyootsah
The train goes as far as...	По́езд сле́дует до ста́нции...	POHeest SLYEHdooeet dah STAHNtseeee
This is the last stop.	По́езд да́льше не пойдёт.	POHeest DAHL'sheh nee pahyDYOHT

Taxi

In addition to being ordered by phone, taxis can be found in front of major hotels and at taxi stands. A small, green light in the front window means that the cab is available. It is common to share a cab with strangers.

| Taxi. | Такси́. | tahkSEE |
| Taxi stand. | Стоя́нка такси́. | stahYAHNkah tahkSEE |

English	Russian	Pronunciation
Where can I get a taxi?	Где мне поймать такси?	gdyeh mnyeh pahy-MAHT' tahkSEE
Where is the nearest taxi stand?	Где ближайшая стоянка такси?	gdyeh bleeZHAY-shahyah stah-YAHNkah tahkSEE
Please call me a taxi.	Пожалуйста, вызовите мне такси.	pahZHAHLstah VIHzahveetyeh mnyeh tahkSEE
Are you free?	Вы свободны?	vih svahBOHdnih
Where do you want to go?	Куда вам?	kooDAH vahm
Here's the address.	Вот адрес.	voht AHdrees
To the Bolshoi Theater, please.	Пожалуйста, к Большому театру.	pahZHAHLstah kbahl'SHOHmoo teeAHtroo
How much will the ride cost?	Сколько этот проезд будет стоит?	SKOHL'kah EHtaht prahYEHST BOOdeet STOHeet
Can you get my bags, please.	Возьмите, пожалуйста, мои чемоданы.	vahz'MEEtyeh pah-ZHAHLstah mahEE chehmahDAHnih
I'm (not) in a hurry.	Я (не) спешу.	yah (nee) speeSHOO
Stop here.	Остановитесь здесь.	ahstahnahVEEtyehs' zdyehs'
Wait for me here.	Подождите меня.	pahdahzhDEEtyeh meenYAH
I'll be back in a couple of minutes.	Я вернусь через несколько минут.	yah veerNOOS' CHEHrees neeSKOHL'kah meeNOOT
Keep the change.	Возьмите себе сдачу.	vahz'MEEtyeh seeBYEH ZDAHchoo
Thank you. Goodbye.	Спасибо. До свидания.	spahSEEbah dah sveeDAHneeyah

Boats

English	Russian	Pronunciation
Boat./Motor boat.	Лодка./Моторная лодка.	LOHTkah/mahTOHR-nahyah LOHTkah

Ship./	Корабль./	kahRAHBL'/
Steamship.	Пароход.	pahrahKHOHT
Hydrofoil.	Судно на подводных крыльях.	SOODnah nah pahdVOHDnihkh KRIHleekh
Ferry.	Паром.	pahrOHM
Cruise.	Круиз.	KROOeez
Tour.	Экскурсия.	ehksKOORseeyah
When does the next ship leave?	Когда отходит следующий пароход?	kahgDAH ahtKHOHdeet SLYEHdooyooshcheey pahrahKHOHT
Where do we get tickets?	Где можно купить билеты?	gdyeh MOHZHnah kooPEET' beelYEHTih
How much are the tickets?	Сколько стоит билеты?	SKOHL'kah STOHeet beelYEHTih
Where is the pier?	Где пристань?	gdyeh PREEstahn'
How long is the trip?	Сколько времены длится путешествие?	SKOHL'kah VRYEHmeenih DLEETsah pooteeshEHSTveeyeh
Where do we stop?	В какие порты мы заходим?	fkahKEEyeh pahrTIH mih zahKHOHdeem
Deck.	Палуба.	PAHloobah
Cabin.	Каюта.	kahYOOtah
Life jacket.	Спасательный пояс.	spahSAHteel'nihy POHyees
Lifeboat.	Спасательная лодка.	spahSAHteel'nahyah LOHTkah
I feel seasick.	Меня тошнит.	meenYAH tahshNEET

Trains

Like all long-distance travel in the Soviet Union, train trips must be reserved in advance. You can usually make reservations through your hotel.

| Train. | Поезд. | POHeest |

English	Russian	Pronunciation
Train station.	Вокзáл.	vahkZAHL
Ticket office.	Билéтная кáсса.	beelYEHTnahyah KAHSsah
When does the ticket office open?	Когдá открóется билéтная кáсса?	kahgDAH ahtKROHeetsah beelYEHTnahyah KAHSsah
Reservation office.	Предварúтельная продáжа билéтов.	preedvahREEtyehl'-nahyah prahDAH-zhah beelYEHTahf
Information office.	Спрáвочное бюрó.	SPRAHvahchnahyeh byooROH
Express long-distance trains	Экспрéсс пóезд.	ehksPRYEHSS POHeest
Standard long-distance trains.	Скóрый пóезд.	SKOHrihy POHeest
Local trains.	Электрúчки.	ehleekTREECHkee
Delux class.	Междунарóдный вагóн.	meezhdoonahROHD-nihy vahgOHN
First class.	Мягкий вагóн.	MYAHKHkeey vahgOHN
Second class.	Купúрованный вагóн.	kooPEERahvahnnihy vahgOHN
Third class.	Плацкáртный вагóн.	plahtsKAHRTnihy vahgOHN
One-way ticket.	Билéт в одúн конéц.	beelYEHT vahdEEN kahnYEHTS
Round-trip ticket.	Билéт тудá и обрáтно.	beelYEHT tooDAH ee ahbRAHTnah
Time table.	Расписáние поездóв	rahspeeSAHneeyeh paheezDOHF
Departure time.	Врéмя отправлéния.	VRYEHmyah aht-prahvLYEHneeyah
Arrival time.	Врéмя прибытия.	VRYEHmyah preeBIHTeeyah

67

English	Russian	Pronunciation
When is the next train to Kiev?	Когда отходит следующий поезд на Киев?	kahgDAH ahtKHOHdeet SLYEHdoo-yooshcheey POHeest nah KEEeef
Is it a direct train?	Это прямой поезд?	EHtah preeMOY POHeest
Do I have to change trains?	Мне надо делать пересадку?	mnyeh NAHdah DYEHlaht' peereeSAHTkoo
What's the fare to Tblisi?	Сколько стоит билет до Тбилиси?	SKOHL'kah STOHeet beelYEHT dah tbeeLEEsee
I'd like to reserve a seat.	Я хотел(а) бы заказать плацкарту.	yah khahtYEHL(ah) bih zahkahZAHT' plahtsKAHRToo
I'd like to reserve a berth in the sleeping car.	Я хотел(а) бы купить билет в спальный вагон.	yah khahtYEHL(ah) bih kooPEET' beelYEHT FSPAHL'nihy vahgOHN
From what platform does the train to Leningrad leave?	С какой платформы отходит поезд на Ленинград?	skahKOY plahtFOHRmih ahtKHOHdeet POHeest nah leeneenGRAHT
When does the train arrive in Erevan?	Во сколько поезд приходит в Ереван?	vahSKOHL'kah POHeest preeKHOHdeet veereeVAHN
Are we on time?	Поезд идёт по расписанию?	POHeest eedYOHT pah rahspeeSAHneeyoo
The train is twenty minutes late.	Поезд опаздывает на двадцать минут.	POHeest ahpAHZdihvaheet nah DVAHtsaht' meeNOOT
Where are we now?	Где мы сейчас?	gdyeh mih seeCHAHS
How long do we stop here?	Сколько поезд стоит здесь?	SKOHL'kah POHeest stahEET zdyehs'

68

English	Russian	Pronunciation
Is there time to get off?	Я успе́ю сойти́?	yah oosPYEHyoo sahyTEE
Is this seat taken?	Это ме́сто за́нято?	EHtah MYEHstah ZAHneetah
This is my seat.	Это моё ме́сто.	EHtah mahYOH MYEHstah
Am I bothering you?	Я вам меша́ю?	yah vahm meeSHAHyoo
Can I open/shut the window?	Мо́жно откры́ть/закры́ть окно́?	MOHZHnah ahtKRIHT'/zahKRIHT' ahkNOH
Can I turn out/on the light?	Мо́жно вы́ключт/включи́т свет?	MOHZHnah VIHKlyoocheet/vklyooCHEET svyeht
I'd like the top/bottom bunk.	Я хоте́л(а) бы ве́рхнюю/ни́жнюю по́лку.	yah khahtYEHL(ah) bih VYEHRKHnyooyoo/NEEZHnyooyoo POHLkoo
We'd like some tea.	Принеси́те нам ча́й.	preeneeSEEtyeh nahm chay
Two glasses, please.	Два стака́на, пожа́луйста.	dvah stahKAHnah pahZHAHLstah
Where is the...	Где...	gdyeh
baggage check?	прие́м багажа́?	preeYOHM bahgahZHAH
lost and found?	бюро́ нахо́док?	byooROH nahKHOHDahk
baggage room?	ка́мера хране́ния?	KAHmeerah khrahNYEHneeyah
snack bar?	буфе́т?	boofYEHT
bathroom?	туале́т?	tooahlYEHT
conductor?	конду́ктор?	kahnDOOKtahr
ticket taker? (m/f)	проводни́к/проводни́ца?	prahvahdNEEK/prahvahdNEEtsah
ticket checker?	контролёр?	kahntrahlYOHR
porter?	носи́льщик?	nahSEEL'shcheek
platform?	платфо́рма?	plahtFOHRmah
gate?	вход?	fkhoht
waiting room?	зал ожида́ния?	zahl ahzheeDAHneeyah

sleeping car?	спа́льный ваго́н?	SPAHL'nihy vahgOHN
dining car?	ваго́н-рестора́н?	vahgOHN-reestahRAHN
smoking car?	ваго́н для куря́щих?	vahgOHN dlyah kooRYAHshch-eekh
my sleeping compart-ment?	моё купе́?	mahYOH kooPYEH
Have a good trip!	Счастли́вого пути́!	shahstLEEvahvah pooTEE

Planes

Intourist can help you make domestic plane reservations on the Soviet airline, Aeroflot.

Plane.	Самолёт.	sahmahlYOHT
Airport.	Аэропо́рт.	ahehrahpOHRT
Arrival.	Прибы́тие.	preeBIHTeeyeh
Departure.	Вы́лет.	VIHlyeht
Boarding pass.	Поса́дочный тало́н.	pahSAHdahchnihy tahlOHN
I'd like to make a res-ervation.	Я хочу́ заказа́ть биле́т.	yah khahCHOO zahkahzAHT beelYEHT
I'd like a flight to Kiev.	Да́йте мне биле́т до Ки́ева.	DAYtyeh mnyeh beelYEHT dah KEEeevah
Is there a direct flight?	Есть ли прямо́й полёт?	yehst' lee preeMOY pahlYOHT
How long is the lay-over?	Как до́лго самолёт бу́дет стои́т?	kahk DOHLgah sahmahlYOHT BOOdeet stahEET
When is the next flight?	Когда́ вылета́ет сле́дующий самолёт?	kahgDAH vihleeTAHeet SLYEHdooyooshch-eey sahmahlYOHT
Is there a connection to Tblisi?	Есль ли переса́дка на Тбли́сы?	yehst' lee peereeSAHTkah nah teebLEEsih

70

English	Russian	Pronunciation
One-way ticket.	Билет в один конец.	beelYEHT vahdEEN kahnYEHTS
Round-trip ticket.	Билет туда и обратно.	beelYEHT tooDAH ee ahbRAHTnah
Is flight (#5) on time?	Рейс (номер пять) идёт по расписанию?	reys (NOHmeer pyaht') eedYOHT pah rahspee-SAHneeyoo
I'd like to change/ confirm my flight.	Я хотел(а) бы поменять/ потвердить рейс.	yah khatYEHL(ah) bih pahmeen-YAHT'/pahtveer-DEET' reys
I'd like to cancel my reserva-tion.	Я хотел(а) бы отказаться от билета.	yah khatYEHL(ah) bih ahtkahzAHT'-sah aht beelYEHTah
How much luggage am I allowed?	Какой вес багажа разрешается провозить?	kahKOY vyehs bahgahZHAH rahzreeSHAHeet-sah prahvahzEET'
What's the flight number?	Какой номер рейса?	kahKOY NOHmeer REYsah
What gate do we leave from?	С какого выхода посадка на наш рейс?	skahKOHvah VIHkhahdah pahSAHTkah nah nahsh reys
Boarding gate.	Выход на посадку.	VIHkhaht nah pahSAHTkoo
What time do we leave/ arrive?	Когда вылет/ прибытие?	kahgDAH VIHlyeht/ preeBIHTeeyeh
What time should I check in?	Во сколько надо регистрировать багаж?	vah SKOHL'kah NAHdah reegeest-REERahvaht' bahgAHSH
Call the stewardess.	Вызовите стюардессу.	VIHzahveetyeh styooahrdYEHSsoo
Fasten your seat belts.	Пристегните ремни.	preesteegNEEtyeh reemNEE
Will there be food served?	Будут ли кормить в самолёте?	BOOdoot lee kahrMEET' fsahmahLYOHtyeh

Can I smoke on board?	Мо́жно кури́ть?	MOHZHnah koorEET'
Is there a bus from the airport into the city?	Есть ли авто́бус с аэропо́рта по го́рода?	yehst' lee ahfTOHboos sahehrahPOHRtah dah GOHrahdah

IX. SIGHTSEEING AND RELAXING

Asking Directions

If the locals can not help you get where you want to go, you can always ask directions at special kiosks marked СПРАВКИ (Information). For five kopecks you will be given a small slip of paper with directions, street names, subway stops or bus numbers to direct you to your desired destination.

I'm lost. (m/f)	Я заблудился/ заблудилась.	yah zahblooDEEL-sah/zahblooDEEL-ahs'
Excuse me.	Простите./ Извините.	prahsTEEtyeh/ eezveeNEEtyeh
Can you tell me how to get to...	Скажите пожалуйста, как попасть...	skahZHEEtyeh pahZHAHLstah kahk pahpAHST'
Gorky Street?	на улицу Горького.	nah OOLeetsoo GOHR'kahvah
the center of town?	в центр города.	vtsehntr GOHrahdah
I'm looking for...	Я ищу...	yah eeshchOO
Am I going in the right direction?	Я иду в правильном направлении?	yah eedOO VPRAHV-eel'nahm nahprah-VLYEHneeee
Do you know where ... is?	Вы знаете где находится...?	vih ZNAHeetyeh gdyeh nahKHOH-deetsah
Is it far?	Это далеко?	EHtah dahleeKOH
Is it close?	Это близко?	EHtah BLEEskah
Can I walk there?	Можно туда пешком?	MOHZHnah tooDAH peeshKOHM
It would be best to take a bus or the metro.	Вам лучше сесть или на метро или на автобус.	vahm LOOCHsheh syehst' eelee nah meetROH eelee nah ahfTOHboos
What bus can I take to get to...?	Каким автобусом можно доехать до...?	kahKEEM ahfTOH-boosahm dah-YEHkhaht' dah

73

What street is this?	Какáя э́то ýлица?	kahKAHyah EHtah OOLeetsah
Please show me on the map where I am.	Покажи́те мне, пожа́луйста, на ка́рте, где я нахожу́сь.	pahkahZHEEtyeh mnyeh pahZHAHL-stah nah KAHR-tyeh gdyeh yah nahkhahZHOOS'
Go straight ahead.	Иди́те пря́мо.	eeDEEtyeh PRYAHmah
Go in this/ that direc-tion.	Иди́те в э́ту/ту сто́рону.	eeDEEtyeh VEHtoo/ftoo STOHrahnoo
Turn left/ right...	Поверни́те нале́во/ напра́во...	pahveerNEEtyeh nahLYEHvah/ nahPRAHvah
at the next corner.	на углу́.	nah oogLOO
at the light.	у светофо́ра.	oo sveetahFOHrah
Take this road.	Поезжа́йте по э́той ýлице.	paheezhZHAYtyeh pah EHtay OOLeetseh
You have to go back.	Вам на́до верни́тесь.	vahm NAHdah veerNEEtyehs'
You're on the wrong bus.	Вы се́ли не на тот авто́бус.	vih SYEHlee nee nah toht ahfTOHboos
Do I have to transfer?	Мне на́до пересе́сть?	mnyeh NAHdah peereeSYEHST'
North./South.	Се́вер./Юг.	SYEHveer/yook
East./West.	Восто́к./За́пад.	vahsTOHK/zahPAHT
It's there...	Э́то там...	EHtah tahm
on the right/left.	напра́во/ нале́во.	nahPRAHvah/ nahLYEHvah
after/ behind...	по́сле/ позади́...	POHslee/ pahzahDEE
next to/ opposite...	ря́дом/ напро́тив...	RYAHdahm/ nahPROHteef
There it is. (m/f/n)	Вот он/она́/ оно́.	voht ohn/ahNAH/ ahNOH
This/That way.	Сюда́./Туда́.	syooDAH/tooDAH

Taking a Bus Trip

The Intourist representative of your hotel can help you sign up for the bus tours available in that city.

English	Russian	Pronunciation
What sights should we see?	Какие здесь достоприме- чательности?	kahKEEyeh zdyehs dahstahpreemee- CHAHteel'nahstee
Where can I sign up for an excursion?	Где можно записаться на экскурсию?	gdyeh MOHZHnah zahpeeSAHTsah nah ehksKOOR- seeyoo
What excursion do you suggest?	Какую экскурсию вы мне посоветуете?	kahKOOyoo ehks- KOORseeyoo vih mnyeh pahsahv- YEHtooeetyeh
I want to take a bus trip around the city.	Я хочу записаться на экскурсию по городу.	yah khahCHOO zah- peeSAHTsah nah ehksKOORseeyoo pah GOHrahdoo
I'd like to sign up for this excursion.	Я хотел(а) бы записаться на эту экскурсию.	yah khahtYEHL(ah) bih zapeeSAHT- sah nah EHtoo ehksKOORseeyoo
Do I have to sign up in advance?	Мне надо заранее заказать билеты?	mnyeh NAHdah zahRAHNeeyeh zahkahzAHT' beeLYEHtih
What does a ticket cost?	Сколько стоит билет?	SKOHL'kah STOHeet beelYEHT
When does it leave?	Когда отходит экскурсию?	kahgDAH ahtKHOH- deet ehksKOOR- seeyoo
How long does it last?	Как долго длится экскурсию?	kahk DOHLgah DLEEtsah ehksKOORseeyoo
When do we get back?	Когда мы вернёмся?	kahgDAH mih veernYOHMsah
Will we stop somewhere for lunch?	Мы где-то обедаем?	mih gdyehtah ahBYEHdaheem

75

From where does the excursion leave?	Откýда отхóдит экскýрсию?	ahtKOOdah ahtKHOHdeet ehksKOORseeyoo
Tour guide.	Экскурсовóд.	ehkskoorsahvOHT
Is there an English-speaking guide?	Есть экскуросовóд, говорáщий по-англи́йски?	yehst' ehkskoorsahv -OHT gahvah- RYAHshcheey pahahngLEEYskee
Will we have free time there?	Бýдет у нас свобóдное врéмя там?	BOOdeet oo nahs svahBOHdnahyeh VRYEHmyah tahm
When should we be back on the bus?	Во скóлько мы должны́ вернýться к автóбусу?	vahSKOHL'kah mih dahlzhNIH veerNYOOtsah kahfTOHboosoo

Taking a Walking Tour

Guided walking tours are available in most larger museums.

When does it open/close?	Когдá открывáется/ закрывáется?	kahgDAH ahtkrih- VAHeetsah/zah- krihVAHeetsah
I want to sign up for a tour.	Я хочý записáться на экскýрсию.	yah khahCHOO zah- peeSAHTsah nah ehksKOORseeyoo
When does it start/end?	Когдá онá начинáется/ конча́ется?	kahgDAH ahNAH nahchehNAHeetsah /kahnCHAHeetsah
What is the cost?	Скóлько стóит билéт?	SKOHL'kah STOHeet beelYEHT
Free admission.	Вход безплáтный.	fkhoht beesPLAHTnihy
Is there an English-speaking guide?	Есть ли экскурсовóд, говорáщий по-англи́йски?	yehst' lee ehkskoor- sahvOHT gahvah- RYAHshcheey pahahngLEEYskee
Do you sell guidebooks in English?	У вас есть путеводи́тель на англи́йском языке́?	oo vahs yehst' poo- teevahDEEteel' nah ahngLEEYskahm yeezIHKyeh

76

Is there a map?	Эсть у вас план?	yehst' oo vahs plahn
In front of...	Впереди́...	vpeereeDEE
To the rear of...	Позади́...	pahzahDEE
In the middle of...	Посереди́не...	pahseereeDEEnyeh
On the left of...	Сле́ва...	SLYEHvah
On the right of...	Спра́ва...	SPRAHvah
Where can I buy post cards?	Где мо́жно купи́ть откры́тки?	gdyeh MOHZHnah kooPEET' ahtKRIHTkee
May I see what post cards you have for sale?	Мо́жно посмотре́ть каки́е у вас откры́тки?	MOHZHnah pahsmahtRYEHT' kahKEEyeh oo vahs ahtKRIHTkee
I'd like to buy this set.	Я куплю́ э́тот компле́кт.	yah koopLYOO EHtaht kahmpLYEHKT
How much is it?	Ско́лько сто́ит?	SKOHL'kah STOHeet
Can I take pictures?	Мо́жно здесь фотографи́ровать?	MOHZHnah zdyehs fahtahgrahFEER-ahvaht'
No cameras allowed.	Фотографи́ровать воспреща́ется.	fahtahgrahFEER-ahvaht' vahspree-SHCHAHeetsah

Taking in the Sights

I want to see the sights.	Я хочу́ осма́тривать достоприме-ча́тельности.	yah khahCHOO ahs-MAHTreevaht' dahstahpreemee-CHAHteel'nahstee
Let's go for a walk.	Дава́йте погуля́ем.	dahVAYtyeh pahgooLYAHeem
What kind of ... is that?	Что э́то за...?	shtoh EHtah zah

English	Russian	Pronunciation
animal/bird/ fish/ flower/ tree.	живо́тное/ пти́ца/ ры́ба/ цвето́к/ де́рево.	zheeVOHTnahyeh/ PTEEtsah/ RIHBah/ tsveeTOHK/ deeRYEHvah
We don't have those at home.	У нас нет таки́х.	oo nahs nyeht tahkEEKH
What a beautiful view!	Како́й прекра́сный вид!	kahKOY preeKRAHSnihy veet
What's that building?	Что э́то за зда́ние?	shtoh EHtah zah ZDAHneeyeh
When was it built?	Когда́ оно́ бы́ло постро́ено?	kahgDAH ahNOH BIHlah pahst- ROHeenah
Who built it?	Кто его́ постро́ил?	ktoh yeeVOH pahstROHeel
Who was the architect/ artist?	Кто был архите́ктором/ худо́жником?	ktoh bihl ahrkheeTYEHK- tahrahm/khood- OHZHneekahm
When did he/she live?	Когда́ он/она́ жил(а́)?	kahgDAH ohn/ahNAH zheel(AH)
Where's the house where ... lived?	Где дом, в кото́ром жил(а́)...?	gdyeh dohm fkah- TOHrahm zheel(AH)
Can we go in?	Мо́жно войти́?	MOHZHnah vahyTEE
Very inter- esting.	О́чень интере́сно.	OHcheen' eenteerYEHSnah
It's...	Это...	EHtah
beautiful.	краси́во.	krahSEEvah
ugly.	безобра́зно.	beezahbRAHZnah
wonderful.	прекра́сно.	preeKRAHSnah
horrible.	ужа́сно.	ooZHAHSnah
great.	великоле́пно.	veeleekahLYEHPnah
terrible.	стра́шно.	STRAHSHnah
amazing.	удиви́тельно.	oodeeveeTYEHL'nah
strange.	стра́нно.	STRAHNnah
cute.	ми́ло.	MEElah
sinister.	жу́тко.	ZHOOTkah

English	Russian	Pronunciation
Let's rest.	Дава́йте отдохнём.	dahVAYtyeh ahtdahkhNYOHM
I'm tired.	Я уста́л(а).	yah oostAHL(ah)
I'm bored.	Мне ску́чно.	mnyeh SKOOCHnah

Worship Services

Most places of worship do not mind visitors, as long as you observe their customs and do not disturb their services. Orthodox churches demand that women wear skirts and cover their heads with a kerchief or hat. Taking pictures inside churches is usually not permitted.

English	Russian	Pronunciation
Worship services.	Богослуже́ния.	bahgahsloozhEHNeeyah
Monastary.	Ла́вра.	LAHVrah
Cathedral.	Собо́р.	sahbOHR
Church.	Це́рковь.	TSEHRkahf'
Synagogue.	Синаго́га.	seenahGOHgah
Temple.	Храм.	khrahm
Mosque.	Мече́ть.	meechEHT'
Orthodox.	Правосла́вный.	prahvahSLAHVnihy
Old-Believers.	Старо-обря́дцы.	stahrah-ahbRYAHTtsih
Saint.	Свято́й.	sveeTOY
Altar.	Алта́рь.	ahlTAHR'
Iconostasis.	Иконоста́с.	eekahnahSTAHS
Icons.	Ико́ны.	eeKOHnih
Incense.	Ла́дан.	LAHdahn
Candle.	Свеча́.	sveeCHAH
Contribution.	Поже́ртвование.	pahzhEHRTvahvahneeyeh
Prayers.	Моли́твы.	mahLEETvih
Prayer book.	Моли́твенник.	mahLEETveenneek
Rabbi.	Равви́н.	rahvVEEN
Priest.	Свяще́нник.	sveeshchEHNneek
When's the service?	Когда́ слу́жба?	kahgDAH SLOOSHbah
I want to look around the church.	Я хочу́ осмотре́ть це́рковь.	yah khahCHOO ahsmahtRYEHT' TSEHRkahf'

English	Russian	Pronunciation
You must cover your head.	Вам надо покрывать голову.	vahm NAHdah pahkrihvAHT' GOHlahvoo
Are women allowed?	Женщины допускают?	ZHEHNshcheenih dahpoosKAHyoot
May I take a picture?	Можно здесь фотографировать?	MOHZHnah zdyehs fahtahgrahFEER-ahvaht'
No cameras allowed.	Фотографировать воспрещается.	fahtahgrahFEER-ahvaht' vahspree-SHCHAHeetsah
Cemetary.	Кладбище.	KLAHTbeeshcheh
Grave.	Могила.	mahGEElah
Tombstone.	Надгробный камень.	nahdGROHBnihy KAHmeen'

Outdoor Recreation

English	Russian	Pronunciation
I enjoy...	Мне нравится...	mnyeh NRAHveetsah
running.	бегать.	BYEHgaht'
cycling.	велоспорт.	veelahSPOHRT
tennis.	теннис.	TYEHNnees
horseback riding.	кататься верхом.	kahTAHTsah veerkhAHM
swimming.	плавание.	PLAHvahneeyeh
sailing.	катанне на парусной лодке.	kahTAHneeyeh nah PAHroosnay LOHTkyeh
mountain climbing.	альпинизм.	ahl'peeNEEZM
skiing.	кататься на лыжах.	kahTAHTsah nah LIHZHahkh
skating.	кататься на коньках.	kahTAHTsah nah kahn'KAHKH
I want to play tennis.	Я хочу играть в теннис.	yah khahCHOO eegRAHT' FTYEHNnees
Can we rent rackets?	Можно взять напрокат ракеты?	MOHZHnah vzyaht' nahprahKAHT rahKYEHtih
Are there courts here?	Эсть ли здесь корты?	yehst' lee zdyehs KOHRtih

Is there a swimming pool here?	Есть ли здесь бассе́йн?	yehst' lee zdyehs bahsSEYN
Can one go swimming here?	Мо́жно здесь купа́ться?	MOHZHnah zdyehs kooPAHTsah
Is it safe to swim here?	Здесь не опа́сно купа́ться?	zdyehs nee ahpAHSnah kooPAHTsah
Is the water here deep?	Вода́ здесь глубока́?	vahDAH zdyehs gloobahKAH
Is the water cold?	Вода́ холо́дная?	vahDAH khahLOHDnahyah
No Swimming.	Купа́ться воспреща́ется.	kooPAHTsah vahs-preeSHCHAHeetsah
I want to lie on the beach.	Я хочу́ лежа́ть на пля́же.	yah khahCHOO leezhAHT' nah PLYAHzheh
I want to sunbathe.	Я хочу́ загора́ть.	yah khahCHOO zahgahrYAHT'
Can I rent...	Мо́жно взять напрока́т...	MOHZHnah vzyaht' nahprahKAHT
a beach chair?	шезло́нг?	shehzLOHNG
a sun umbrella?	зо́нтик?	ZOHNteek
a row boat?	ло́дку?	LOHTkoo
water skis?	во́дные лы́жи?	VOHDnihyeh LIHZHee
skiing equipment?	лы́жное снаряже́ние?	LIHZHnahyeh snah-reeZHEHneeyeh
skates?	коньки́?	KOHN'kee
What's the charge per hour/per day?	Ско́лько сто́ит на час/день?	SKOHL'kah STOHeet nah chahs/dyehn'
Is there a skating rink here?	Есть ли здесь като́к?	yehst' lee zdyehs kahTOHK
Where can I go skiing?	Где мо́жно ката́ться на лы́жах?	gdyeh MOHZHnah kahTAHTsah nah LIHZHahkh

81

Camping

English	Russian	Pronunciation
Camping.	Кéмпинг.	KYEHMpeeng
Camping equipment.	Оборýдование для кéмпинга.	ahbahROOdahvah-neeyeh dlyah KYEHMpeengah
Camping permit.	Разрешéние на кéмпинг.	rahzreeSHEHneeyeh nah KYEHMpeeng
Can we camp here?	Мóжно здесь устрóить стоя́нку?	MOHZHnah zdyehs' oosTROHeet' stahYAHNkoo
What's the charge per day?/per person?	Скóлько стóит на день?/на человéка?	SKOHL'kah STOHeet nah dyehn'/nah chehlahVYEHKah
Are there showers/ toilets?	Эсть душ/ убóрная?	yehst' doosh/ oobOHRnahyah
Where are the toilets?	Где убóрная?	gdyeh ooBOHRnahyah
Can we light a fire here?	Мóжно здесь разжéчь костёр?	MOHZHnah zdyehs' rahzZHEHCH kahstYOHR
Is there electricity?	Эсть электри́чество?	yehst' ehleekTREE-chehstvah
Is swimming allowed?	Мóжно здесь купáться?	MOHZHnah zdyehs' kooPAHTsah
Can we fish here?	Мóжно здесь ловѝть рыбу?	MOHZHnah zdyehs' lahvEET' RIHBoo
Do we need a liscense to fish?	Нáдо имéть разрешéние на рыбную лóвлю?	NAHdah eemYEHT' rahzreeSHEHnee-yeh nah RIHBnoo-yoo LOHVlyoo
Can we rent equipment?	Мóжно взять напрокáт оборýдование для кéмпинга?	MOHZHnah vzyaht' nahprahKAHT ahbahROOdahvah-neeyeh dlyah KYEHMpeengah
Where can we get (a) ...	Где мóжно достáть...	gdyeh MOHZHnah dahsTAHT'
corkscrew?	штóпор?	SHTOHpahr
candles?	свéчки?	SVYEHCHkee

can opener?	консéрвный нож?	kahnSYEHRVnihy nohsh
charcoal?	древéсный ýголь?	dreeVYEHSnihy OOGahl'
compass?	кóмпас?	KOHMpahs
cooking utensils?	кýхонные принадлéжности?	KOOkhahnnihyeh preenahdLYEHZHnahstee
cooler?	сýмка- тéрмос?	SOOMkah- TYEHRmahs
fire wood?	дровá?	drahVAH
first-aid kit?	аптéчку?	ahpTYEHCHkoo
flashlight?	кармáнный фонáрь?	kahrMAHNnihy fahnAHR'
groundsheet?	постúлку под палáтку?	pahsTEELkoo paht pahLAHTkoo
kerosene?	керосúн?	keerahSEEN
lantern?	фонáрь?	fahnAHR'
mattress?	матрáс?	mahtRAHS
sleeping bag?	спáльный мешóк?	SPAHL'nihy meeshOHK
tent?	палáтку?	pahLAHTkoo
thermos?	тéрмос?	TYEHRmahs

Public Baths

Russian public baths usually have saunas and pools where you can relax Russian-style. After sitting for awhile in the sauna, it is a Russian custom to beat oneself lightly with dried birch switches.

Public bath.	Бáня.	BAHNyah
Men.	Мужчúны.	mooshCHEEnih
Women.	Жéнщины.	ZHEHNshcheenih
What's the admission?	Скóлько стóит вход?	SKOHL'kah STOHeet fxoht
I'd like to rent...	Я хотéл(а) бы взять напрокáт...	yah khahtYEHL(ah) bih vzyaht' nahprahKAHT
a towel.	полотéнце.	pahleeTYEHNtseh
a sheet.	простыню́.	prahstihnYOO

83

It's too hot/cold here.	Здесь слишком жа́рко/ хо́лодно.	zdyehs SLEESHkahm ZHAHRkah/ KHOHlahdnah
Shower.	Душ.	doosh
Pool.	Бассе́йн.	bahsSEYN
Bathing cap.	Купа́льная ша́почка.	kooPAHL'nahyah SHAHPahchkah
Bathing suit.	Купа́льный костю́м.	kooPAHL'nihy kahstYOOM
Soap.	Мы́ло.	MIHlah
Bucket.	Ведро́.	veedROH
Steam room.	Пари́льня	pahrEEL'nyah
Birch switches.	Берёзовые пру́тья.	beerYOHZahvihyeh PROOt'yah
Massage.	Масса́ж.	mahsSAHSH

X. ENTERTAINMENT

Tickets

Tickets can be purchased most easily from Intourist for dollars. You can also try your luck at buying tickets from kiosks on the street, but do not expect to get your first choice. Russians are avid theatergoers and most performances sell out quickly. If you really want to see a particular performance, you can go down to the theater a little early and try to buy spare tickets (ли́шние биле́ты) from people outside the theater. This is not only accepted behavior, it is actually quite common.

English	Russian	Pronunciation
Tickets.	Биле́ты.	beelYEHTih
(Theater) box office.	(Театра́льная) ка́сса.	(teeahTRAHL'nahyah) KAHSsah
Ticket window.	Биле́тная ка́сса.	beelYEHTnahyah KAHSsah
Can you recommend a(n) opera/ concert/ play?	Мо́жете ли вы мне рекоменд- ова́ть о́перу/ конце́рт/ пье́су?	MOHZHehtyeh lee vih mnyeh reehk- ahmeendahvAHT' OHPeeroo/kahnts- EHRT/P'YEHsoo
Have you any tickets for tonight's performance?	У вас есть биле́ты на сего́дняшний спекта́кль?	oo vahs yehst' beelYEHTih nah seeVOHDneesh- neey speekTAHKL'
How much are they?	Ско́лько сто́ит?	SKOHL'kah STOHeet
I'd like two for...	Я хоте́л(а) бы два на...	yah khahtYEHL(ah) bih dvah nah
We're sold out.	Все биле́ты про́даны.	vsyeh beelYEHTih PROHdahnih
What time does it begin?	Во ско́лько начина́ет спекта́кль?	vah SKOHL'kah nahcheeNAHeet speekTAHKL'
How do I get to this theater?	Как мне дойти́ до э́того теа́тра?	kahk mnyeh dahy- TEE dah EHtahvah teeAHtrah

The Bolshoi Theater.	Большой Театр.	bahl'SHOY teeAHTR
The Kremlin Palace of Congresses.	Кремлёвский Дворец съездов.	kreemLYOHFskeey dvahrYEHTS S"YEHSdahf
Chaikovsky Conservatory.	Концертный зал имени Чайковского.	kahntsEHRTnihy zahl EEMeennee chayKOHFskahvah
No admittance after the third bell.	Вход в зрительный зал после третьего звонка воспрещён.	fxoht VZREEteel'-nihy zahl POHslee TRYEHt'ehvah zvahnKAH vahspreeshchOHN
Orchestra stalls.	Партер.	pahrtYEHR
Amphitheater.	Амфитеатр.	ahmfeeteeAHTR
Balcony.	Балкон.	bahlKOHN
Box.	Ложа.	LOHzhah
Left side.	Левая сторона.	LYEHvahyah stahrahNAH
Right side.	Правая сторона.	PRAHvahyah stahrahNAH
Middle.	Середина.	seereeDEEnah
Lobby.	Фойе.	foyYEH
Snack bar.	Буфет.	boofYEHT
Smoking room.	Курительная комната.	kooREEteel'nahyah KOHMnahtah
Cloakroom.	Гардероб.	gahrdeerOHP
Cloakroom attendant. (f)	Гардеробщик/ Гардеробщица.	gahrdeerOHP-shcheek/gahrdeer-OHPshcheetsah
Entrance to auditorium.	Вход в зрительный зал.	fxoht VZREEteel'-nihy zahl
Exit.	Выход.	VIHkhat

Theater and Movies

Movies are shown all day long and cost very little. No one is admitted after the lights are turned off and Russians typically keep their coats on in the theater.

Play.	Пьеса.	P'YEHsah
Performance.	Спектакль.	speekTAHKL'
Movie.	Кино.	keeNOH
Theater.	Театр.	teeAHTR
What's at the... ?	Что идёт в... ?	shtoh eedYOHT f
What kind of play/movie is it?	Что это за пьеса/ фильм?	shtoh EHtah zah P'YEHsah/ feel'm
It's a...	Это...	EHtah
cartoon.	мультфильм.	mool'tFEEL'M
comedy.	комедия.	kahMYEHdeeyah
documen- tary.	документальный фильм.	dahkoomeentAHL'- nihy feel'm
drama.	драматический фильм.	drahmahTEEchehs- keey feel'm
Who's the director?	Кто режиссёр?	ktoh reezheesSYOHR
Who's playing the lead?	Кто играет главную роль?	ktoh eegRAHeet GLAHVnooyoo rohl'
Are there any tickets left?	Остались лишние билеты?	ahSTAHlees' LEESHneeyeh beelYEHTih
Is there a matinee?	Есть дневной спектакль?	yehst' dneevNOY speekTAHKL'
When does the show begin?	Когда начинается спектакль?	kahgDAH nahcheeNAHeet- sah speekTAHKL'
Do you have any extra tickets?	У вас есть лишние?	oo vahs yehst' LEESHneeyeh

Opera, Concerts and Ballet

Tickets to the Bolshoi Theater are practically impossible to get unless you buy them for dollars through the Intourist office in your hotel.

Opera.	Опера.	OHPeerah
Concert.	Концерт.	kahntsEHRT
Ballet.	Балет.	bahlYEHT
Orchestra.	Оркестр.	ahrkYEHSTR

English	Russian	Pronunciation
Folk songs/ dances.	Наро́дные пе́сни/ та́нцы.	nahROHDnihyeh PYEHSnee/ TAHNtsih
Here is my ticket.	Вот моя́ биле́т.	voht moy beelYEHT
Where is my seat?	Где моё ме́сто?	gdyeh mahYOH MYEHstah
Follow me.	Сле́дуйте за мной.	SLYEHdooytyeh zah mnoy
How much for a program?	Ско́лько сто́ит програ́мму?	SKHOL'kah STOHeet prahgRAHMmoo
May I have a program, please?	Да́йте, пожа́луйста, програ́мму.	DAYtyeh pahZHAHLstah prahgRAHMmoo
Want to rent opera glasses?	Бино́кль вам ну́жен?	beeNOHKL' vahm NOOZHehn
No, thank you. I don't need them.	Нет, спаси́бо. Они́ мне не на́до.	nyeht spahSEEbah ahNEE mnyeh nee NAHdah
Who is the conductor?	Кто дирижёр?	ktoh deereezhOHR
Who is dancing the lead?	Кто танцу́ет гла́вную па́ртию?	ktoh tahnTSOOeht GLAHVnooyoo PAHRteeyoo
Who is the soloist?(f)	Кто соли́ст(ка)?	ktoh sahlEEST(kah)
When is the inter- mission?	Когда́ антра́кт?	kahgDAH ahnTRAHKT
How long is the inter- mission?	Как до́лго антра́кт?	kahk DOHLgah ahnTRAHKT
Pardon me, can I get by?	Прости́те, мо́жно пройти́?	prahsTEEtyeh MOHZHnah prahyTEE
That's my seat.	Это моё ме́сто.	EHtah mahYOH MYEHstah

Circus and Puppet Show

Circus.	Цирк.	tseerk

Puppet theater.	Кукольный театр.	KOOkahl'nihy teeAHTR
Do you have tickets for the circus/ puppet theater?	У вас есть билеты на цирк/ кукольный театр?	oo vahs yehst' beelYEHTih nah tseerk/ KOOkahl'nihy teeAHTR
How do I get to the circus?	Как мне пойти до парка?	kahk mnyeh dahyTEE dah TSEERkah
Is there a matinee today?	Есть ли сегодня дневной спектакль?	yehst' lee seeVOHdnyah dneevNOY speekTAHKL'
Do you have a spare ticket?	У вас есть лишний билет?	oo vahs yehst' LEESHneey beelYEHT
Give me a program, please.	Дайте мне, программу, пожалуйста..	DAYtyeh mnyeh prahgRAHMmoo pahZHAHLstah

Sporting Events

Sporting events.	Спортивные соревнование.	spahrTEEVnihyeh sahreevnahVAHneeyeh
Sports fan. I want to see a hockey/ soccer game.	Болельщик. Я хочу посмотреть хоккейный/ футбольный матч.	bahlYEHLshcheek yah khahCHOO pahsmahTRYEHT' khahkKEYnihy/ footBOHL'nihy mahtch
How much are the tickets?	Сколько стоит билеты?	SKOHL'kah STOHeet beelYEHTih
Are there any tickets for today's game?	Есть билеты на сегодняшний матч?	yehst' beelYEHTih nah seeVOHdnyeeshneey mahtch
How do I get to Lenin Stadium?	Как мне поехать до Ленинского стадиона?	kahk mnyeh dahYEHkhat' dah leenEENskahvah stahdeeOHNah

Who is playing?	Какие команды играют?	kahKEEyeh kahMAHNdih eegRAHyoot
Scoreboard.	Табло.	tahbLOH
Who is winning?	Кто выигрывает?	ktoh vihEEGrih-vaheet
What's the score?	Какой счёт?	kahKOY shchoht
Dynamo are ahead 3-1.	Три один в пользу Динамо.	tree ahdEEN FPOHL'zoo deeNAHmoh
It's score-less.	Это нулевой.	EHtah nooleeVOY
Score a point.	Выиграть очко.	VIHeegraht' ahchKOH
Score a goal.	Забить гол.	zahBEET' gohl
Who won?	Кто выиграл?	ktoh VIHeegrahl
Scoreless tie.	Нулевая ничья.	nooleeVAHyah neechYAH
Do you want to play chess?	Вы хотите играть в шахматы?	vih khahTEEtyeh eegRAHT' FSHAHKHmahtih
Check mate.	Мат.	maht

90

XI. STORES

Moscow has two large department stores, known as GUM (State Department Store) and TSUM (Central Department Store), which are open from 8 am to 9:30 pm. Food stores typically open at 9 am and close at 8 pm. Other shops, like bookstores and souvenir shops, are open from 11 am to 8 pm. Most stores, except those selling food, are closed on Sundays.

Finding the Right Store

The easiest and most convenient, although also the most expensive, stores for foreigners are the hard-currency stores or Beryozkas. Specifically set aside for foreigners, these stores accept only foreign currency and credit cards. The staff usually speaks some English and the shelves are stocked with items unavailable in Soviet stores.

Where can I buy...?	Где можно купить...?	gdyeh MOHZHnah kooPEET'
Where can I find a...?	Где мне найти...?	gdyeh mnyeh nahyTEE
Is there a ... near here?	Есть ли поблизости...	yehst' lee pahbLEEzahstee
bakery.	булочная.	BOOlahchnahyah
bookstore.	книжный магазин.	KNEEZHnihy mahgahZEEN
candy shop.	кондитерская.	kahnDEEteerskahyah
clothes store.	одежда./дом моды.	ahdYEHZHdah/dohm MOHdih
dairy.	молочная.	mahLOHCHnahyah
department store.	универмаг.	ooneeveerMAHK
drug store.	аптека.	ahpTYEHkah
farmers' market.	рынок.	RIHnahk
fish market.	рыбный магазин.	RIHBnihy mahgahZEEN

91

fruit and vegetable store.	фру́кты и о́вощи.	FROOKtih ee OHVahchshee
furrier.	меха́.	meeKHAH
gift shop.	пода́рки.	pahdAHRkee
greengrocer.	зеленщи́к.	zeeleenSHCHEEK
grocery.	проду́кты.	prahDOOKtih
Beryozka.	Берёзка.	beerYOHSkah
hat shop.	магази́н головны́х убо́ров.	mahgahZEEN gahlahvNIHKH ooBOHrahf
jeweler.	ювели́рный магази́н.	yooveelEERnihy mahgahZEEN
liquor store.	вино́.	veeNAH
newsstand.	союзпеча́ть.	sahyoozpeeCHAHT'
record store.	грампласти́нки.	grahmplahstEENkee
secondhand bookstore.	букинисти́ческий магази́н.	bookeeneestEECHeh-skeey mahgahZEEN
secondhand store.	комиссио́нный магази́н.	kahmeesseeOHNnihy mahgahZEEN
shoe store.	Обувы.	OHBoovih
souvenirs.	сувени́ры.	sooveeNEErih
stationary.	канцтова́ры.	kahntstahVAHrih
tobacconist.	таба́к.	tahBAHK
toy store.	магази́н игру́шек.	mahgahZEEN eegROOSHehk

Looking Around

Service.	Обслужива́ние.	ahploozheeVAH-neeyeh
Can you help me...	Бу́дьте добры́...	BOOt'tyeh dahbRIH
Where's the ... department?	Где нахо́дится отде́л...	gdyeh nahKHOHdee-tsah ahtTYEHL
Can I help you?	Слу́шаю вас.	slooSHAHyoo vahs
Do you have...	Есть ли у вас...	yehst' lee oo vahs
What kind of ... would you like?	Како́й ... вы хоти́те?	kahKOY ... vih khahTEEtyeh

(handwritten: Please give me)

(handwritten: I listen)

(handwritten next to Обслужива́ние: Be so kind)

92

I'd like...	Я хотéл(а) бы...	yah khahtYEHL(ah) bih
I'm sorry, we don't have any.	Простúте, этого у нас нет.	prahsTEEtyeh EHtahvah oo nahs nyeht
We're sold out.	Всё распрóдано.	vsyoh rahsPROH-dahnah
Anything else?	Ещё чтó-нибудь?	yeeSHCHOH SHTOH-neeboot'
Show me (this/that), please.	Покажúте мне (это/тó), пожáлуйста.	pahkahZHEEtyeh mneyh (EHtah/toh) pahZHAHLstah
No, not that, but that there...next to it.	Нет, не это, а вот это...рáдом.	nyeht nee EHtah ah voht EHtah... RYAHdahm
It's not what I want.	Это не тó, чтó я хочý.	EHtah nee toh shtoh yah khahCHOO
I don't like it.	Это мне не прáвится.	mnyeh EHtah nee NRAHveetsah
I'm just looking.	Я тóлько смотрю́.	yah TOHL'kah smahtRYOO
I prefer...	Я предпочитáю...	yah preetpahchee-TAHyoo
Something not too expensive.	Чтó-нибудь не óчень дорогóе.	shtahneeBOOT' nee OHcheen' dahrah-GOHyeh
How much is it?	Скóлько это стóит?	SKHOL'kah EHtah STOHeet
Repeat that, please.	Повторúте, пожáлуйста.	pahftahREEtyeh pahZHAHLstah
Please write it down.	Пожáлуйста, напишúте.	pahZHAHLstah nahpeeSHEEtyeh

Making a Purchase

Shopping in the Soviet Union is an adventure. There are usually several steps involved in making a purchase. First, you choose your merchandise and take note of the price. Next, you go to the register and pay for it, receiving a чек (receipt) in return. Finally, you take this receipt to another counter where you receive your purchase.

Have you decided?	Вы решили?	vih reeSHEElee
Yes, I want this.	Да, я хочу́ э́то.	dah yah khahCHOO EHtah
I'll take it.	Я возьму́ э́то.	yah vahz'MOO EHtah
Will I have problems with customs?	Бу́дут ли у меня́ тру́дности на тамо́жне?	BOOdoot lee oo meenYAH TROOdnahstee nah tahMOHZHnyeh
Pay at the cashier.	Плати́те в ка́ссу.	plahTEEtyeh FKAHSsoo
Do you accept traveler's checks/ credit cards/ dollars?	Вы берёте доро́жные че́ки/ креди́тные ка́рточки/ до́ллары?	vih beeRYOHtyeh dahROHZHnihyeh SHEHkee/ kreeDEETnihyeh KAHRtahchkee/ DOHLlahrih
Can I have a receipt, please.	Да́йте, пожа́луйста, квита́нцию.	DAYtyeh pahZHAHLstah kveeTAHNtseeyoo
Wrap it up for me, please.	Заверни́те, пожа́луйста.	zahveerNEEtyeh pahZHAHLstah
Please give me a bag.	Да́йте мне су́мку, пожа́луйста.	DAYtyeh mnyeh SOOMkoo pahZHAHLstah

XII. SHOPPING

Gifts and Souvenirs

Before buying gifts for hard currency at the Beryozkas, you might try shopping in a Подарки or Сувинеры store, where you can often find the same merchandise for cheaper prices in rubles.

Amber.	Янтарь.	yeenTAHR'
Balalaika.	Балалайка.	bahlahLAYkah
Books.	Книги.	KNEEgee
Box of candy.	Коробка конфét.	kahROHPkah kahnFYEHT
Caviar.	Икрá.	eekRAH
Ceramics.	Керáмика.	keeRAHmeekah
Chess set.	Шáхматы.	SHAHKHmahtih
Chocolate.	Шоколáд.	shahkahLAHT
Cigarettes.	Сигарéты.	seegahRYEHtih
Cigarette case.	Папирóсница.	pahpeeROHSneetsah
Cigarette lighter.	Зажигáлка.	zahzheeGAHLkah
Coins.	Монéты.	mahNYEHtih
Fur hat.	Меховáя шáпка.	meekhahVAHyah SHAHPkah
Icon.	Икóна.	eeKOHnah
Jewelry.	Драгоцéнности.	drahgahTSEHNahstee
Lace.	Кружевá.	kroozhehVAH
Nested wooden doll.	Матрёшка.	mahtRYOHSHkah
Palekh boxes.	Пáлехские шкатýлы.	PAHleekhskeeyeh shkahTOOlih
Perfume.	Духú.	dooKHEE
Postcards.	Открытки.	ahtKRIHTkee
Posters.	Плакáты.	plahKAHtih
Records.	Пластúнки.	plahstEENkee
Samovar.	Самовáр.	sahmahVAHR
Scarf.	Шáрф.	shahrf
Shawl.	Платóк.	plahTOHK
Stamps.	Мáрки.	MAHRkee

Tapes.	Кассе́ты.	kahsSYEHtih
Tea caddy.	Ча́йница.	CHAYneetsah
Toys.	Игру́шки.	eegROOSHkee
Vodka.	Во́дка.	VOHTkah
Wine.	Вино́.	veeNOH
Wood carvings.	Резьба́ по де́реву.	rees'BAH pah DYEHreevoo
Wooden spoons and bowls.	Деревя́нные ло́жки и ми́ски.	deereevYAHNnihyeh LOSHkee ee MEESkee

Jewelry

Jewelry department.	Ювели́рные изде́лия.	yooveelEERnihyeh eezDYEHleeyah
Jewelry.	Драгоце́нности.	drahgahTSEHN-nahstee
Bracelet.	Брасле́т.	brahsLYEHT
Brooch.	Брошь.	brohsh
Chain.	Цепо́чка.	tseePOHCHkah
Charm.	Брело́к.	breeLOHK
Clips.	Клипс.	kleeps
Cufflinks.	За́понки.	ZAHpahnkee
Earrings.	Се́рьги.	SYEHR'gee
Money clip.	Де́нежная скре́пка.	DYEHneezhnahyah SKRYEHPkah
Necklace.	Ожере́лье.	ahzheeRYEHL'yeh
Pendant.	Куло́н.	kooLOHN
Ring.	Кольцо́.	kahl'TSOH
Tie pin.	Була́вка для га́лстука.	booLAHFkah dlyah GAHLstookah
Watch.	Часы́.	cheeSIH

Stones and Metals

What's it made of?	Из чего́ э́то сде́лано?	ees cheeVOH EHtah ZDYEHlahnah
Is it real silver/gold?	Это настоя́щее серебро́/ зо́лото?	EHtah nahstahYAH-shchehyeh seereebROH/ ZOHlahtah

English	Russian	Pronunciation
How many carats is this?	Ско́лько здесь кара́тов?	SKOHL'kah zdyehs' kahRAHTahf
What kind of metal/ stone is it?	Что э́то за мета́лл/ ка́мень?	shtoh EHtah zah meetAHL/ KAHmeen'
Amber.	Янта́рь.	yeenTAHR'
Amethyst.	Амети́ст.	ahmeetEEST
Copper.	Медь.	myeht'
Coral.	Кора́лл.	kahrAHL
Crystal.	Хруста́ль.	khroosTAHL'
Diamond.	Бриллиа́нт.	breelleeAHNT
Ebony.	Чёрное де́рево.	CHOHRnahyeh DYEHreevah
Emerald.	Изумру́д.	eezoomROOT
Garnet.	Грана́т.	grahNAHT
Gilded.	Позоло́ченный.	pahzahLOHCH-ehnneey
Glass.	Стекло́.	steekLOH
Gold.	Зо́лото.	ZOHlahtah
Ivory.	Слоно́вая кость.	slahNOHvahyah kohst'
Jade.	Нефри́т.	neefREET
Onyx.	Они́кс.	ahnEEKS
Pearl.	Же́мчуг.	ZHEHMchook
Pewter.	О́лово.	OHlahvah
Platinum.	Пла́тина.	PLAHteenah
Ruby.	Руби́н.	rooBEEN
Sapphire.	Сапфи́р.	sahpFEER
Silver.	Серебро́.	seereeBROH
Silver plated.	Сере́бряный.	seeREEbreenihy
Topaz.	Топа́з.	tahPAHS
Turquoise.	Бирюза́.	beeryooZAH

Books and Stationary Supplies

English	Russian	Pronunciation
Bookstore.	Кни́жный магази́н.	KNEEZHnihy mahgahZEEN
Newsstand.	Газе́тный кио́ск.	gahzYEHTnihy keeOHSK
Secondhand bookstore.	Букинисти́ческий магази́н.	bookeeneestEECHeh-skeey mahgahZEEN

Stationary store.	Канцтовáры.	kahntstahVAHrih
Do you have any books in English?	Есть ли у вас кнúги на англúйском язы́ке?	yehst' lee oo vahs KNEEgee nah ahngLEEYskahm yeeZIHkyeh
Do you have any children's books /art books?	Есть ли у вас дéтские кнúги/ кнúги по искýсству?	yehst' lee oo vahs DYEHTskeeyeh KNEEgee/KNEEgee pah eesKOOSTvoo
Where are the guide-books/dic-tionaries?	Где нахóдятся путеводúтели/ словарú?	gdyeh nahKHOH-deetsah pootee-vahDEEteelee/ slahvahREE
How much is this book?	Скóлько стóит э́та кнúга?	SKOHL'kah STOHeet EHtah KNEEgah
Where do I pay?	Где мне платúть?	gdyeh mnyeh plahTEET'
Have you got...	Есть ли у вас...	yehst' lee oo vahs
calendars?	календáры?	kahleenDAHrih
envelopes?	конвéрты?	kahnVYEHRtih
magazines in English?	журнáлы на англúйском язы́ке?	zhoorNAHlih nah ahngLEEYskahm yeeZIHkyeh
maps?	плáны/кáрты?	PLAHnih/KAHRtih
notebooks?	блокнóты.	blahkNOHtih
paper?	бумáгу?	booMAHgoo
pens?	рýчки?	ROOCHkee
pencils?	карандашú?	kahrahndahSHEE
post cards?	откры́тки?	ahtKRIHTkee
stationary?	почтóвую бумáгу?	pachTOHvooyoo booMAHgoo

Records

Records.	Пластúнки.	plahstEENkee
Cassettes.	Кассéты.	kahsSYEHtih
Have you got any rec-ords by...	Есть ли у вас пластúнки...	yehst' lee oo vahs plahstEENkee
Do you have any...	Есть ли у вас...	yehst' lee oo vahs

98

Russian folk songs?	рýсские нарóдные пéсни?	ROOskeeyeh nah-ROHDnihyeh PYEHsnee
music of the peoples of the USSR?	мýзыку нарóдов СССР?	MOOzihkoo nahROHDahf eseseser
poets reading their work?	поэ́ты, чита́ют свои́ стихи́?	pahEHtih cheeTAH-yoot svahEE steeKHEE
classical music?	класси́ческую мýзыку?	klahsSEEchehskoo-yoo MOOzihkoo
popular music?	эстра́дную мýзыку?	ehstRAHDnooyoo MOOzihkoo
recordings of operas and plays?	за́писи óпер и спекта́клей?	ZAHpeesee OHpeer ee speekTAHkley
rock?	рок-н-ролл?	rohk-n-rohl
Can I listen to this record?	Мóжно прослýшать э́ту пласти́нку?	MOHZHnah prahs-LOOshaht' EHtoo plahstEENkoo

Toys

Toys./Games.	Игрýшки./Игры.	eegROOshkee/EEGrih
For a boy.	Для ма́льчика.	dlyah MAHL'cheekah
For a girl.	Для де́вочки.	dlyah DYEHvahchkee
Ball.	Мяч.	myahch
Blocks.	Кýбики.	KOObeenkee
Cards.	Игра́льные ка́рты.	eegRAHL'nihyeh KAHRtih
Checkers.	Ша́шки.	SHAHSHkee
Chess.	Ша́хматы.	SHAHKHmahtih
Doll.	Кýкла.	KOOklah
Electronic game.	Электрóнная игра́.	ehleekTROHNnahyah eegRAH
Stuffed animal.	Чýчело.	CHOOchehlah
Teddy bear.	Ми́шка.	MEESHkah
Wooden toys.	Деревя́нные игрýшки.	deereeVYAHNnihyeh eegROOSHkee

Clothes

Clothes.	Одéжда.	ahDYEHZHdah

99

English	Russian	Pronunciation
Where can I find a...	Где мне найти...	gdyeh mnyeh nahyTEE
bathing cap?	купáльную шáпку?	koopAHL'nooyoo SHAHPkoo
bathing suit?	купáльник?	koopAHL'neek
bathrobe?	халáт?	khahlAHT
belt?	пóяс?	POHyees
blouse?	блýзку?	BLOOSkoo
bra?	бюстгáльтер?	byoozKHAHL'teer
children's clothes?	дéтскую одéжду?	DYEHTskooyoo ahdYEHZHdoo
coat?	пальтó?	pahl'TOH
dress?	плáтье?	PLAHt'yeh
fur coat?	шýбу?	SHOOboo
fur hat?	мехóвую шáпку?	meekhahVOOyoo SHAHPkoo
gloves?	перчáтки?	peerCHAHTkee
handkerchief?	носовóй платóк?	nahsahVOY plahTOHK
hat?	шляпу?	SHLYAHpoo
jacket?	кýртку?	KOORTkoo
panties?	трýски?	TROOSkee
pants?	брюки?	BRYOOkee
pygamas?	пижáму?	peeZHAHmoo
raincoat?	плащ?	plahshch
scarf?	шарф?	shahrf
shirt?	рубáшку?	rooBAHSHkoo
shorts?	шóрты?	SHOHRtih
skirt?	юбку?	YOOPkoo
slip?	комбинáцию?	kahmbeeNAHtseeyoo
socks?	носки?	nahsKEE
stockings?	чулки?	choolKEE
suit?	костюм?	kahstYOOM
sweater?	свúтер?	SVEEteer
sweatsuit?	тренирóвочный костюм?	treeneeROHVahchnihy kahstYOOM
swimming trunks?	плáвки?	PLAHFkee
tie?	гáлстук?	GAHLstook
t-shirt?	мáйку?	MAYkoo
underwear?	нúжнее бельё?	NEEZHnehyeh beel'YOH

100

Fit

English	Russian	Pronunciation
I don't know my size.	Размер не знаю.	rahzMYEHR nee ZNAHyoo
I take a size...	У меня размер...	oo meenYAH rahzMYEHR
Is there a mirror?	Есть ли у вас зеркало?	yehst' lee oo vahs ZYEHRkahlah
Can I try it on?	Можно померить?	MOHZHnah pahMYEHreet'
Where is the fitting-room?	Где примерочная?	gdyeh preemYEHR-ahchnahyah
Does it fit?	Вам годится?/ Хорошо сидит?	vahm gahDEEtsah/ khahrahSHOH seeDEET
It fits well.	Очень хорошо сидит.	OHcheen' khahrah-SHOH seeDEET
It doesn't suit me.	Не годится.	nee gahDEEtsah
It's too...	Слишком...	SLEESHkahm
big/small.	велик/мало.	veeLEEK/MAHlah
long/short.	длинно/коротко.	DLEENnah/ KOHRahtkah
loose/tight.	широко/узко.	sheerahKOH/OOSkah

Colors

English	Russian	Pronunciation
Color.	Цвет.	tsvyeht
What color is it?	Это какого цвета?	EHtah kahKOHvah TSVYEHtah
I don't like the color.	Мне не нравится этот цвет.	mnyeh nee NRAH-veetsah EHtaht tsvyeht
Do you have other colors?	Есть ли у вас другие цветы?	yehst' lee oo vahs drooGEEyeh TSVYEHtih
I'd like something bright.	Я хотел(а) бы что-нибудь яркое.	yah khahtYEHL(ah) bih SHTOHneeboot' YAHRkahyeh
Do you have anything in red?	У вас что-нибудь красного цвета?	oo vahs SHTOH-neeboot' KRAHS-nahvah TSVYEHtah
Red.	Красный.	KRAHSnihy

101

Pink.	Ро́зовый.	ROHzahvihy
Violet.	Фиоле́товый.	feeahLYEHtahvihy
Purple.	Пурпу́рный.	poorPOORnihy
Blue.	Си́ний.	SEEneey
Light blue.	Голубо́й.	gahlooBOY
Green.	Зелёный.	zeeLYOHnihy
Orange.	Ора́нжевый.	ahrAHNzhehvihy
Yellow.	Жёлтый.	ZHOHLtihy
Brown.	Кори́чневый.	kahrEECHneevihy
Beige.	Бе́жевый.	BYEHzhehvihy
Grey.	Се́рый.	SYEHrihy
Black.	Чёрный.	CHOHRnihy
White.	Бе́лый.	BYEHlihy
Light- (+color).	Све́тло-...	SVYEHTlah-
Dark- (+color).	Тёмно-...	TYOHMnah-

Materials and Fabrics

Aluminum.	Алюми́ний.	ahlyooMEEneey
Brass.	Лату́нь.	lahtOON'
Ceramics.	Кера́мика.	keeRAHmeekah
Chiffon.	Шифо́н.	sheeFOHN
China.	Фарфо́р.	fahrFOHR
Copper.	Медь.	myeht'
Corduroy.	Вельве́т.	veel'VYEHT
Cotton.	Хлопчато- бума́жный.	khlahpchahtah- booMAHZHnihy
Crepe.	Креп.	kryehp
Crystal.	Хруста́ль	khroosTAHL'
Fabric.	Ткань.	tkahn'
Felt.	Фетр.	fyehtr
Flannel.	Ба́йка.	BAYkah
Fur.	Мех.	myehkh
Glass.	Стекло́.	steekLOH
Gold.	Зо́лото.	ZOHlahtah
Iron.	Желе́зо.	zheeLYEHzah
Lace.	Кружева́.	kroozhehVAH
Leather.	Ко́жа.	KOHzhah
Linen.	Полотно́.	pahlahtNOH
Metal.	Мета́лл.	meetAHL
Nylon.	Нейло́н.	neyLOHN

Plastic.	Платмácca.	plahtMAHSsah
Satin.	Атлáс.	ahtLAHS
Silk.	Шёлк.	shohlk
Silver.	Серебрó.	seereeBROH
Steel.	Стáль.	stahl'
Stone.	Кáмень.	KAHmeen'
Suede.	Зáмша.	ZAHMshah
Synthetic.	Синтéтика.	seenTYEHteekah
Terrycloth.	Махрóвая ткань.	mahkhROHvahyah tkahn'
Velvet.	Бáрхат.	BAHRkhaht
Wood.	Дéрево.	DYEHreevah
Wool.	Шéрсть.	shehrst'

Shoes

Shoes.	Обувь.	OHboovee
Boots.	Сапогú.	sahpahGEE
Felt boots.	Вáленки.	VAHleenkee
Sandals.	Сандáлии.	sahnDAHleeee
Slippers.	Тáпочки.	TAHpahchkee
Children's shoes.	Дéтские óбувь.	DYEHTskeeyeh OHboovee
Shoelaces.	Шнýрки.	SHNOORkee
Are these made of cloth/ suede/ leather/ rubber?	Онú сдéланны из ткáни/ зáмши/ кóжи/ резúны?	ahNEE ZDYEHlahnnih ees TKAHNee/ ZAHMshee/ KOHzhee/ reeZEEnih
I take a size...	У меня нóмер...	oo meenYAH NOHmeer
I don't know my size.	Нóмера не знáю.	NOHmeerah nee ZNAHyoo
Can I try these on in a size...	Дáйте мне эти по нóмеру....	DAYtyeh mnyeh EHtee pah NOHmeeroo
These are too big/ small/ narrow/ wide.	Онú слúшком бóльшие/ малéнькие/ úзкие/ шúрóкие.	ahNEE SLEESHkahm bahl'SHEEyeh/ mahlYEHN'keeyeh/ OOSkeeyeh / sheeROHkeeyeh

Groceries

Groceries.	Проду́кты.	prahDOOKtih
I'd like...	Я хоте́л(а) бы...	yah khahtYEHL(ah) bih
a piece of that.	кусо́к э́того.	koosOHK EHtahvah
a half kilo...	полкило́...	pohlkeeLOH
a kilo...	килогра́мм...	keelahgRAHMM
one-and-a-half kilos...	полтора́ кило́...	pohltahRAH keeLOH
50 grams...	пятьдеся́т грамм...	peet'deesYAHT grahm
100 grams...	сто грамм...	stoh grahm
a liter of...	литр...	leetr
a bottle of...	буты́лку...	bootIHLkoo
ten eggs.	деся́ток яиц.	deeSYAHtahk yaheets
a packet of cookies/ tea.	па́чку пече́нья/ ча́я.	PAHCHkoo peechEHN'yah/ CHAHyah
a can of pears.	ба́нку гру́шев.	BAHNkoo GROOSHehf
a jar of sour cream.	ба́нку смета́ны.	BAHNkoo smeeTAHnih
a loaf of bread.	буха́нку хле́ба.	bookhAHNkoo KHLYEHbah
a box of candy.	коро́бку конфе́т.	kahROHPkoo kahnFYEHT
a bar of chocolate.	пли́тку шокола́да.	PLEETkoo shahkah-LAHdah

Health and Beauty Aides

Absorbent cotten.	Ва́та.	VAHtah
Antiseptic.	Антисепти́ческая мазь.	ahnteeseepTEECH-eeskahyah mahs'
Aspirin.	Аспири́н.	ahspeerEEN
Ace-bandage.	Эласти́чный би́нт.	ehlahsTEECHnihy beent
Band-Aides.	Пла́стырь.	PLAHStihr'
Bobby-pins.	Зако́лки.	zahKOHLkee
Comb.	Расчёска.	rahsCHOHSkah

English	Russian	Pronunciation
Condoms.	Пресервати́вы.	preeseervahTEEvih
Contraceptives.	Противозачаточные сре́дства.	prahteevahzahCHAHtahchnihyeh SRYEHTstvah
Cough drops.	Табле́тки от ка́шля.	tahbLYEHTkee aht KAHSHlyah
Curlers.	Бигуди́.	beegooDEE
Deodorant.	Дезодора́тор.	deezahdahRAHtahr
Diapers.	Пелёнки.	peelYOHNkee
Disinfectant.	Дизинфици́рующее сре́дство.	deezeenfeeTSEERooyooshchehyeh SRYEHTstvah
Ear drops.	Ушны́е ка́пли.	ooshNIHyeh KAHPlee
Eye drops.	Глазны́е ка́пли.	glahzNIHyeh KAHPlee
Eye liner.	Тушь для век.	toosh dlyah vyehk
Eye shadow.	Те́ни для век.	TYEHnee dlyah vyehk
Hair brush.	Щётка для во́лос.	SHCHOHTkah dlyah VOHlahs
Hair dye.	Кра́ска.	KRAHSkah
Hair spray.	Лак.	lahk
Hand cream.	Крем для рук.	kryehm dlyah rook
Insect repelent.	Сре́дство от комаро́в.	SRYEHTstvah aht kahmahrOHF
Iodine.	Йод.	yoht
Laxative.	Слаби́тельное.	slahBEEteel'nahyeh
Lipstick	Губна́я пома́да.	goobNAHyah pahMAHdah
Make-up.	Косме́тика.	kahsMYEHteekah
Mascara.	Тушь для ресни́ц.	toosh dlyah reesNEETS
Nail clipper.	Но́жницы для ногте́й.	NOHZHneetsih dlyah nahkTEY
Nail file.	Пи́лочка.	PEElahchkah
Nail polish.	Лак для ногте́й.	lahk dlyah nahkTEY
Nail polish remover.	Ацето́н.	ahtseeTOHN
Pacifier.	Со́ска.	SOHSkah
Perfume.	Дух.	dookh
Razor.	Бри́тва.	BREETvah
Razor blades.	Ле́звия.	LYEHZveeyah

English	Russian	Pronunciation
Rouge.	Румя́на.	roomYAHnah
Safety pins.	англи́йские була́вки.	ahngLEEYskeeyeh boolAHFkee
Sanitary napkins.	Гигиени́ческие салфе́тки.	geegeeehnEECHeeskeeyeh sahlFYEHTkee
Shampoo.	Шампу́нь.	shahmpOON'
Shaving cream.	Крем для бри́тва.	kryehm dlyah BREETvah
Sleeping pills.	Снотво́реное.	snahTVOHreenahyeh
Soap.	Мы́ло.	MIHlah
Sponge.	Гу́бка.	GOOPkah
Sun-tan lotion.	Ма́сло для загара.	MAHslah dlyah zahGAHrah
Thermometer.	Гра́дусник.	GRAHdoosneek
Throat lozengers.	Табле́тки для го́рла.	tahbLYEHTkee dlyah GOHRlah
Toilet paper.	Туале́тная бума́га.	tooahlYEHTnahyah booMAHgah
Tooth brush.	Зубна́я щётка.	zoobNAHyah SHCHOHTkah
Tooth paste.	Зубна́я па́ста.	zoobNAHyah PAHStah
Tranquillizer.	Успокои́тельное.	oospahkahEETeel'nahyeh
Tweezers.	Пинце́т.	peentsEHT
Vitamins.	Витами́ны.	veetahMEEnih

XIII. ACCIDENTS AND EMERGENCIES

Help

I need help.	Мне надо помочь.	mnyeh NAHdah POHmahch
There's been an accident.	Произошёл несчастный случай.	praheezahSHOHL neeSHAHSTnih SLOOchay
Please call the...	Позовите, пожалуйста...	pahzahVEEtyeh pahZHAHLstah
American/ British/ Canadian embassy.	американское/ английское/ канадское посольство.	ahmeereeKAHN-skahyeh/ahngLEEY -skahyeh/kah-NAHTskahyeh pahSOHL'stvah
consulate.	консульство.	KOHNsool'stvah
ambulance.	скорую помочь.	SKOHrooyoo POHmahch
Please get...	Пожалуйста, вызовите...	pahZHAHLstah VIHzahveetyeh
a doctor.	врача.	vrahCHAH
the police.	милиции.	meeLEEtseey
Please notify...	Пожалуйста, сообщите...	pahZHAHLstah sahahpSHCHEEtyeh
my husband.	моему мужу.	maheeMOO MOOzhoo
my wife.	моей жене.	maheey zhehNYEH
my family.	моей семьё.	maheey seem'YEH
my hotel.	моей гостинице.	maheey gahsteeNEE-tseh
I've had my ... stolen.	У меня украли...	oo meenYAH ookRAHlee
I've lost my...	Я потерял(а)...	yah pahteer-YAHL(ah)
passport.	паспорт.	PAHSpahrt
wallet.	бумажник.	booMAHZHneek
purse.	сумку.	SOOMkoo
keys.	ключи.	KLYOOchee
money.	деньги.	DYEHN'gee

Illness and Injury

English	Russian	Pronunciation
He/She is hurt.	Он болен./Она больна.	ohn BOHleen/ ahNAH bahl'NAH
He/She is bleeding badly.	У него/неё сильное кровотечёние.	oo neeVOH/neeYOH SEEL'nahyeh krahvahtee-CHEHneeyeh
He/She is unconscious.	Он/Она потерял(а) сознание.	ohn/ahNAH pahteer-YAHL(ah) sahz-NAHneeyeh
He/She is seriously injured.	У него/неё серьёзное повреждёние.	oo neeVOH/neeYOH seer'YOHZnahyeh pahvreezhDYEH-neeyeh
I'm in pain.	Мне больно.	mnyeh BOHL'nah
My ... hurts.	У меня болит...	oo meenYAH bahlEET
I can't move my...	Я не могу двинуть...	yah nee mahGOO DVEEnoot'
I'm ill. (f)	Я болен/ больна.	yah BOHleen/ (bahl'NAH)
I'm dizzy.	У меня кружится голова.	oo meenYAH KROOZHeetsah gahlahVAH
I'm nauseous.	Меня тошнит.	meenYAH tahshNEET
I feel feverish.	Меня лихорадит.	meenYAH leekhah-RAHdeet
I've vomited.	Меня вырвало.	meenYAH VIHR-vahlah
I've got food poisoning.	У меня отравлёние едой.	oo meenYAH ahtrahvLYEH-neeyeh yeeDOY
I've got diarrhea.	У меня понос.	oo meenYAH pahNOHS
I'm constipated.	У меня запор.	oo meenYAH zahpOHR
It hurts to swallow.	Мне больно глотать.	mnyeh BOHL'nah glahtAHT'
I'm having trouble breathing.	Мне трудно дышать.	mnyeh TROOdnah dihshAHT'
I have chest pain.	У меня боль в груди.	oo meenYAH bohl' fgrooDEE

English	Russian	Pronunciation
I've got indigestion.	У меня несварéние желýдка.	oo meenYAH neesvahRYEHneeyeh zheelOOTkah
I've got a bloody nose.	У меня кровотечéние из нóса.	oo meenYAH krahvahteeCHEH-neeyeh ees NOHsah
I've got sun stroke.	У меня сóлнечный удáр.	oo meenYAH SOHLneechnihy ooDAHR
I'm sunburned.	Я загорáл(а).	yah zahgahrAHL(ah)
I've got a cramp/cramps.	У меня сýдорога/схвáтки.	oo meenYAH SOOdahrahgah/SKHVAHTkee
I've got a bladder/vaginal infection.	У меня воспалéние пузыря́/влагáлища.	oo meenYAH vahspahlYEHNee-yeh poozihRYAH/vlahGAHleeshchah
I've broken my arm.	Я сломáл(а) себé рýку.	yah slahMAHL(ah) seeBYEH ROOkoo
I've sprained my ankle.	Я подвернýл(а) себé нóгу.	yah pahdveerNOOL-(ah) seeBYEH NOHgoo
I've dislocated my shoulder.	Я вы́вихнул(а) себé лопáтку.	yah VIHveekhnool-(ah) seeBYEH lahPAHTkoo
I've been stung by a wasp/bee.	Меня укýсила осá/пчелá.	meenYAH ooKOO-seelah ahSAH/pchehLAH
I've got...	У меня...	oo meenYAH
arthritis.	артрúт.	ahrtREET
asthma.	áстма.	AHSTmah
diabetis.	диабéт.	deeahbYEHT
high blood pressure.	высóкое давлéние.	VIHsahkahyeh dahvLYEHneeyeh
an ulcer.	я́зва.	YAHZvah

Parts of the Body

English	Russian	Pronunciation
Ankle.	Лоды́жка.	lahDIHSHkah
Appendix.	Аппéндикс.	ahPYEHNdeeks
Arm.	Рукá.	rooKAH
Back.	Спинá.	speeNAH

Bladder.	Мочевóй пузы́рь.	mahchehVOY poozIHR'
Blood.	Крóвь.	krohf'
Body.	Тéло.	TYEHlah
Bone.	Кóсть.	kohst'
Breasts.	Грýди.	GROOdee
Calf.	Икрá	eekRAH
Cheek.	Щекá.	shchehKAH
Chest cavity.	Грýдная пóлость.	GROOdnahyah POHlahst'
Ear/Ears.	Ухо/Уши.	OOkhah/OOshee
Elbow.	Лóкоть.	LOHkaht'
Eye.	Глаз.	glahs
Face.	Лицó.	leeTSOH
Finger.	Пáлец.	PAHleets
Foot.	Ногá.	nahGAH
Gall bladder.	Жёлчный пузы́рь.	ZHOHLCHnihy poozIHR'
Genitals.	Половы́е óрганы.	pahlahVIHyeh OHRgahnih
Glands.	Жéлезы.	ZHEHlehzih
Hand.	Рукá.	rooKAH
Heart.	Сéрдце.	SYEHRTtseh
Heel.	Пя́тка.	PYAHTkah
Hip.	Бедрó.	beedROH
Intestines.	Кишки́.	keeshKEE
Jaw.	Чéлюсть.	CHEHlahst'
Joint.	Сустáв.	soosTAHF
Kidney.	Пóчка.	POHCHkah
Knee.	Колéно.	kahLYEHnah
Leg.	Ногá.	nahGAH
Lip.	Губá.	gooBAH
Liver.	Пéчень.	PYEHchehn'
Lungs.	Лёгкие.	LYOHKHkeeyeh
Mouth.	Рот.	roht
Muscle.	Мы́шца.	MIHSHtsah
Neck.	Шéя.	SHEHyah
Nerve.	Нерв.	nyehrf
Nose.	Нос.	nohs
Rib.	Ребрó.	reebROH
Shoulder.	Плечó.	pleeCHOH
Skin.	Кóжа.	KOHzhah
Spine.	Позвонóчник.	pahzvahNOHCHneek

Stomach.	Живо́т.	zheeVOHT
Teeth.	Зу́бы.	ZOObih
Tendon.	Сухожи́лие.	sookhahZHEEleeyeh
Throat.	Го́рло.	GOHRlah
Thumb.	Большо́й па́лец.	bahl'SHOY PAHleets
Toe.	Па́лец ноги́.	PAHleets nahGEE
Tongue.	Язы́к.	yeezIHK
Tonsils.	Минда́лины.	meenDAHleenih
Vein.	Ве́на.	VYEHnah
Wrist.	Запя́стье.	zahPYAHST'yeh

Seeing a Doctor

Except for the cost of the medicine, health care in the Soviet Union is free.

I'd like an appointment...	Я хочу́ записа́ться на приём...	yah khahCHOO zapeeSAHTsah nah preeYOHM
for tomorrow.	на за́втра.	nah ZAHFtrah
as soon as possible.	как мо́жно скоре́е.	kahk MOHZHnah skahRYEHyee
Where does it hurt?	Что у вас боли́т?	shtoh oo vahs bahLEET
Is the pain sharp/dull /constant?	Боль о́страя/ ту́пая/ постоя́нная?	bohl' OHStrahyah/ TOOpahyah/pahs- tahYAHnahyah
How long have you felt this way?	Вы давно́ так себе́ чу́вствуете?	vih dahvNOH tahk seeBYEH CHOOST- vooyehtyeh
I'll take your temperature.	Я изме́рю ва́шу темпера- ту́ру.	yah eezMYEHryoo vashoo teempee- rahTOOroo
I'll measure your blood pressure.	Я изме́рю ва́ше давле́ние.	yah eezMYEHryoo vahsheh dahv- LYEHneeyeh
I'll take your pulse.	Я пощу́паю ваш пульс.	yah pahSHOOpahyoo vahsh pools'
Roll up your sleeve.	Засучи́те рука́в.	zahsooCHEEtyeh rookAHF

111

Undress to the waist.	Разде́нтесь до по́яса.	rahzDYEHNtees' dah POHyeesah
Breathe deeply.	Сде́лайте глубо́кий вдох.	ZDYEHlaytyeh glooBOHkeey vdohkh
Open your mouth.	Откро́йте рот.	ahtKROYtyeh roht
Cough.	Поканшля́йте.	pahkahshLYAYtyeh
I'll need an X-ray.	На́до сде́лать ре́нтген.	NAHdah ZDYEHlaht' RYEHNTgeen
Is it serious?	Это серьёзно?	EHtah seer'YOHZnah
Do I need surgery?	Мне на́до опера́ция?	mnyeh NAHdah ahpeeRAHTSeeyah
It's broken/ sprained.	Это сло́мано/ подверну́то.	EHtah slahMAHnah/ pahdveerNOOtah
You need a cast.	Вам на́до гипс.	vahm NAHdah geeps
You've pulled a muscle.	Вы растя́нули мы́шцу.	vih rahsTYAHnoolee MIHSHtsoo
It's infected.	У вас зараже́ние.	oo vahs zahrah-ZHEHneeyeh
It's not contagious.	Это не зара́зано.	EHtah nee zahRAHzahnah
Get well!	Поравля́йтесь!	pahprahvLYAYtees'

Seeing a Dentist

Dentist.	Зубно́й врач.	zoobNOY vrahch
I need a dentist.	Мне на́до идти́ к зубно́му врачу́.	mnyeh NAHdah eedTEE kzoob-NOHmoo vrahCHOO
What are the clinic's hours?	Когда́ приёмные часы́ поликли́ники?	kahgDAH preeYOHMnihyeh cheeSIH pahlee-KLEEneekee
I want to make an appoint-ment.	Я хочу́ записа́ться на приём.	yah khahCHOO zahpeeSAHTsah nah preeYOHM
Will I have to wait long?	Мне придётся до́лго ждать?	mnyeh preedYOHT-sah DOHLgah zhdaht'
I have...	У меня́...	oo meenYAH

112

an abscess.	нарыв.	nahrIHF
a broken tooth.	сломался зуб.	slahMAHLsah zoop
a broken denture.	сломался протез.	slahMAHLsah prahTYEHS
lost a filling.	выпала пломба.	VIHpahlah PLOHMbah
a toothache.	болят зуб.	bahLEET zoop
a cavity.	дупло.	doopLOH
sore and bleeding gums.	дёсны очень воспалёны и кровоточат.	DYOHSnih OHcheen' vahspahLYOHnih ee krahvahtahch-AHT
Don't pull it out.	Не вырывайте его.	nee vihrihVAYtyeh yeeVOH
Can you fix it temporarily?	Можно ли вы его времмено залечить?	MOHZHnah lee vih yeeVOH VRYEHMmeenah zahlee-CHEET'
When will my denture be ready?	Когда протез будет готов?	kahgDAH prahtYEHZ BOOdeet gahTOHF
May I have an anesthetic?	Можно сделать обезболивание?	MOHZHnah ZDYEHlaht' ahbeesBOHleevahneeyeh

Treatment

I'm taking medication.	Я принимаю лекарство.	yah preeneeMAHyoo leekAHRSTvah
What medicine are you taking?	Какое лекарство вы принимаете?	kahKOHyeh leekAHRstvah vih preeneeMAHeetyeh
I'm taking antibiotics.	Я принимаю антибиотики.	yah preeneeMAHyoo ahnteebeeOHteekee
I'm on the Pill.	Я принимаю противозачаточные пилюли.	yah preeneeMAHyoo prahteevahzahch-AHTahchnihyeh peelYOOlee
I'm allergic to penicillin.	Я имею аллергию к пенициллину.	yah eeMYEHyoo ahlleegGEEyoo k peeneetseelLEEnoo

113

English	Russian	Pronunciation
I'll prescribe an antibiotic/a pain-killer.	Я пропишу́ вам антибио́тик/ болеутоля́ющее сре́дство.	yah prahpeeSHOO vahm ahnteebee-OHteek/bahleeoo-tahLYAHyooshch-ehyeh SRYEHT-stvah
Where can I have this prescription filled?	Где мо́жно доста́ть лека́рство по э́тому реце́пту?	gdyeh MOHZHnah dahsTAHT' leekAHRSTvah pah ehtahMOO reetsEHPtoo
When should I take the medicine?	Когда́ мне принима́ть это лека́рство?	kahgDAH mnyeh preeneemAHT' EHtah leek-AHRSTvah
Take...	Принима́йте...	preeneeMAYtyeh
2 pills.	по две табле́тки.	pah dvyeh tahbLYEHTkee
3 teaspoons.	по три ча́йных ло́жки.	pah tree CHAY-nihkh LOHSHkee
every 2/6 hours.	ка́ждые два часа́/шесть часо́в.	KAHZHdihyeh dvah cheeSAH/shehst' cheesOHF
twice a day.	два ра́за в день.	dvah RAHzah vdyehn'
before meals.	пе́ред едо́й.	PYEHreet yeeDOY
after meals.	по́сле еды́.	POHSlee yeeDIH
as needed.	когда́ вам на́до.	kahgDAH vahm NAHdah
for 5/10 days	пять/де́сять дней	pyaht'/DYEHsaht' dnyay
I feel better/ worse/ the same.	Я чу́вствую себя́ лу́чше/ ху́же/ так же.	yah CHOOSTvooyoo seeBYAH LOOCH-sheh/KHOOzheh/ tahk zheh
Can I travel on Friday?	Могу́ ли я путеше́ствовать в пя́тницу?	mahGOO lee yah pooteeshEHSTvah-vaht' FPYAHTnee-tsoo

114

At the Hospital

English	Russian	Pronunciation
Hospital.	Больница.	bahl'NEEtsah
Clinic.	Поликлиника.	pahleeKLEEneekah
Doctor.	Врач.	vrahch
Surgeon.	Хирург.	kheerOORK
Gynecologist.	Гинеколог.	geeneeKOHlahk
Ophtha-mologist.	Офтальмолог.	ahftahl'MOHlahk
Pediatrician.	Педиатр.	peedeeAHTR
Nurse.	Медсестра.	meedseesTRAH
Patient. (f)	Пациент(ка).	pahtseeEHNT(kah)
Anesthesia.	Анестезия.	ahneesteeZEEyah
Bedpan.	Подкладное судно.	pahtklahdNOHyeh SOODnah
Injection.	Укол.	ookOHL
Operation.	Операция.	ahpeerAHTSeeyah
Transfusion.	Переливание крови.	peereeleeVAH-neeyeh KROHvee
Thermo-meter.	Градусник.	GRAHdoosneek
I can't sleep/eat.	Я не могу спать/есть.	yah nee mahGOO spaht'/yehst'
When will the doctor come?	Когда придёт врач?	kahgDAH preedYOHT vrahch
When can I get out of bed?	Когда я смогу вставать.	kahgDAH yah smahGOO fstahVAHT'
When are visiting hours?	Когда часы посещений?	kahgDAH cheeSIH pahseeshchEHN-eey

115

XIV. NUMBERS AND TIME EXPRESSIONS

Cardinal Numbers

Russian numbers are highly irregular. The number "one" agrees in gender with the noun it modifies, so that it can be either masculine, feminine or neuter. The number "two" has two forms: one serves as both masculine and neuter, while the other form is reserved for feminine subjects. All the remaining numbers have only one form.

0	Ноль/Нуль.	nohl'/nool'
1 (m/f/n)	Один/Одна/Одно.	ahdEEN/ahdNAH/ ahdNOH
2 (m/n, f)	Два/Две.	dvah/dvyeh
3	Три.	tree
4	Четыре.	chehTIHree
5	Пять.	pyaht'
6	Шесть.	shehst'
7	Семь.	syehm'
8	Восемь.	VOHseem'
9	Девять.	DYEHveet'
10	Десять.	DYEHseet'
11	Одиннадцать.	ahDEENnahtsaht'
12	Двенадцать.	dveeNAHtsaht'
13	Тринадцать.	treeNAHtsaht'
14	Четырнадцать.	chehTIHRnahtsaht'
15	Пятнадцать.	peetNAHtsaht
16	Шестнадцать.	sheesNAHtsaht'
17	Семнадцать.	seemNAHtsaht'
18	Восемнадцать.	vahseemNAHtsaht'
19	Девятнадцать.	deeveetNAHtsaht'
20	Двадцать.	DVAHtsaht'
21	Двадцать один.	DVAHtsaht' ahdEEN
22	Двадцать два.	DVAHtsaht' dvah
23	Двадцать три.	DVAHtsaht' tree
24	Двадцать четыре.	DVAHtsaht' chehTIHree
25	Двадцать пять.	DVAHtsaht' pyaht'
26	Двадцать шесть.	DVAHtsaht' shehst'

27	Двадцать семь.	DVAHtsaht' s‿ ‿
28	Двадцать восемь.	DVAHtsaht' VOHseem'
29	Двадцать девять.	DVAHtsaht' DYEHveet'
30	Тридцать.	TREEtsaht'
31	Тридцать один.	TREEtsaht' ahdEEN
40	Сорок.	SOHrahk
41	Сорок один.	SOHrahk ahdEEN
50	Пятьдесят.	peet'deesYAHT'
60	Шестьдесят.	sheezdeesYAHT'
70	Семьдесят.	SYEHM'deeseet
80	Восемьдесят.	VOHseem'deeseet
→90	Девяносто.	deeveeNOHstah
100	Сто.	stoh
200	Двести.	DVYEHstee
300	Триста.	TREEstah
400	Четыреста	chehTIHreestah
500	Пятьсот.	peet'SOHT
600	Шестьсот.	sheesSOHT
700	Семьсот.	seem'SOHT
800	Восемьсот.	vahseem'SOHT
900	Девятьсот.	deeveet'SOHT
1,000	Тысяча.	TIHseechah
2,000	Две тысячи.	dvyeh TIHseechee
5,000	Пять тысяч.	pyaht' TIHseech
100,000	Сто тысяч. ⁴	stoh TIHseech
1,000,000	Миллион.	meelleeOHN

ch = childh (handwritten)

billion (handwritten)

meelard / *meelyard* (handwritten)

Ordinal Numbers

Since they act as adjectives grammatically, all ordinal numbers have masculine (-ый, -ой), feminine (-ая) and neuter forms (-ое), which can be identified by their endings. The number "three" has irregular ("soft") endings.

First.	Первый. (-ая, -ое)	PYEHRvihy
Second.	Второй. (-ая, -ое)	vtahROY
Third.	Третий. (-ья, ье)	TRYEHteey
Fourth.	Четвёртый.	chehtVYOHRtihy
Fifth.	Пятый.	PYAHtihy
Sixth.	Шестой.	sheesTOY

English	Russian	Pronunciation
eventh.	Седьмóй.	seed'MOY
Eighth.	Восьмóй.	vahs'MOY
Ninth.	Девя́тый.	deevYAHtihy
Tenth.	Деся́тый.	deesYAHtihy
Eleventh.	Оди́ннадцатый.	ahDEEnahtsahtihy
Twelfth.	Двена́дцатый.	dveeNAHtsahtihy
Thirteenth.	Трина́дцатый.	treeNAHtsahtihy
Fourteenth.	Четы́рнадцатый.	chehTIHRnaht-sahtihy
Fifteenth.	Пятна́дцатый.	peetNAHtsahtihy
Sixteenth.	Шестна́дцатый.	sheesNAHtsahtihy
Seventeenth.	Семна́дцатый.	seemNAHtsahtihy
Eighteenth.	Восемна́дцатый.	vahseemNAH-tsahtihy
Nineteenth.	Девятна́дцатый.	deeveetNAHtsahtihy
Twentieth.	Двадца́тый.	dvahTSAHtihy
Thirtieth.	Тридца́тый.	treeSAHtihy
Fourtieth.	Сороковóй.	sahrahkahVOY
Hundredth.	Сóтый.	SOHtih
Thousandth.	Ты́сячный.	TIHseechnihy

Quantities and Measurements

English	Russian	Pronunciation
Quantity.	Колúчество.	kahLEEchehstvah
A lot./Much.	Мнóго.	MNOHgah
A little./	Мáло./	MAHlah/
Few.	Нéсколько.	NYEHskahl'kah
More./	Бóльше./	BOHL'sheh/
Less.	Мéньше.	MYEHN'sheh
Most/	Бóльше/	BOHL'sheh/
least/	мéньше/	MYEHN'sheh/
best/ better	лу́чше/	LOOCHsheh/
worst	ху́же	KHOOzheh
of all.	всегó.	vseeVOH
Majority./	Большинствó./	bahl'sheenstVOH/
Minority.	Меньшинствó.	meen'sheenstVOH
Enough./	Достáточно./	dahsTAHtahchnah/
Too much.	Слúшком мнóго.	SLEESHkahm MNOHgah
A third.	Трéть.	tryeht'
A quarter.	Чéтверть.	CHEHTveert'
A half.	Половúна.	pahlahVEEnah

118

English	Russian	Pronunciation
Three-quarters.	Три четверти.	tree CHEHTveertee
The whole.	Це́лое.	TSEHlahyeh
Once.	Ра́з.	rahs
Twice.	Два ра́за.	dvah RAHzah
Three times.	Три ра́за.	tree RAHzah
Five times.	Пять ра́з.	pyaht' rahs
Early./Late.	Ра́но./По́здно.	RAHnah/POHZnah
Now.	Сейча́с.	seeCHAHS
Still. *yet*	Ещё.	yeeSHCHOH
Never.	Никогда́.	neekahgDAH
Seldom.	Ре́дко.	RYEHTkah
Sometimes.	Иногда́.	eenahgDAH
Usually.	Обы́чно.	ahbIHCHnah
Often.	Ча́сто.	CHAHStah
Always.	Всегда́.	FSYEHGdah
In the past.	В про́шлом.	FPROHSHlahm
In the future.	В бу́дущем.	FBOOdooshchehm
A long time ago.	Да́вным давно́.	DAHVnihm dahvNOH
A short while ago.	Не так давно́.	nee tahk dahvNOH

Days and Weeks

English	Russian	Pronunciation
Sunday.	Воскресе́нье.	vahskreeSYEHN'yeh
Monday.	Понеде́льник.	pahneedYEHL'neek
Tuesday.	Вто́рник.	FTOHRneek
Wednesday.	Среда́.	sreeDAH — *middle*
Thursday.	Четве́рг.	chehtVYEHRK
Friday.	Пя́тница.	PYAHTneetsah
Saturday.	Суббо́та.	soobBOHtah
On Wednesday.	В сре́ду.	FSRYEHdoo
On Monday.	В понеде́льник.	fpahneedYEHL'neek
Last Saturday.	В про́шлую суббо́ту.	FPROHSHlooyoo soobBOHtoo
Next Thursday.	В бу́дущий четве́рг.	FBOOdooshcheey chehtVYEHRK
From Monday to Friday.	С понеде́льника до пя́тницы.	spahneedYEHL'neekah dah PYAHTneetsih

119

English	Russian	Pronunciation
What day is it today?	Какой сегодня день недели?	kahKOY seeVOHdnyah dyehn' neeDYEHlee
It's Tuesday.	Сегодня вторник.	seeVOHdnyah FTOHRneek
Week.	Неделя.	neeDYEHlyah
Last week.	На прошлой неделе.	nah PROHSHlay neeDYEHlyeh
This week.	На этой неделе.	nah EHtay neeDYEHlyeh
Next week.	На будущей неделе.	nah BOOdooshchey neeDYEHLyeh
In two weeks.	Через две недели.	CHEHrees dvyeh neeDYEHlee
In five weeks.	Через пять недель.	CHEHrees pyaht' neeDYEHL'
Every week.	Каждую неделю.	KAHZHdooyoo neeDYEHlyoo
For 3 weeks.	На три недели.	nah tree neeDYEHlee
Two weeks ago.	Две недели назад.	dvyeh neeDYEHlee nahzAHT

Months

English	Russian	Pronunciation
Month.	Месяц.	MYEHseets
This month.	В этом месяце.	VEHtahm MYEHseetseh
Last month.	В прошлом месяце.	FPROHSHlahm MYEHseetseh
Next month.	В будущем месяце.	FBOOdooshchehm MYEHseetseh
Every month.	Каждый месяц.	KAHZHdihy MYEHseets
In a month.	Через месяц.	CHEHrees MYEHseets
January.	Январь.	yeenVAHR'
February.	Февраль.	feevRAHL'
March.	Март.	mahrt
April.	Апрель.	ahpRYEHL'
May.	Май.	may
June.	Июнь.	eeYOON'
July.	Июль.	eeYOHL'
August.	Август.	AHVgoost
September.	Сентябрь.	seenTYAHBR'

October.	Октябрь.	ahkTYAHBR'
November.	Ноябрь.	nahYAHBR'.
December.	Декабрь.	deeKAHBR'
In July...	В июне...	veeYOONyeh
Since January...	С января...	syeenvahrYAH
In the beginning of October...	В начале октября...	vnahCHAHlyeh ahkteebRYAH
In the middle of December...	В середине декабря...	fseereeDEEnyeh deekahbRYAH
In the end of April...	В конце апреля...	fkahnTSEH ahpRYEHlyah
We'll be here from June to August.	Мы здесь будем от июня по августа.	mih zdyehs' BOOdeem aht eeYOONyah dah AHVgoostah
We'll be here from the 3rd of May through the 19th of July.	Мы здесь будем с третьего мая по девятнадцатое июля.	mih zdyehs' BOOdeem STRYEHt'eevah MAHyah pah deeveetNAHtsahtahyeh eeYOOL'yah
I've been here since October 14th.	Я здесь с четырнадцатого октября.	yah zdyehs' schehtIHRnahtsahtahvah ahkteebRYAH
What's the date?	Какое сегодня число?	kahKOHyeh seeVOHdnyah cheesLOH
It's January 22nd.	Сегодня двадцать второе января.	seeVOHdnyah DVAHtsaht' vtahROHyeh yeenvahrYAH
When did he come?	Когда он приехал?	kahgDAH ohn preeYEHkhahl
He arrived on May 20th.	Он приехал двадцатого мая.	ohn preeYEHkhahl dvahTSAHtahvah MAHyah

121

Years

Year.	Гóд.	goht
Decade.	Десятилéтие.	deeseeteeLYEH-teeyeh
Century.	Вéк.	vyehk
This year.	В э́том годý.	VEHtahm gahDOO
Next year.	В бýдущем годý.	FBOOdooshchehm gahDOO
Last year.	В прóшлом годý.	FPROHSHlahm gahDOO
In a year.	Чéрез год.	CHEHrees goht
For a year.	Нá год.	NAH goht
Three years ago.	Трú гóда назáд.	tree GOHdah nahzAHT
Year round.	Крýглый год.	KROOGlihy goht
In the 19th century.	В девятнáдцатом вéке.	vdeeveetNAHtsahtahm VYEHkyeh
In the 20th century.	В двадцáтом вéке.	vdvahTSAHtahm VYEHkyeh
In the 21st century.	В двáдцать пéрвом вéке.	VDVAHtsaht' PYEHRvahm VYEHkyeh
In 2010.	В две тýсячи десятом годý.	vdvyeh TIHseechee deeSYAHtahm gahDOO
In 1991.	В тýсяча девятсóт девянóсто пéрвом годý.	FTIHseechah deeveetSOHT deeveeNOHstah PYEHRvahm gahDOO
In 1985.	В тýсяча девятсóт вóсемьдесят пя́том годý.	FTIHseechah deeveetSOHT VOHseem'deeseet PYAHTahm gahDOO
How old are you?	Скóлько вам лéт?	SKOHL'kah vahm lyeht

122

English	Russian	Pronunciation
I'm 28/51 years old.	Мне двáдцать вóсемь лет /пятьдеся́т одúн год.*	mnyeh DVAHtsaht' VOHseem' lyeht/ peet'deeSYAHT ahDEEN goht
When was he/she born?	Когдá он роди́лся?/ Когдá онá роди́лáсь?	kahgDAH ohn rahDEELsah/ kahgDAH ahNAH rahdeeLAHS'
He was born in...1936/ 1960.	Он роди́лся в... ты́сяча девятьсóт три́дцать шестóм годý/ ты́сча девятьсóт шестидеся́том годý.	ohn rahDEELsah VTIHseechah deeveet'SOHT TREEtsaht' shehs- TOHM gahDOO/ TIHseechah deev- eetSOHT sheezdee- deeSYAHtahm gahDOO

Other Time Expressions

English	Russian	Pronunciation
Today.	Сегóдня.	seeVOHdnyah
Tomorrow.	Зáвтра.	ZAHFtrah
Yesterday.	Вчерá.	fchehRAH
Day after tomorrow.	Послезáвтра.	pahsleeZAHFtrah
Day before yesterday.	Позавчерá.	pahzahvchehRAH
The next day.	На другóй день.	nah drooGOY dyehn'
Three/Five days ago.	Три дня́/Пять дней назáд.	tree dnyah/pyaht' dnyey nahzAHT
Morning.	Утро.	OOtrah
In the morning.	Утром.	OOtrahm
This morning.	Сегóдня ýтром.	seeVOHdnyah OOtrahm

2 Days ago

---

* The word for year changes depending on the number that precedes it. For one year or numbers that end in a one (41, 621 etc) the word for year is год (goht). For two, three, four and numbers that end in any of those numbers, the word is гóда and for five and above, as well as numbers that end in five or higher, the word for year is лет (lyeht).

123

English	Russian	Pronunciation
Yesterday morning.	Вчера́ у́тром.	vchehRAH OOtrahm
Tomorrow morning.	За́втра у́тром.	ZAHFtrah OOtrahm
All morning.	Всё у́тро.	fsyoh OOtrah
Every morning.	Ка́ждое у́тро.	KAHZHdahyeh OOtrah
Day.	Де́нь.	dyehn'
In the afternoon.	Днём./ По́сле обе́да.	dnyohm/POHSlee ahBYEHdah
This afternoon.	Сего́дня по́сле обе́да.	seeVOHdnyah POHSlee ahBYEHdah
Yesterday afternoon.	Вчера́ по́сле обе́да.	vchehRAH POHSlee ahBYEHdah
Tomorrow afternoon.	За́втра по́сле обе́да.	ZAHFtrah POHSlee ahBYEHdah
All day.	Ве́сь де́нь.	vyehs' dyehn'
Every day.	Ка́ждый де́нь.	KAHZHdihy dyehn'
Evening.	Ве́чер.	VYEHchehr
In the evening.	Ве́чером.	VYEHchehrahm
This evening.	Сего́дня ве́чером.	seeVOHdnyah VYEHchehrahm
Yesterday evening.	Вчера́ ве́чером.	vchehRAH VYEHchehrahm
Tomorrow evening.	За́втра ве́чером.	ZAHFtrah VYEHchehrahm
All evening.	Ве́сь ве́чер.	vyehs' VYEHchehr
Every evening.	Ка́ждый ве́чер.	KAHZHdihy VYEHchehr
Night.	Но́чь.	nohch
At night.	Но́чью.	NOHCHyoo
Tonight.	Сего́дня но́чью.	seeVOHdnyah NOHCHyoo
All night.	Всю́ но́чь.	fsyoo nohch
Every night.	Ка́ждая но́чь.	KAHZHdahyah nohch
Weekend.	Коне́ц неде́ли.	kahnYEHTS neeDYEHlee
Holiday.	Пра́здник.	PRAHZneek
Vacation.	О́тпуск.	OHTpoosk
School holiday.	Кани́кулы.	kahNEEkoolih

124

Birthday.	Дéнь рождéния.	dyehn' rahzhDYEH-neeyah

Telling Time

Moscow is eight hours ahead of Eastern Standard Time and has no Daylight Savings Time. The USSR has eleven time zones.

English	Russian	Pronunciation
Time.	Врéмя.	VRYEHmyah
Half hour.	Полчасá.	pahlcheeSAH
Hour.	Чáс.	chahs
Minute.	Минýта.	meeNOOtah
Second.	Секýнда.	seekOONdah
Early./Late.	Рáно./Пóздно.	RAHnah/POHZnah
I'm sorry, I'm late.	Простúте за опоздáние.	prahsTEEtyeh zah ahpahzDAHneeyeh
On time.	Вóвремя.	VOHvreemyah
What time is it?	Скóлько врéмени?	SKOHL'kah VRYEHmeenee
It's...	Сейчáс...	seeCHAHS
one o'clock.	чáс.	chahs
five past three.	пять минýт четвёртого.	pyaht' meeNOOT chehtVOHRtahvah
ten past six.	дéсять минýт седьмóго.	DYEHseet' mee-NOOT seedMOHvah
quarter after four.	пятнáдцать минýт пятого.	peetNAHtsaht' meeNOOT PYAHTahvah
twenty past twelve.	двáдцать минýт пéрвого.	DVAHtsaht' mee-NOOT PYEHR-vahvah
twenty-five after two.	двáдцать пять минýт трéтьего.	DVAHtsaht' pyaht' meeNOOT TRYEH-t'ehvah
seven thirty.	половúна восьмóго.	pahlahVEEnah vahs'MOHvah
twenty-five to nine.	без двадцатú пятú дéвять.	byehs dvahtsahTEE peeTEE DYEHveet'
twenty to eleven.	без двадцатú одúннадцать.	byehs dvahtsahTEE ahDEENnahtsaht'
quarter to one.	без четвертú чáс.	byehs chehtveerTEE chahs

125

English	Russian	Pronunciation
ten of eight.	без десяти́ во́семь.	byehs deeseeTEE VOHseem'
five of two.	без пяти́ два.	byehs peeTEE dvah
twelve o'clock.	двена́дцать часо́в.	dveeNAHtsaht' cheeSOHF
midnight.	по́лночь.	POHLnahch
noon.	по́лдень.	POHLdeen'
A.M.	Утра́.	ootRAH
P.M.	Ве́чера.	VYEHchehrah
At what time?	В кото́ром часу́?	fkahTOHrahm cheeSOO
At one.	В час.	fchahs
At 3:05.	В пять мину́т четвёртого.	fpyaht' meeNOOT chehtVOHRtahvah
At 2:10.	В де́сять мину́т тре́тьего.	VDYEHsaht' mee-NOOT TRYEH-t'ehvah
At 5:30.	В полови́не шесто́го.	vpahlahVEENyeh sheesTOHvah
At 7:40	Без двадцати́ во́семь.	byehs dvahstahTEE VOHseem'
At 12:50	Без десяти́ час.	byehs deeseeTEE chahs

Seasons

English	Russian	Pronunciation
Seasons.	Времена́ го́да.	vreemeeNAH GOHdah
Spring./In the spring.	Весна́./Весно́й.	veesNAH/veesNOY
Summer./In the summer.	Ле́то./Ле́том.	LYEHtah/LYEHtahm
Fall./In the fall.	Осень./Осенью.	OHseen'/OHseen'yoo
Winter./In the winter.	Зима́./Зимо́й.	zeeMAH/zeeMOY

XV. REFERENCE

Soviet National Holidays

Jan. 1	New Years Day.	Но́вый го́д.
Mar. 8	International Women's Day.	Междунаро́дный де́нь же́нщин.
May 1-2	May Day.	Пе́рвое ма́я.
May 9	V-E Day.	Де́нь Побе́ды.
Oct. 7	Constitution Day.	Де́нь конститу́ции.
Nov. 7-8	Anniversary of the Great October Socialist Revolution.	Пра́здник Октя́брьской Револю́ции.

Weather

The weather.	Пого́да.	pahGOHdah
What is it like outside?	Кака́я сего́дня пого́да?	kahKAHyah seeVOHdnyah pahGOHdah
What's the forecast (for tomorrow)?	Како́й прогно́с пого́ды (на за́втра?)	kahKOY prahgNOHS pahGOHdih (nah ZAHFtrah)
Tomorrow it will rain.	За́втра бу́дет до́ждь.	ZAHFtrah BOOdeet dohsht'
Today it's...	Сего́дня...	seeVOHdnyah
sunny.	све́тит со́льнце.	SVYEHteet SOHN'tseh
overcast.	па́смурно.	PAHsmoornah
cool.	прохла́дно.	prahkhLAHdnah
warm.	тепло́.	teepLOH
hot.	жа́рко.	ZHAHRkah
cold.	хо́лодно.	KHOHlahdnah
humid.	вла́жно.	VLAHZHnah
foggy.	тума́н.	tooMAHN
windy.	ве́тер.	VYEHteer
What's it usually like here?	Кака́я пого́да быва́ет здесь?	kahKAHyah pahGOHdah bihVAHeet zdyehs'
It's raining/ snowing.	Идёт до́ждь/ снег.	eedYOHT dohsht'/ snyehk

| What a beau-
tiful day! | Какóй прекрáсный
день! | kahKOY preeKRAHS-
nihy dyehn' |
| What awful
weather! | Какáя ужáсная
погóда! | kahKAHyah
oozhAHSnahyah
pahGOHdah |

Directions

North.	Сéвер.	SYEHveer
In the north.	На сéвере.	nah SYEHveeryeh
To the north.	На сéвер.	nah SYEHveer
Northward.	К сéверу.	KSYEHveeroo
South.	Юг.	yook
In the south.	На юге.	nah YOOgyeh
To the south.	На юг.	nah yook
Southward.	К югу.	KYOOgoo
East.	Востóк.	vahsTOHK
In the east.	На востóке.	nah vahsTOHKyeh
To the east.	На востóк.	nah vahsTOHK
Eastward.	К востóку.	kvahsTOHKoo
West.	Зáпад.	ZAHpaht
In the west.	На зáпаде.	nah ZAHpahdyeh
To the west.	На зáпад.	nah ZAHpaht
Westward.	К зáпаду.	KZAHpahdoo

Family

Family.	Семья.	seem'YAH
Relatives.	Рóдственники.	ROHTSTveeneekee
Children.	Дéти.	DYEHtee
Adults.	Взрóслые.	VZROHSlihyeh

Wife./
  Spouse. (f)
	Женá./
	  Супрýга.
		zhehNAH/
		  soopROOgah

Husband./
  Spouse. (m)
	Мýж./
	  Супрýг.
		moosh/
		  soopROOK

Mother.	Мáть.	maht'
Father.	Отéц.	ahtYEHTS
Baby.	Ребёнок.	reebYOHnahk
Daughter.	Дóчь.	dohch
Son.	Сын.	sihn
Sister.	Сестрá.	seesTRAH
Brother.	Брáт.	braht
Grandmother.	Бáбушка.	BAHbooshkah
Grandfather.	Дéдушка.	DYEHdooshkah

Grand-daughter.	Внучка.	VNOOCHkah
Grandson.	Внук.	vnook
Aunt.	Тётя.	TYOHtyah
Uncle.	Дядя.	DYAHdyah
Niece.	Племянница.	pleemYAHNneetsah
Nephew.	Племянник.	pleemYAHNneek
Cousin. (m/f)	Двоюродный брат/ Двоюродная сестра.	dvahYOOrahdnihy braht/dvahYOO-rahdnahyah seesTRAH
Husband's mother.	Свекровь.	sveekROHF'
Husband's father.	Свёкор.	SVYOHKahr
Wife's mother.	Тёща.	TYOHshchah
Wife's father.	Тесть.	tyehst'

(margin handwriting: ТУОТУЛ ДУА ДУА)

Signs

Information.	Справки./ Справочное бюро.	SPRAHFkee/SPRAH-vahchnahyeh byooROH
Bathroom (M/W).	Туалет (М/Ж).	tooahlYEHT
Don't touch.	Не трогайте.	nee trahGAYtyeh
Push./ Pull.	От себя./ К себе.	ahtseeBYAH/ kseeBYEH
No admit-tance.	Не входить.	neefkhahDEET'
Entrance.	Вход.	fkhoht
Exit.	Выход.	VIHkhaht
No entry.	Нет входа.	nyeht FKHOHdah
No exit.	Нет выхода.	nyeht VIHkhahdah
Emergency exit.	Запасной выход.	zahpahsNOY VIHkhaht
Employees' entrance.	Служебный вход.	sloozhEHBnihy fkhoht
Elevator.	Лифт.	leeft
Stairs.	Лестницы.	LYEHSTneetsih
Up./Down.	Вверх./Вниз.	vyehrkh/vnees

129

Keep to the left/right.	Держи́тесь к ле́вой /пра́вой стороне́.	deerZHEEtyehs k LYEHvay/PRAHvay stahrahNYEH
Don't lean.	Не прислоня́ться.	nee preeslahn-YAHTsah
Stop.	Стоп.	stohp
Wait.	Сто́йте.	STOYtyeh
Go.	Иди́те.	eeDEEtyeh
Careful!	Осторо́жно!	ahstahROHZHnah
Attention!	Внима́ние!	vneeMAHneeyeh
Prohibited.	Воспреща́ется.	vahspreeSHCHAH-eetsah
Danger!	Опа́сно!	ahPAHSnah
Police.	Мили́ция.	meeLEEtseeyah
Quiet!	Не шуме́ть.	nee shoomYEHT'
Self-serve.	Самообслу́живание.	sahmahahpSLOO-zheevahneeyeh
Occupied.	За́нято.	ZAHneetah
No smoking.	Не кури́ть.	nee kooREET'
Closed for lunch/ repairs/ cleaning.	Закры́то на обе́д/ремо́нт/ санита́рный день.	zahKRIHtah nah ahbYEHT/reem-OHNT/sahnee-TAHRnihy dyehn'
Closed for a break from 1 to 2.	Переры́в с 1 до 2.	peereeRIHF SCHAH-soo dahdVOOKH
Office hours.	Приёмные часы́.	preeYOHMnihyeh cheeSIH
Men working.	В ремо́нте.	vreeMOHNtyeh
Watch out for cars.	Береги́сь автомоби́ля.	beereeGEES' ahftahmahBEElyah

Abbreviations and Acronyms

АЗС	автозапра́вочная ста́нция.	gas station.
бульв.	бульва́р.	boulevard.
ВДНХ	Вы́ставка дости-же́ния наро́дного хозя́йство.	Exhibition of Economic Achieve-ments (in Moscow).
в.	век.	century.
г.	год./го́род./грамм./ гора́./господи́н.	year./city./gram./ mountain./Mr.
г-жа.	госпожа́.	Mrs.

гр.	граждани́н.	citizen.
ГУМ	Госуда́рственный универса́льный магагзи́н.	State Department Store (in Moscow).
д.	дом.	house.
до н.э.	до на́шей э́ры.	B.C.
ж.	же́нский	women.
и т. д.	и так да́лее.	etc.
им.	и́мени.	named after...
к., коп.	копе́йка.	kopeck.
к., корп.	ко́рпус.	corpus.
кв.	кварти́ра.	apartment.
КПСС	Коммунисти́ческая па́ртия Сове́тского Сою́за.	The Communist Party of the Soviet Union.
ЛГУ	Ленингра́дский госуда́рственный университе́т.	Leningrad State University.
м.	метр./мужско́й.	meter./men.
МГУ	Моско́вский госуда́рственный университе́т.	Moscow State University.
наб.	на́бережная.	embankment.
напр.	наприме́р.	for example.
н.э.	на́шей э́ры.	A.D.
обл.	о́бласть	oblast.
оз.	о́зеро.	lake.
пл.	пло́щадь.	square.
пр., просп.	проспе́кт.	prospect.
р.	рубль.	rouble.
РСФСР	Росси́йская Сове́тская Федерати́вная Социалисти́ческая Респу́блика.	RSFSR - Russian Soviet Federal Socialist Republic.
с., стр.	страни́ца.	page.
СССР	Сою́з Сове́тских Социалисти́ческих Респу́блик.	USSR - Union of Soviet Socialist Republics.
США	Соединённые Шта́ты Аме́рики.	USA - United States of America.
ТАСС	Телегра́фное аге́нство Сове́тского Сою́за.	Telegraph Agency of the Soviet Union.

т.е.	то есть.	that is, ie.
тов.	товáрищ.	comrade.
ул.	улица.	street.
ЦК	Центрáльный комитéт	The Central Committee.
ЦУМ	Центрáльный универсáльный магазúн.	Central Department Store (in Moscow).
ч.	час.	hour.

Metric Conversions

Temperature:

To convert Celsius into Fahrenheit, multiply degree Celsius by 1.8 and add 32. To convert Fahrenheit into Celsius, subtract 32 from degree Fahrenheit and divide by 1.8.

Distance:

To convert miles into kilometers, divide miles by 5 and multiply by 8. To convert kilometers into miles, divide kilometers by 8 and multiply by 5.

1 km = 5/8 mile
1 centimeter = 0.39 inches
1 meter = 3.28 feet
1 kilometer = .675 mile
1 inch = 2.54 centimeters
1 foot = 30.5 centimeters
1 mile = 1609 meters

Weight:

1 kilogram = 2.2 pounds
1 gram = 0.0352 ounces
1 ounce = 28.35 grams
1 pound = 453.60 grams

Volume:

1 liter = 0.264 gallons
1 liter = 1.06 quarts
1 quart = .95 liter
1 gallon = 3.8 liters

As in all standard dictionaries, verbs are listed in the infinitive form. Adjectives are given in the masculine form and are marked by the abbreviation (adj). Nouns are given without articles. When both masculine and feminine forms exist, the masculine form is given first, followed by the feminine (f) version.

Russian-English Dictionary

А

авáрия ahVAHreeyah - breakdown; accident.

авеню ahveenYOO - avenue.

авиапóчта ahveeahPOHCH-tah - airmail.

автóбус ahfTOHboos - bus.

автозапрáвочная стáнция ahftahzahPRAHvahch-nahyah STAHNtseeyah - service station.

автомáт ahftahMAHT - vending machine.

автомабилúст ahftahmah-beeLEEST - motorist.

автомобúль ahftahmah-BEEL' - car.

áвтор AHFtahr - author.

адвокáт ahdvahKAHT - lawyer.

администрáтор ahdmee-neesTRAHtahr - manager.

áдрес AHdrees - address.

áзбука AHSbookah - alphabet.

аккурáтный ahkooRAHT-nihy - neat, tidy, punctual (adj).

áкт ahkt - act.

актёр ahkTYOHR - actor.

актрúса ahkTREEsah - actress.

актуáльный ahktooAHL'-nihy - current (adj).

акушёр ahkooSHOHR - obstetrician.

акцéнт ahkTSEHNT - accent.

алкогóль ahlkahGOHL' - alcohol.

аллéргия ahlLYEHRgeeyah - allergy.

аллó ahlLOH - hello (on the telephone).

амбулатóрия ahmboolah-TOHreeyah - outpatient clinic.

американец/(-кáнка) ahmeereeKAHneets/ (-KAHNkah) - American/ (f).

американский ahmeeree-KAHNskeey - American (adj).

ананáс ahnahNAHS - pineapple.

англúйская булáвка ahng-LEEskahyah booLAHFkah - safety pin.

англúйский ahngLEEYskeey - English, British (adj).

англичáнин/(-чáнка) ahn-gleeCHAHneen (-CHAHN-kah) Englishman/(f).

анкéта ahnKYEHtah - form, blank, survey.

антибиóтик ahnteebeeOH-teek - antibiotic.

антра́кт ahnTRAHKT - intermission.

апельси́н ahpeel'SEEN - orange.

аппе́ндикс ahPYEHNdeeks - appendix.

аппендици́т ahppeendeeTSEET - appendicitis.

аппети́т (прия́тного аппети́та!) ahpeeTEET (preeYAHTnahvah ahpeeTEEtah!) appetite (Hearty appetite!)

апте́ка ahpTYEHkah - drugstore.

апте́чка ahpTYEHCHkah - first-aid kit.

арбу́з ahrBOOZ - watermelon.

арома́тный ahrahMAHTnihy - fragrant (adj).

арте́ль ahrTYEHL' - workers' cooperative.

арте́рия ahrTYEHreeyah - artery.

арти́ст ahrTEEST - performer.

артри́т ahrtREET - arthritis.

архите́ктор ahrkheeTYEHKtahr - architecht.

архитекту́ра ahrkheeteekTOOrah - architechture.

аспира́нт/(-ка) ahspeeRAHNT/(-kah) - graduate student/(f).

аспири́н ahspeeREEN - aspirin.

а́стма AHSTmah - asthma.

атеи́зм ahteeEEZM - atheism.

атле́тика ahtLYEHTeekah - athletics.

атлети́ческий ahtLYEHTeechskeey - athletic (adj).

афи́ша ahFEEshah - poster; play bill.

аэропо́рт ahehrahPOHRT - airport.

Б

ба́бушка BAHbooshkah - grandmother.

бага́ж bahgAHSH - baggage.

база́р bahZAHR - market; bazaar.

баклажа́н bahklahzhAHN - eggplant.

балала́йка bahlahLAYkah - balalaika.

бале́т bahLYEHT - ballet.

балко́н bahlKOHN - balcony.

бана́н bahNAHN - banana.

бандеро́ль bahndeeROHL' - wrapping for mailing printed matter.

банк bahnk - bank.

ба́нка BAHNkah - jar; can.

банке́т bahnKYEHT - banquet.

ба́ня BAHNyah - public bath.

бара́нина bahRAHneenah - mutton; lamb.

бассе́йн bahsSEYN - pool.

батаре́я bahtahREEyah - battery.

ба́шня BAHSHnyah - tower.

бег byehk - run; race.

бе́гать BYEHgaht' - to run.

беда́ beeDAH - misfortune.

бе́дный BYEHDnihy - poor (adj).

бедро́ beedROH - hip; thigh.

без byehs - without

безалкого́льный beezahl-kahGOHL'nihy - nonalcoholic (adj).

безбо́жие beesBOH-zheeyeh - atheism.

безбо́жник beesBOHZH-neek - atheist.

безви́нный beezVEENnihy - innocent (adj).

безвку́сный beezVKOOS-nihy - tasteless (adj).

безопа́сно beezahPAHSnah - safely.

безусло́вно beezoosLOHV-nah - certainly; absolutely.

беко́н beeKOHN - bacon.

бе́лый BYEHlihy - white (adj).

бельё beel'YOH - laundry; linen.

бензи́н beenZEEN - gas.

бензоба́к beenzahBAHK - gas tank.

бензозапра́вочная ста́нция beenzahzahPRAHvahch-nahyah STAHNtseeyah - gas station.

бе́рег BYEHreek - coast; bank; shore.

береги́сь beereeGEES' - caution.

берёза beerYOHzah - birch.

Берёзка beerYOHSkah - hard-currency store.

бере́менная beeRYEHmeen-nahyah - pregnant (adj).

бере́чь beeRYEHCH - to save, keep; to guard.

бе́с byehs - demon.

бесе́да beeSYEHdah - conversation.

бесе́довать beeSYEH-dahvaht' - to talk, chat.

беспереса́дочный bees-peereeSAHdahchnihy - without transfer (adj).

беспла́тный beesPLAHT-nihy - free of charge (adj).

беспоко́ить beespahKOH-eet' - to worry, trouble, bother, disturb.

беспоко́йный beespah-KOYnihy - worried; troubled (adj).

беспо́лезный beespahl-YEHZnihy - useless (adj).

беспоса́дочный beespah-SAHdahchnihy - nonstop (of a flight) (adj).

беспо́шлинный bees-POHSHleennihy - duty-free (adj).

бессозна́тельный bees-sahzNAHteel'nihy - unconscious (adj).

бессо́нница beesSOHNeetsah - insomnia.

бесцве́тный beesTSVYEHT-nihy - colorless; dull (adj).

библиоте́ка beebleeah-TYEHkah - library.

би́блия BEEbleeyah - Bible.

бизнесме́н/(-ка) beezneesMYEHN/(-kah) - businessman/(f).

биле́т beeLYEHT - ticket.

биле́тная ка́сса beeLYEHT-nahyah KAHSsah - ticket office.

бино́кль beeNOHKL' - binoculars; opera glasses.

би́нт beent - bandage.

би́ть beet' - to beat, strike.

би́ться BEETsah - to fight.

бифштéкс beefSHTYEHKS - steak.

благодарúть blahgahdah-REET' - to thank.

благодáрный blahgah-DAHRnihy - thankful; grateful (adj).

благополýчно blahgah-pahLOOCHnah - safely; without mishap.

благословéние blahgah-slahVYEHneeyeh - blessing.

блáнк blahnk - form; blank.

блéдный BLYEHDnihy - pale (adj).

ближáйший bleeZHAY-sheey - nearest; next (adj).

блúзко BLEESkah - near; close; nearby.

блúн bleen - pancake.

блондúн/(-ка) blahnDEEN/(-kah) - blonde/(f).

блýзка BLOOSkah - blouse.

блюдо BLYOOdah - dish; food; course.

бóг bohkh- God.

богáтый bahGAHtihy - rich (adj).

богослужéние bahgahsloo-ZHEHneeyeh - worship service.

бóдрый BOHdrihy - cheerful (adj).

бóк bohk - side.

бóком BOHKahm - sideways.

бóлее BOHleeyeh - more.

болéзнь bahLYEHZN' - illness; disease.

болéльщик bahlYEHL'-shcheek - sports fan.

болéть bahlYEHT' - to be ill.

болеутолáющее срéдство bahleeootahlYAHyooshch-ehyeh SRYEHTstvah - painkiller.

болтлúвый bahltLEEvihy - talkative (adj).

бóль bohl' - pain.

больнúца bahl'NEEtsah - hospital.

больнóй bahl'NOY - sick (adj).

бóльше BOHL'sheh - larger; bigger; greater.

большинствó bahl'sheenst-VOH - majority.

большóй bahl'SHOY - big; large; great (adj).

большóй пáлец bahl'SHOY PAHleets - thumb.

большóе спасúбо bahl'-SHOHyeh spahSEEbah - thanks a lot!

бородá bahrahDAH - beard.

бóрщ bohrshch - borsch; beet soup.

борьбá bahr'BAH - fight, struggle.

ботанúческий сáд bahtah-NEEchehskeey saht - botanical garden.

боáться bahYAHTsah - to fear, be afraid.

брáк brahk - marriage.

брáт braht - brother

брáть braht' - to take, seize.

бриллиáнт breeleeAHNT - diamond.

брúтва BREETvah - razor.

брúться BREETsah - to shave; get a shave.

бровь brohf' - eyebrow.
брошь brohsh - brooch.
брюки BRYOOkee - pants.
брюнет/(-ка) bryooNYEHT/
(-kah) - brunette/(f).
будильник booDEEL'neek -
alarm clock.
будний день BOODneey
dyehn' - weekday.
будущий BOOdooshcheey -
the future.
буква BOOKvah - letter of
the alphabet.
букинист bookeenEEST -
secondhand book dealer.
булавка booLAHFkah - pin.
булка BOOLkah - roll; bun.
булочная BOOlahchnahyah
- bakery.
бульвар bool'VAHR -
boulevard.
бульон bool'OHN -
bouillon.
бумага booMAHgah - paper.
бумажник booMAHZHneek
- wallet; billfold.
бурный BOORnihy -
stormy; violent (adj).
буря BOORyah - storm.
бусы BOOsih - beads.
бутерброд booteerBROHT -
sandwich.
бутылка booTIHLkah -
bottle.
буфет boofYEHT - snack
bar.
буханка bookhAHNkah -
loaf of bread.
бывший BIHFsheey -
former (adj).
быстро BIHStrah - fast;
quickly; rapidly.
бюро byooROH - office;

bureau.
бюро Интуриста byooROH
eentooREESTah - Intourist
office.
бюстгальтер byoozKHAHL'-
teer - bra.

В

в v - in, at, for, to.
в один конец vahDEEN
kahNYEHTS - one-way
(ticket).
вагон vahGOHN - railroad
car.
важность VAHZHnahst' -
importance.
важный VAHZHnihy -
important (adj).
вазелин vahzeeLEEN -
vaseline.
вальдшнеп VAHL'Tshneep -
woodcock.
валюта vahLYOOtah - hard-
currency.
валютный курс vahLYOO-
tnihy koors - rate of
exchange.
ваниль vahNEEL' - vanilla.
ванна VAHNnah - bathtub.
ванная VAHNnahyah -
bathroom.
вареник vahRYEHneek -
filled dumpling.
варёный vahRYOHnihy -
boiled (adj).
варенье vahRYEHN'yeh -
jam.
варить vahrEET' - to cook,
boil.
вата VAHtah - absorbent
cotton.
введение vveeDYEHneeyeh
- introduction.

137

вверх vvyehrkh - up, upwards (destination).

вверху vveerKHOO - above; overhead (location).

вдали vdahLEE - in the distance.

вдова vdahVAH - widow.

вдовец vdahvYEHTS - widower.

вдруг vdrook - suddenly.

вегетарианец veegeetahreeAHNeets - vegetarian.

ведро veedROH - bucket.

веер VYEHeer - fan.

вежливый VYEHZHleevihy - polite; courteous (adj).

везде veezDYEH - everywhere.

век vyehk - century; age.

великий veeLEEkeey - great (adj).

велосипед veelahseePYEHT - bicycle.

вена VYEHnah - vein.

вера VYEHrah - belief; faith.

верблюд veerBLYOOT - camel.

верёвка veeRYOHFkah - rope; string; cord.

верить VYEHreet' - to believe, have faith.

верный VYEHRnihy - true; faithful (adj).

вероятно veerahYAHTnah - probably.

верх vyehrkh - top

верхний VYEHRkhneey - upper; top (adj).

вес vyehs - weight.

веселиться veeseeLEEtsah - to enjoy oneself; have fun.

весенний veesYEHNneey - spring (adj).

весна veesNAH - spring.

весь vyehs' - all; the whole.

ветер VYEHteer - wind.

ветреный VYEHTreenihy - windy (adj).

ветровое стекло veetrahvOHyeh steekLOH - windshield.

ветчина veetcheeNAH - ham.

вечер VYEHcheer - evening.

вечерний veeCHEHRneey - evening (adj.).

вечно VYEHCHnah - eternally.

вешалка VYEHshahlkah - hanger.

взаимопонимание vzaheemahpahneeMAHneeyeh - mutual understanding.

взгляд vzglyaht - look; glance.

вздор vzdohr - nonsense.

взлёт vzlyoht - takeoff (in a plane).

взрослый VZROHSlihy - adult.

взятка VZYAHTkah - bribe.

взять напрокат vzyaht' nahprahKAHT - to rent.

вид veet - appearance.

видение VEEdeeneeyeh - sight; vision.

видеть VEEdeet' - to see.

видимо VEEdeemah - apparently; evidently.

видно VEEDnah - visible; clear; obvious.

виза VEEzah - visa.

вилка VEELkah - fork.

вина veeNAH - guilt.

винегрет veeneegRYEHT -

vegetable salad.

вино́ veeNOH - wine.

винова́тый veenahVAHtihy - guilty (adj).

виногра́д veenahGRAHT - grapes.

ви́рус VEEroos - virus.

витами́ны veetahMEEnih - vitamins.

ви́шня VEESHnyah - sour cherries.

включа́ть vklyooCHAHT' - to turn, switch on.

вку́сный VKOOSnihy - tasty (adj).

влага́лище vlahGAH-leeshcheh - vagina.

вла́жность VLAHZHnahst' - humidity.

вла́жный VLAHZHnihy - humid (adj).

влия́ние vleeYAHneeyeh - influence.

влия́тельный vleeYAHTeel'-nihy - influential (adj).

вме́сте VMYEHStyeh - together.

вме́сто VMYEHStah - instead of.

вне́ vnyeh - outside; out of.

вне́шний VNYEHSHneey - outward; external (adj).

вни́з vnees - down; downward (destination).

внизу́ vneeZOO - down below (location).

внима́ние vneeMAHneeyeh - attention.

внук vnook - grandson.

вну́тренний VNOOtreen-neey - internal (adj).

внутри́ vnooTREE - inside.

вну́чка VNOOCHkah -

granddaughter.

во́время VOHvreemyah - on time.

вода́ vahDAH - water.

води́тель vahDEEteel' - driver.

во́дка VOHTkah - vodka.

водопа́д vahdahPAHT - waterfall.

водопрово́дчик vahdah-prahVOHTcheek - plumber.

вое́нный vahYEHNnihy - military (adj).

возбуждённый vahzboozh-DYOHNnihy - excited.

возвраща́ть vahzvrah-SHCHAHT' - to return.

во́здух VOHZdookh - air.

возмо́жность vahzMOHZH-nahst' - opportunity.

возмущённый vahzmoo-shchOHNnihy - out-raged (adj).

возраже́ние vahzrahZHEH-neeyeh - objection.

во́зраст VOHZrahst - age.

война́ voyNAH - war.

вокза́л vahkZAHL - station.

вокру́г vahkROOK - around (location).

волна́ vahlNAH - wave.

волнова́ться vahlnahVAH-tsah - to be worried, agitated.

во́лосы VOHlahsih - hair.

во́льно VOHL'nah - freely; voluntarily.

вольта́ж vahl'TAHSH - voltage.

во́ля VOHLyah - freedom.

воображе́ние vahahbrah-ZHEHneeyeh - imagin-

ation.
вообще́ vahahpSHCHEH - in
general.
вопро́с vahpROHS -
question.
во́р vohr - thief.
воро́та vahROHtah - gate.
воспале́ние vahspahLYEH-
neeyeh - inflamation.
воспале́ние влага́лища
vahspahLYEHneeyeh
vlahGAHleeshchah -
vaginal infection.
воспале́ние лёгких
vahspahLYEHneeyeh
LYOHKHkeekh -
pneumonia.
воспомина́ние vahspah-
meeNAHneeyeh - memory;
recollection.
воспреща́ться vahspree-
SHCHAHtsah - to be
forbidden.
восста́ние vahsSTAH-
neeyeh - uprising; revolt.
восто́к vahsTOHK - east.
восто́чный vahsTOHCHnihy
- eastern (adj).
восхо́д vahsKHOHT -
sunrise.
во́т voht - here (is).
впервы́е fpeerVIHyeh - for
the first time; first.
вперёд fpeeRYOHT -
forward; ahead.
впереди́ fpeereeDEE - in
front; ahead.
впечатле́ние fpeechaht-
LYEHneeyeh - impres-
sion.
вполне́ fpahlNYEH - fully;
completely; quite.
впуск fpoosk - admission;

admittance.
впуска́ть fpoosKAHT' - to
admit, let in.
вра́г vrahk - enemy.
вра́ть vraht' - to lie, tell
lies.
вра́ч vrahch - doctor.
вре́дный VRYEHDnihy -
harmful (adj).
вре́менно VRYEHmeennah -
temporarily.
вре́мя VRYEHmyah - time.
всегда́ fseegDAH - always.
всео́бщий fseeOHPshcheey
- universal; general (adj).
всё-таки VSYOHtahkee -
still; all the same.
вслу́х fslookh - aloud.
встава́ть fstahVAHT' - to
get, stand up.
встре́ча FSTRYEHchah -
meeting; encounter.
встреча́ть fstreechAHT' - to
meet.
вхо́д fkhoht - entrance.
входи́ть fkhahDEET' - to
enter.
вчера́ fcheeRAH -
yesterday.
вчера́шний fcheeRAHSH-
neey - yesterday's (adj).
вы́бор VIHbahr - choice;
assortment; selection.
вы́боры VIHbahrih -
elections.
вы́годный VIHgahdnihy -
profitable; favorable (adj).
вы́золоченный VIHzahlah-
chehnnihy - gilded (adj).
выключа́ть vihklyooCHAHT'
- to turn out, switch off.
вы́пуск VIHpoosk - issue;
edition; output.

высо́кий vihSOHkeey -
high; tall; lofty (adj).
высота́ vihsahTAH - height;
altitude.
вы́ставка VIHstahfkah -
exhibition; display.
вы́ход VIHkhaht - exit.
выходи́ть vihkhahDEET' -
to leave, go out, exit.
выходно́й день vihkhahd-
NOY dyehn' - day off.
вы́шитый VIHsheetihy -
embroidered (adj).

Г

га́дкий GAHTkeey - nasty;
foul; vile (adj).
газе́та gahZYEHtah - newspaper.
газоме́р gahzahMYEHR - gas
meter.
гало́ши gahLOHshee -
rubbers; galoshes.
га́лстук GAHLstook - tie.
гара́ж gahRAHSH - garage.
гардеро́б gahrdeeROHP -
cloakroom.
гардеро́бщик gahrdee-
ROHPsheek - cloakroom
attendant.
гастри́т gahstREET -
gastritis.
гастроно́м gahstrahNOHM -
grocery store.
гвозди́ка gvahzDEEkah -
carnation.
гвоздь gvohst' - nail, tack.
где gdyeh - where.
где-нибудь GDYEHneeboot'
- somewhere.
геморро́й geemahrROY -
hemorrhoids.
гемофилия geemahfeeLEE-

yah - hemophilia.
гепати́т geepahTEET -
hepatitis.
гериатри́ческий geeree-
ahtREEcheeskeey -
geriatric (adj).
герма́нец/(-ма́нка) geer-
MAHneets/(-MAHNkah) -
German/(f).
герма́нский geerMAHN-
skeey - German (adj).
геро́й geeROY - hero.
ги́бкий GEEPkeey - flexible
(adj).
гид geet - guide.
гинеко́лог geeneeKOHlahk -
gynecologist.
гипертони́я geepeertah-
NEEyah - high blood
pressure.
гипс geeps - cast.
гита́ра geeTAHrah - guitar.
гла́вный GLAHVnihy -
main; principle (adj).
глаго́л glahGOHL - verb.
гла́дить GLAHdeet' - to
iron.
гла́дкий GLAHTkeey -
smooth (adj).
глаз glahs - eye.
гла́нды GLAHNdih - ton-
sils.
гли́на GLEEnah - clay.
глота́ть glahTAHT' - to
swallow.
глубо́кий glooBOHkeey -
deep; in depth (adj).
глу́пый GLOOpihy - stupid;
silly (adj).
глухо́й glooKHOY - deaf
(adj).
гнев gnyehf - anger.
говори́ть gahvahrEET' - to

speak, talk (about).

говя́дина gahvYAHDeenah - beef.

год goht - year.

голова́ gahlahVAH - head.

головна́я бо́ль gahlahv-NAHyah bohl' - headache.

го́лод GOHlaht - hunger.

голо́дный gahLOHDnihy - hungry (adj).

го́лос GOHlahs - voice.

голосова́ть gahlahsahVAHT' - to vote.

голубо́й gahlooBOY - light blue (adj).

голубцы́ gahloopTSIH - stuffed cabbage.

го́лубь GOHloop' - pigeon; dove.

го́лый GOHlihy - naked (adj).

гомосексуали́зм gahmah-seeksooahlEEZM - homo-sexuality.

гора́ gahRAH - mountain.

гора́здо gahRAHZdah - much, far.

го́рдый GOHRdihy - proud (adj).

го́ре GOHRyeh - grief.

го́рло GOHRlah - throat.

го́рничная GOHRneech-nahyah - maid.

го́род GOHraht - city.

горо́х gahROHKH - peas.

горчи́ца gahrCHEEtsah - mustard.

го́рький GOHR'keey - bitter (adj).

горя́чий gahrYAHcheey - hot (of food and drink) (adj).

господи́н gahspahDEEN -

Mr. (pre-revolutionary).

госпожа́ gahspahZHAH - Mrs. (pre-revolutionary).

гости́ница gahsTEEneetsah - hotel.

го́сть gohst' - guest.

госуда́рственный gahsoo-DAHRstveennihy - state; government (adj).

госуда́рство gahsooDAHR-stvah - the State.

гото́вить gahTOHveet' - to prepare.

гото́вый gahTOHvihy - ready (adj).

гра́дус GRAHdoos - temp-erature.

гра́дусник GRAHdoosneek - thermometer.

граждани́н grahzhdahNEEN - citizen.

гражда́нка grahzhDAHNkah - citizeness.

гражда́нский grahzhDAHN-skeey - civil; civilian (adj).

гражда́нство grahzhDAHN-stvah - citizenship.

гра́мм grahm - gram.

грамма́тика grahmMAHtee-kah - grammar.

грампласти́нка grahmplahs-TEENkah - record.

грана́т grahNAHT - garnet.

грани́ца grahNEEtsah - border.

гребёнка greebYOHNkah - comb.

гре́йпфрут GREYPfroot - grapefruit.

гре́х gryehkh - sin.

грибы́ greeBIH - mush-rooms.

грипп greep - flu.
гроза grahZAH - thunder-
storm.
грозный GROHZnihy -
threatening (adj).
гром grohm - thunder.
громкий GROHMkeey - loud
(adj).
грубый GROObihy - rude;
course (adj).
грудь groot' - chest; breast.
грузовик groozahVEEK -
truck.
группа GROOPpah - group.
группа крови GROOPpah
KROHvee - blood type.
грустный GROOSTnihy -
sad; melancholy (adj).
груша GROOshah - pear.
грыжа GRIHzhah - hernia.
грязный GRYAHZnihy -
dirty; filthy (adj).
грязь gryahs' - dirt; filth.
губа gooBAH - lip.
гудок gooDOHK - horn;
whistle.
гулять goolYAHT' - to
stroll, walk.
гуляш goolYAHSH -
goulash.
густой goosTOY - thick,
dense (adj).
гусь goos' - goose.

Д

да dah - yes.
давай dahVAY - let's; go
ahead!
давать dahVAHT' - to give.
давление dahvLYEHneeyeh
- (blood) pressure.
давно dahvNOH - long ago.
далее DAHleeyeh - further;

farther.
далеко dahleeKOH - far
away.
дальше DAHL'sheh -
farther; continue.
дамский DAHMskeey -
ladies (adj).
дарить dahrEET' - to give
(as a gift).
дары моря DAHrih
MOHryah - sea food.
дача DAHchah - cottage.
дверь dvyehr' - door.
движение dveeZHEHnee-
yeh - movement; traffic.
дворец dvahrYEHTS -
palace.
двоюродный брат dvah-
YOOrahdnihy braht -
cousin (m).
двоюродная сестра dvah-
YOOrahdnahyah sees-
TRAH - cousin (f).
двуспальный dvoo-
SPAHL'nihy - double
occupency (adj).
девочка DYEHvahchkah -
little girl.
девушка DYEHvooshkah -
young lady; waitress.
дедушка DYEHdooshkah -
grandfather.
дежурная deezhOORnahyah
- hall monitor.
дезинфицировать deezeen-
feetsEERahvaht' - to
disinfect.
дезодаратор deezahdah-
RAHtahr - deoderant.
действие DEYSTveeyeh -
action.
действительно deystVEE-
teel'nah - really; truly.

143

действительный deystVEE-teel'nihy - real; actual; effective (adj).
действовать DEYSTvahvaht' - to act, take action.
делать DYEHlaht' - to do.
делить deelEET' - to share, divide.
дело DYEHlah - matter; affair; business.
деловой deelahVOY - business (adj).
денежный перевод DYEH-neezhnihy peereeVOHT - money order.
день dyehn' - day.
день рождения dyehn' rahzhDYEHneeyah - birthday.
деньги DYEHN'gee - money.
деревня deeRYEHVnyah - countryside.
дерево DYEHreevah - tree.
деревянный deereevYAHN-nihy - wooden (adj).
держать deerZHAHT' - to hold, keep, support.
десерт deeSYEHRT - dessert.
детектив deeteekTEEF - mystery (story/movie).
дети DYEHtee - children.
детский DYEHTskeey - children's (adj).
дефицит deefeeTSEET - deficit.
дешёвый deeSHOHvihy - inexpensive; cheap (adj).
джинсы DZHEENsih - jeans.
диабет deeahBYEHT - diabetes.
диагноз deeAHGnahs - diagnosis.

диван deeVAHN - sofa.
диета deeYEHtah - diet.
дикий DEEkeey - wild (adj).
директор deeRYEHKtahr - director; manager.
дирижёр deereezhOHR - conductor (music).
дичь deech' - wild game.
длина dleeNAH - length.
длинный DLEENnihy - long (physically) (adj).
длиться DLEEtsah - to last.
для dlyah - for.
дневной dneevNOY - daytime (adj).
до dah - to; before; until.
до свидания dahsveeDAH-neeyah - goodbye.
доброта dahbrahTAH - kindness.
добрый DOHbrihy - good; kind (adj).
довольно dahVOHL'nah - rather; fairly.
договор dahgahVOHR - contract; agreement.
дождь dohsht' - rain.
дозировка dahzeeROHFkah - dosage.
долгий DOHLgeey - long (in time) (adj).
долго DOHLgah - for a long time.
должен DOHLzhehn - should; must; ought to.
долина dahLEEnah - valley.
доллар DOHLlahr - dollar.
доля DOHLyah - share; lot.
дом dohm - house; home.
дорога dahROHgah - road.
дорогой dahrahGOY - dear; expensive; valuable (adj).

144

достáточно dahsTAHtahch-nah - enough.
достóинство dahsTOHeen-stvah - value; worth.
дóступ DOHstoop - access.
доход dahKHOHT - income.
дочь dohch - daughter.
драгоцéнность drahgah-TSEHNnahst' - jewel.
драматýрг drahmahTOORK - playwright.
дрéвний DRYEHVneey - ancient (adj).
друг drook - friend.
другóй drooGOY - other; another; the other.
дрýжба DROOZHbah - friendship.
дрýжный DROOZHnihy - friendly; amicable (adj).
дуплó dooplLOH - cavity.
дýра DOOrah - fool (f).
дурáк dooRAHK - fool (m).
духи dooKHEE - perfume.
душ doosh - shower.
душá dooSHAH - soul.
душéвный dooshEHVnihy - mental; emotional (adj).
дýшно DOOSHnah - stuffy.
дым dihm - smoke.
дымный DIHMnihy - smokey (adj).
дыня DIHNyah - melon.
дырá dihRAH - hole.
дыхáние dihKHAHneeyeh - breathing; respiration.
дышáть dihshAHT' - to breath.
дюжина DYOOzheenah - dozen.
дюйм dyooym - inch.
дядя DYAHdyah - uncle.

Е

еврéй/(-ка) yeevREY/(-kah) - Jew/(f).
еврéйский yeevREYskeey - Jewish; Hebrew (adj).
европéец/(-пéйка) yeev-rahPYEHeets/(-PEYkah) - European (f).
европéйский yeevrah-PEYskeey - European (adj).
егó yeeVOH - his; its.
едá yeeDAH - food.
едвá yeedVAH - hardly; scarsely; barely.
её yeeYOH - her; its.
ёж yohsh - hedgehog.
ежевика yeezhehVEEkah - blackberries.
ежегóдный yeezhehGOHD-nihy - yearly; annual (adj).
ежеднéвный yeezhehd-NYEHVnihy - daily (adj).
ежемéсячный yeezheh-MYEHseechnihy - monthly (adj).
ездá yeezDAH - ride; drive.
éздить YEHZdeet' - to drive.
ёлка YOHLkah - spruce; Christmas tree.
ермóлка yeerMOHLkah - skullcap.
éсли YEHSlee - if; when; whereas.
естéственно yeestYEHST-veennah - naturally.
есть yehst' - to eat.
éхать YEHkhaht' - to drive.
ещё yeeSHCHOH - still; yet; else; more; another.
ещё раз yeeSHCHOH rahs - once again.

Ж

жа́дный ZHAHDnihy - greedy (adj).

жа́жда ZHAHZHdah - thirst.

жале́ть zhahLYEHT' - to feel sorry for; pity.

жа́лоба ZHAHlahbah - complaint.

жаль zhahl' - pity.

жар zhahr - fever.

жа́рить ZHAHReet' - to fry, roast, broil.

жа́ркий ZHAHRkeey - hot (of the weather) (adj).

ждать zhdaht' - to wait.

железа́ zhehleeZAH - gland.

жёлтый ZHOHLtihy - yellow (adj).

же́мчуг ZHEHMchook - pearl.

жена́ zhehNAH - wife.

жена́т zhehNAHT - married (men) (adj.)

же́нский ZHEHNskeey - feminine; woman's (f.)

же́нщина ZHEHNshchee-nah - woman.

жесто́кий zhehsTOHkeey - cruel; brutal (adj).

жечь zhehch - to burn.

жи́вопись ZHEEvahpees' - painting.

живо́т zheeVOHT - stomach.

живо́тное zheeVOHTnah-yeh - animal.

жи́знь zheezn' - life.

жи́ла ZHEElah - vein.

жиле́т zheeLYEHT - vest.

жир zheer - fat; grease.

жи́рный ZHEERnihy - fatty; greasy; oily (adj).

жи́тель ZHEEteel' - resident.

жить zheet' - to live.

журна́л zhoorNAHL - magazine.

журнали́ст zhoornahLEEST - journalist.

З

за zah - behind; beyond; past; for; in; after.

заболе́ть zahbahLYEHT' - to fall ill.

забо́та zahBOHtah - care; concern.

забыва́ть zahbihVAHT' - to forget.

забы́тый zahBIHTihy - forgotten (adj).

заведе́ние zahveeDYEH-neeyeh - institution.

заве́дующий zahVYEHdoo-yooshcheey - manager.

завод zahVOHT - factory.

за́втра ZAHFtrah - tomorrow.

за́втрак ZAHFtrahk - breakfast.

за́втракать ZAHFtrahkaht' - to eat breakfast.

за́втрашний ZAHFtrahsh-neey - tomorrow's (adj).

зага́р zahGAHR - sunburn; sun tan.

за́дний ZAHDneey - rear; back; hind (adj).

зажига́лка zahzhee-GAHLkah - cigarette lighter.

заказа́ть zahkahzAHT' - to order.

146

заключе́ние zahklyooCHEH
-neeyeh - conclusion.
зако́н zahKOHN - law.
зако́нный zahKOHNnihy -
legal; legitimate (adj).
зако́нченный zahKOHN-
chehnnihy - finished;
completed (adj).
закры́тый zahKRIHtihy -
closed (adj).
заку́ска zahKOOSkah -
appetizer; snack.
заку́сочная zahKOOsahch-
nahyah - snackbar.
зал zahl - hall.
зали́в zahLEEF - bay; gulf.
заме́на zahMYEHnah -
substitution.
заме́тка zahMYEHTkah -
note; mark; notice.
замо́к zahMOHK - lock.
за́мужем ZAHmoozhehm -
married (women).
за́навес ZAHnahvees -
curtain.
заня́тие zahnYAHteeyeh -
occupation; work; studies.
заня́тый zahnYAHtihy -
busy; occupied (adj).
за́пад ZAHpaht - west.
за́падный ZAHpahdnihy -
western (adj).
за́пах ZAHpahkh - smell.
записа́ться zahpeeSAHTsah
- to sign up (for).
за́пись ZAHpees' -
recording (record/tape).
запо́р zahPOHR - constip-
ation.
запреща́ть zahpreeshch-
AHT' - to forbid.
зараже́ние zahrahZHEH-
neeyeh - infection.

зара́нее zahRAHnehyeh -
in advance.
за́яц ZAHeets - hare.
звезда́ zvyehzDAH - star.
звук zvook - sound; noise.
зда́ние ZDAHneeyeh -
building.
здесь zdyehs' - here.
здоро́вый zdahROHvihy -
healthy (adj).
здоро́вье zdahROHv'yeh -
health.
зеленщи́к zeeleenSHCHEEK
- greengrocer.
зелёный zeeLYOHnihy -
green (adj).
земля́ zeemLYAH - ground;
dirt; earth.
земляни́ка zeemleeNEEkah
- strawberries.
зе́ркало ZYEHRkahlah -
mirror.
зерно́ zeerNOH - grain.
зима́ zeeMAH - winter.
зи́мний ZEEMneey - winter
(adj).
зло́бный ZLOHBnihy -
malicious; spiteful (adj).
злой zloy - evil; wicked;
mean; malicious (adj).
знак znahk - sign; signal.
знако́мство znahKOHM-
stvah - acquaintance.
знако́мый znahKOHMihy -
acquainted; familiar (adj).
знамени́тый znahmeeNEE-
tihy - famous (adj).
зна́ние ZNAHneeyeh -
knowledge.
знать znaht' - to know.
значе́ние znahCHEHneeyeh
- meaning; sense.
значи́тельный znahCHEE-

teel'nihy - considerable; significant (adj).
знáчить ZNAHcheet' - to mean.
значóк znahCHOHK - badge.
зóлото ZOHlahtah - gold.
золотóй zahlahTOY - gold (adj).
зóнтик ZOHNteek - umbrella.
зоопáрк zahahPAHRK - zoo.
зрéлый ZRYEHlihy - ripe; mature (adj).
зрéние ZRYEHneeyeh - eyesight.
зрúтель ZREEteel' - spectator.
зуб zoop - tooth.
зубнáя бóль zoobNAHyah bohl' - toothache.
зубнáя пáста zoobNAHyah PAHStah - toothpaste.
зубнáя щётка zoobNAHyah SHCHOHTkah - toothbrush.
зубнóй врáч zoobNOY vrahch - dentist.
зять zyaht' - son-in-law; brother-in-law.

И

и ee - and; also.
игóлка eeGOHLkah - needle.
игрá eegRAH - game.
игрáть eegRAHT' - to play.
игрýшка eegROOSHkah - toy.
идéя eedYEHyah - idea.
идти EETtee - to go, walk.
избá eesBAH - peasant's hut; cabin.
извéстие eezVYEHSteeyeh - news.

извинúте eezveeNEEtyeh - sorry; excuse me.
извинять eezveenYAHT' - to excuse, pardon.
из-за eezzah - because of.
излúшний eezLEESHneey - excessive; superfluous (adj).
изумрýд eezoomROOT - emerald.
изюм eezYOOM - raison.
икóна eekOHnah - icon.
иконостáс eekahnahSTAHS - iconostasis.
икрá eekRAH - caviar.
или EElee - or.
úменно EEMeennah - exactly; precisely.
имýщество eemOOSHCHehstvah - property.
úмя EEMyah - first name.
инáче eeNAHcheh - differtly; otherwise.
инвалúд eenvahLEET - disabled person.
инвалúдность eenvahLEEDnahct' - disability.
индéйка eenDEYkah - turkey.
инженéр eenzheeNYEHR - engineer.
иногдá eenahgDAH - sometimes.
инострáнец eenahsTRAHneets - foreigner.
инострáнный eenahsTRAHNnihy - foreign (adj).
инстрýкция eenSTROOKtseeyah - instructions.
инсýльт eenSOOL'T - stroke.
интерéсный eenteeRYEHS-

nihy - interesting (adj).
искренний EESkreenneey -
sincere (adj).
искусственный eesKOOST-
veennihy - artificial (adj).
искусство eesKOOSTvah -
art; skill.
испорченный eesPOHR-
chehnnihy - spoiled;
rotten; tainted (adj).
исследование eesSLYEH-
dahvahneeyeh - research.
история eesTOHreeyah -
history; story.

Й
йод yoht - iodine.

К
к k - to; toward.
кабина kahBEEnah - booth;
cubicle.
каблук kahbLOOK - heel.
каждый KAHZHdihy -
every (adj).
как kahk - how.
как далеко kahk dahlee-
KOH - how far.
как долго kahk DOHLgah -
how long.
какао kahKAHoh - cocoa.
какой kahKOY - which.
как-то KAHKtah -
somehow.
календарь kahleenDAHR' -
calendar.
калория kahLOHreeyah -
calorie.
кальсоны kahl'SOHnih -
long underwear.
камбала KAHMbahlah -
flounder; sole.
камень KAHmeen' - rock.

камера хранения KAHmee-
rah khrahNYEHneeyah -
baggage room.
канадец/(-надка)
kahNAHdeets/(-NAHT-
kah) Canadian/(f).
канадский kahNAHTskeey -
Canadian (adj).
канал kahNAHL - canal.
каникулы kahNEEkoolih -
school vacation.
капля KAHPlyah - drop.
капуста kahPOOStah -
cabbage.
карандаш kahrahnDAHSH -
pencil.
карат kahRAHT - carat.
караул kahrahOOL - guard;
sentry.
карман kahrMAHN -
pocket.
карманный фонарь kahr-
MAHNnihy fahNAHR' -
flash light.
карнавал kahrnahVAHL -
carnival.
карта KAHRtah - map.
картина kahrTEEnah -
picture; drawing.
картофель kahrTOHfeel' -
potato.
касса KAHSsah - ticket
office; cashier's booth.
кассета kahsSYEHtah -
cassette.
кассир kahsSEER - cashier.
кастрюля kahstRYOOLyah -
pot; sausepan.
каток kahTOHK - skating
rink.
кафе kahFYEH - cafe.
кафедра KAHfeedrah -
department.

ка́чество KAHchehstvah -
quality.
ка́шель KAHSHehl' - cough.
квадра́тный kvahdRAHT-
nihy - square (adj).
кварта́л kvahrTAHL - block
(in a city).
кварти́ра kvahrTEERah -
apartment.
квас kvahs - kvass
(fermented drink).
ке́ды KYEHdih - sneakers.
ке́мпинг KYEHMpeeng -
camping.
кефи́р keeFEER - a yogurt-
like drink.
килогра́мм keelahgRAHM -
kilogram.
киломе́тр keelahMYEHTR -
kilometer.
кино́ keeNOH - movie; the
cinema.
кинотеа́тр keenahteeAHTR
- movie theater.
кио́ск keeOHSK - kiosk.
кислоро́д keeslahROHT -
oxygen.
ки́слый KEESlihy - sour
(adj).
кишка́ keeshKAH -
intestine.
кла́дбище KLAHTbee-
shcheh - cemetary.
класси́ческий klahsSEECH-
ehskeey - classical (adj).
клей kley - glue.
кли́мат KLEEmaht -
climate.
кли́пс kleeps - clip-on
earrings.
клоп klohp - bedbug.
клуб kloop - club.
клю́ква KLYOOKvah -

cranberries.
ключ klyooch - key.
кни́га KNEEgah - book.
кни́жный магази́н
KNEEZHnihy mahgahZEEN
- book store.
кно́пка KNOHPkah - push
button; snap.
ковёр kahVYOHR - rug.
когда́ kahgDAH - when.
ко́жа KOHzhah - skin;
leather.
ко́жаный KOHzhahnihy -
leather (adj).
колбаса́ kahlbahSAH -
sausage.
коле́но kahLYEHnah - knee.
колесо́ kahleeSOH - wheel.
коли́чество kahlEECHehst-
vah - quantity.
ко́локол KOHlahkahl - bell.
колхо́з kahlKHOHS -
collective farm.
кома́нда kahMAHNdah -
sports team.
командиро́вка kahmahn-
deeROHFkah - business
trip; assignment.
кома́р kahMAHR -
mosquito.
комбина́ция kahmbeen-
AHTSeeyah - slip.
коме́дия kahMYEHdeeyah -
comedy.
коммуна́льный kahmmoon-
AHL'nihy - communal
(adj).
ко́мната KOHMnahtah -
room.
компле́кт kahmpLYEHKT -
complete set.
компози́тор kahmpahZEE-
tahr - composer.

компью́тер kahmP'YOOteer
- computer.
конве́рт kahnVYEHRT -
envelope.
конди́терская kahnDEEteer
-skahyah - confectionery
shop.
кондиционе́р kahndeetsee-
ahNYEHR - air condit-
ioner.
коне́ц kahnYEHTS - end.
коне́чно kahnYEHSHnah - of
course.
ко́нкурс KOHNkoors -
competition; contest.
консе́рвный нож kahn-
SYEHRVnihy nohsh - can
opener.
консе́рвы kahnSYEHRvih -
canned goods.
ко́нсульство KOHNsool'-
stvah - consulate.
конта́ктная ли́нза kahn-
TAHKTnahyah LEENzah -
contact lens.
конто́ра kahnTOHrah -
office.
конфе́ты kahnFYEHtih -
candy.
конце́рт kahnTSEHRT -
concert.
коньки́ kahn'KEE - skates.
конья́к kahn'YAK - cognac;
brandy.
кооперати́в kahahpeerah-
TEEF cooperative store.
копе́йка kahPEYkah -
kopeck.
кора́бль kahRAHBL' - ship.
корзи́на kahrZEEnah -
basket.
кори́нка kahrEENkah -
currants.

кори́ца kahREEtsah -
cinnamon.
кори́чневый kahREECH-
neevihy - brown (adj).
коро́бка kahrOHPkah - box.
коро́ткий kahROHTkeey -
short (adj).
косме́тика kahsMYEHteekah
- make up.
костёр kahsTYOHR -
campfire.
кость kohst' - bone.
костю́м kahsTYOOM - suit.
котле́та kahtLYEHtah -
cutlet.
ко́фе KOHfyeh - coffee.
коше́рный kahshEHRnihy -
kosher (adj).
ко́шка KOHSHkah - cat.
край kray - edge; rim;
country.
кран krahn - faucet.
краси́вый krahsEEVihy -
beautiful; pretty (adj).
кра́сный KRAHSnihy - red
(adj).
красота́ krahsahTAH -
beauty.
крахма́л krahkhMAHL -
starch.
креди́тная ка́рточка kree-
DEETnahyah KAHRtahch-
kah - credit card.
крем kryehm - cream;
lotion.
кре́пкий KRYEHPkeey -
strong; durable (adj).
кре́сло KRYEHSlah - arm
chair.
крест kryehst - cross.
криво́й kreeVOY - crooked
(adj).
кри́зис KREEzees - crisis.

151

крик kreek - shout; cry.
кровать krahVAHT' - bed.
кровоизлияние krahvah-
eezleeYAHneeyeh -
hemorrhage.
кровоточить krahvah-
taCHEET' - to bleed.
кровь krohf' - blood.
кролик KROHleek - rabbit.
кроме KROHmyeh - except
for; but; besides.
круг krook - circle.
круглый KROOGlihy -
ciruclar; round (adj).
круиз krooEEZ - cruise.
крыша KRIHshah - roof.
крышка KRIHshkah - lid;
cover.
кстати KSTAHtee -
incidentally; by the way.
кто ktoh - who.
кто-нибудь KTOHneeboot' -
anyone; someone.
куда kooDAH - where to.
кукла KOOKlah - doll;
puppet.
культура kool'TOOrah -
culture.
купальная шапочка
kooPAHL'nahyah SHAHP-
ahchkah - bathing cap.
купальник koopAHL'neek -
bathing suit.
купе koopYEH - train
compartment.
купить kooPEET' - to buy.
курить kooREET' - to
smoke.
курица KOOreetsah -
chicken.
курорт koorOHRT - resort.
кусок kooSOHK - piece.
кухня KOOKHnyah -
kitchen.

Л
лавра LAHVrah -
monastery.
лагерь LAHgeer' - camp.
ладно LAHDnah - ok.
ладонь lahDOHN' - palm.
лак lahk - polish; lacquer.
лампа LAHMpah - lamp.
лампочка LAHMpahchkah -
light bulb.
лапша lahpSHAH - soup
noodle.
левый LYEHvihy - left
(direction).
легальный leeGAHL'nihy -
legal (adj).
лёгкий LYOHKHkeey - easy
(adj).
легко leekhKOH - easily.
лёгкое LYOHKHkahyeh -
lung.
лёд lyoht - ice.
лезвия LYEHZveeyah -
razor blades.
лекарство leeKAHRstvah -
medicine.
лекция LYEHKtseeyah -
lecture.
лес lyehs - forest.
лестница LYEHSTneetsah -
stairs.
летний LYEHTneey -
summer (adj).
лето LYEHtah - summer.
лечение leeCHEHneeyeh -
medical treatment.
ли lee - if; whether.
либо LEEbah - or.
лимон leeMOHN - lemon.
лимонад leemahnAHT -
lemonade.

152

липкий LEEPkeey - sticky (adj).
листок leesTOHK - leaf; sheet (of paper).
литература leeteerahTOOrah - literature.
литр leetr - liter.
лифт leeft - elevator.
лицо leetsOH - face.
личный LEECHnihy - personal; private (adj).
лишний LEESHneey - spare; extra (adj).
лоб lohp - forehead.
лодка LOHTkah - boat.
лодыжка lahDIHSHkah - ankle.
ложа LOHzhah - theater box.
ложка LOHSHkah - spoon.
ложный LOHZHnihy - false (adj).
локоть LOHkaht' - elbow.
лососина lahsahSEEnah - salmon.
лошадь LOHSHaht' - horse.
лужа LOOZHah - puddle.
лук look - onion.
луна looNAH - moon.
лучше LOOCHsheh - better.
лучший LOOCHsheey - better; the best (adj).
лыжи LIHzhee - skis.
любить lyoobEET' - to love.
любовь lyoobOHF' - love.
любой lyoobOY - any.
любопытный lyoobahPIHTnihy - curious (adj).
люди LYOOdee - people.

М

мавзолей mahvzahLEY - mausoleum.

магазин mahgahZEEN - store.
магнитофон mahgneetah-FOHN - tape recorder.
майка MAYkah - t-shirt.
мак mahk - poppy.
малахит mahlahKHEET - malachite.
маленький MAHLeen'keey - small (adj).
малина mahLEEnah - raspberries.
мало MAHlah - a little; not enough.
мальчик MAHL'cheek - boy.
мандарин mahndahREEN - tangerine.
маринованный mahree-NOHvahnnihy - marinated (adj).
марка MAHRkah - stamp.
маслина mahsLEEnah - olives.
масло MAHSlah - butter.
мат maht - check mate.
матрёшка mahtRYOHSHkah - wooden, nested dolls.
матч mahtch - sports match.
мать maht' - mother.
мачеха MAHchehkhah - step-mother.
машина mahSHEEnah - car; machine.
мебель MYEHbeel' - furniture.
мёд myoht - honey.
медленный MYEHDleen-nihy - slow (adj).
медсестра meedseesTRAH - nurse.
между MYEHZHdoo - between.

международный meezhdoo-
nahROHDnihy - inter-
national.
мелочь MYEHlahch - small
change.
менструация meenstroo-
AHtseeyah - menstru-
ation.
меньше MYEHN'sheh - less.
меню meenYOO - menu.
мера MYEHrah - measure;
extent; degree.
мёртвый MYOHRTvihy -
dead (adj).
местный MYEHSTnihy -
local (adj).
место MYEHStah - place;
seat; site.
месяц MYEHSeets - month.
метр myehtr - meter.
метро meeTROH - subway.
мех myehkh - fur.
механизм meekhahnEEZM -
mechanism.
меховая шапка meekhah-
VAHyah SHAHPkah - fur
hat.
меховой meekhahVOY - fur
(adj).
мешок meeSHOHK - bag;
sack.
маленький MEEleen'keey -
dear; sweet (adj).
милиционер meeleetseeah-
NYEHR - policeman.
милиция meeLEEtseeyah -
the police.
миллион meelleeOHN -
million.
милый MEElihy - nice;
sweet; dear; darling (adj).
мимо MEEmah - by; past.
миндалина meenDAHlee-

nah - tonsil.
минута meenOOTah -
minute.
мир meer - world; peace.
миска MEESkah - bowl.
мишка MEESHkah - teddy
bear.
младенец mlahDYEHneets -
baby; infant.
младший MLAHTsheey -
younger (adj).
мнение MNYEHneeyeh -
opinion.
много MNOHgah - a lot.
многообразный mnahgah-
ahbRAHZnihy - diverse
(adj).
многоцветный mnahgah-
TSVYEHTnihy - multi-
colored (adj).
могила mahGEElah - grave.
могучий mahGOOcheey -
powerful.
мода MOHdah - fashion;
style.
модный MOHDnihy -
fashionable; stylish (adj).
может быть MOHZHeht
biht' - maybe; perhaps.
можно MOHZHnah - may;
can.
мозг mohsk - brain.
мокрый MOHKrihy - wet
(adj).
молитва mahLEETvah -
prayer book.
молния MOHLneeyah -
lightning; zipper.
молодёжь mahlahDYOHSH -
young people.
молодой mahlahDOY -
young (adj).
молоко mahlahKOH - milk.

154

моло́чная mahLOHCH-
nahyah - dairy.
молча́ние mahlCHAH-
neeyeh - silence.
монасты́рь mahnahsTIHR' -
monastary.
моне́та mahNYEHtah - coin.
мо́ре MOHRyeh - sea.
морко́вь mahrKOHF' -
carrot.
моро́женое mahROHZH-
ehnahyeh - ice cream.
моро́женый mahROHZH-
ehnnihy - frozen (adj).
моро́з mahROHS - frost.
моско́вский mahsKOHF-
skeey - Moscow (adj).
мост mohst - bridge.
мото́р mahTOHR - motor.
мотоци́кл mahtahTSEEKL -
motorcycle.
моча́ mahCHAH - urine.
мочево́й пузы́рь mahchee-
VOY poozIHR' - bladder.
мо́щный MOHSHCHnihy -
powerful (adj).
муж moosh - husband.
му́жество MOOZHehstvah -
courage.
мужско́й mooshSKOY -
men's (adj).
мужчи́на mooshCHEEnah -
man.
музе́й mooZEY - museum.
му́зыка MOOZihkah -
music.
мука́ mooKAH - flour.
му́льтфильм MOOL'Tfeel'm
- cartoon.
му́скул MOOSkool - muscle.
му́сор MOOsahr - trash;
rubbish.
му́ха MOOkhah - fly.

мы mih - we.
мы́ло MIHlah - soap.
мысль mihsl' - thought;
idea.
мышь mihsh - mouse.
мя́гкий MYAHKHkeey - soft
(adj).
мя́со MYAHsah - meat.
мяч myahch - ball.

Н

на nah - on; in.
наби́тый nahBEEtihy -
tightly packed (adj).
наве́рно nahVYEHRnah -
probably.
наве́рх nahVYEHRKH - up;
upwards (location).
наверху́ nahveerKHOO -
above (destination).
наводне́ние nahvahdNYEH-
neeyeh - flood.
на́волочка NAHvahlahchkah
- pillowcase.
навсегда́ nahfseegDAH -
forever.
награ́да nahGRAHdah -
reward.
над naht - over; above.
надгро́бный ка́мень nahd-
GROHBnihy KAHmeen' -
tombstone.
наде́жда nahDYEHZHdah -
hope.
на́до NAHdah - must.
на́дпись nahtPEES' -
inscription.
наза́д nahzAHT - back;
backwards.
назва́ние nahzVAHneeyeh
- name; title.
называ́ть nahzihVAHT' - to
be called, named.

155

наизу́сть naheezOOST' - by heart.

найти́ nayTEE - to find.

наказа́ние nahkahzAHN-eeyeh - punishment.

наконе́ц nahkahnYEHTS - at last; finally.

накра́сть nahkRAHST' - to steal.

нале́во nahLYEHvah - on the left.

нало́г nahLOHK - tax.

наме́рение nahMYEHree-neeyeh - intention.

наоборо́т nahahbahROHT - the other way around; on the contrary.

напи́ток nahPEEtahk - drink.

напо́р nahPOHR - pressure.

напра́во nahPRAHvah - on the right.

напра́сно nahPRAHSnah - in vain; for nothing.

наприме́р nahpreeMYEHR - for example; for instance.

напро́тив nahPROHteef - opposite; facing.

напряже́ние nahpreeZHEH-neeyeh - tension; stress; strain.

нарко́з nahrKOHS - anesthesia.

наро́д nahROHT - a people;

наро́дный nahROHDnihy - national; folk (adj).

наро́ст nahROHST - growth; tumor.

наро́чно nahROHCHnah - deliberately; on purpose.

нары́в nahRIHF - abscess.

насеко́мое nahseeKOHmah-yeh - insect.

населе́ние nahseeLYEHnee-yeh - population.

наси́лие nahSEEleeyeh - violence.

наслажде́ние nahslahzh-DYEHneeyeh - enjoyment; pleasure; delight.

на́сморк NAHsmahrk - head cold.

настоя́щий nahstahYAH-shcheey - present; real; true (adj).

настрое́ние nahstrahYEH-neeyeh - mood.

нау́шник nahOOSHneek - earmuff; headphone.

находи́ться nahkhahDEET-sah - to be found, located.

национа́льность nahtseeah-NAHL'nahst' - national-ity.

на́ция NAHtseeyah - nation.

нача́ло nahCHAHlah - beginning.

нача́льник nahCHAHL'-neek - chief; head; boss.

начина́ть nahcheeNAHT' - to begin, start.

неблагополу́чный neeblah-gahpahLOOCHnihy - un-fortunate; unhappy (adj).

не́бо NYEHbah - sky; heaven.

небоскрёб neebahSKRYOHP - skyscraper.

небре́жный neeBRYEHZH-nihy - careless; negligent; sloppy; slipshod (adj).

нева́жный neeVAHZHnihy - unimportant (adj).

невероя́тный neeveerah-YAHTnihy - incredible;

unbelievable (adj).

невéста neeVYEHStah - bride.

невéстка neeVYEHSTkah - daughter-in-law; sister-in-law.

невóльный neeVOHL'nihy - unintentional; involuntary (adj).

невыгодный neeVIHgahdnihy - unprofitable; unfavorable (adj).

недáвно needAHVnah - not long ago; recently.

недалёкий needahLYOHkeey - nearby (adj).

недалекó needahleeKOH - not far; close by.

недéля needYEHlyah - week.

недоброкáчественный needahbrahKAHCHehstveennihy - poor-quality (adj).

недовóльный needahvOHL'nihy - dissatisfied (adj).

недóлго neeDOHLgah - not long; brief.

недоразумéние needahrahzooMYEHneeyeh - misunderstanding.

недостáток needahsTAHtahk - shortage; scarcity; defect; deficiency.

недостáточно needahsTAHtahchnah - insufficient.

недостижáмый needahsteeZHEEmihy - unattainable (adj).

неестéственный neeeestEHSTveennihy - unnatural (adj).

нéжный NYEHZHnihy - tender; gentle (adj).

незавáсимость neezahVEEseemahst' - independence.

незакóнный neezahKOHNnihy - illegal (adj).

незамéтно neezahMYEHTnah - unnoticable (adj).

незнакóмец neeznahKOHMeets - stranger.

незнакóмый neeznahKOHmihy - unfamiliar (adj).

незрéлый neezRYEHlihy - unripe; not mature (adj).

неизвéстный neeeezVYEHSTnihy - unknown (adj).

нейтрáльный neytRAHL'nihy - neutral (adj).

некрáсивый neeKRAHSeevihy - ugly (adj).

непóвкий neeLOHFkeey - awkward; clumsy (adj).

нельзя neel'ZYAH - impossible; one can not.

немнóго neemNOHgah - a little; not much.

необходáмый neeahpkhahDEEmihy - necessary; essential (adj).

необыкновéнный neeahbihknahVYEHNnihy - unusual; uncommon (adj).

неопределённый neeahpreedeeLYOHNnihy - vague; indefinite (adj).

неóпытный neeOHpihtnihy - inexperienced (adj).

неохóтно neeahKHOHTnah - reluctantly.

непонятный neepahnYAHTnihy - incomprehensible; unintelligible (adj).

непрáвда neePRAHVdah - untruth; falsehood; lie.

неправильный neePRAH-
veel'nihy - wrong;
incorrect (adj).
неприличный neepree-
LEECHnihy - improper;
indecent (adj).
неприятный neepree-
YAHTnihy - unpleasant;
disagreeable (adj).
нерв nyehrf - nerve.
нервный NYEHRVnihy -
nervous; irritable (adj).
несгораемый шкаф nee-
zgahRAHeemihy shkahf -
safe.
несколько neeSKOHL'kah -
a few; some; several.
неслышный neeSLIHSHnihy
- inaudible (adj).
несправедливый neesprah-
veedLEEvihy - unfair;
injust (adj).
несчастный neeSHAHST-
nihy - unhappy; unfor-
tunate (adj).
несчастный случай nee-
SHAHSTnihy SLOOchay -
accident.
не nee - not.
нет nyeht - no.
нетерпение neeteerPYEH-
neeyeh - impatience.
неудобный neeooDOHBnihy
- uncomfortable (adj).
неуспешный neeoos-
PYEHSHnihy - unsuccess-
ful (adj).
нечестный neeCHEHSTnihy
- dishonest (adj).
нечистый neeCHEEStihy -
unclean; dirty (adj).
неясный neeYAHSnihy -
unclear (adj).

нижнее бельё NEEZH-
neeyeh beel'YOH -
underwear.
нижний NEEZHnihy - lower
(adj).
никак neeKAHK - no way.
никогда neekahgDAH -
never.
никто neekTOH - no one.
нитка NEETkah - thread.
ничего neecheeVOH -
nothing.
но noh - but; however.
новый NOHvihy - new (adj).
Новый год NOHvihy goht -
New Year.
нога nahGAH - leg; foot.
нож nohsh - knife.
ножницы NOHZHneetsih -
scissors.
ноль nohl' - zero.
номер NOHmeer - hotel
room; number; issue.
номерок nahmeeROHK -
(coat check) ticket.
нормальный NOHRmahl'-
nihy - normal (adj).
нос nohs - nose.
носилки nahSEELkee -
stretcher.
носильщик nahSEEL'-
shcheek - porter.
носки nahsKEE - socks.
ночь nohch - night.
нравиться NRAHveetsah -
to enjoy.
нравы NRAHvih - customs.
ну noo - well; well then.
нужда noozhDAH - need.
нужно NOOZHnah - (one)
must, has to.

О

о oh - about.

о́ба OHbah - both.

обе́д ahBYEHT - lunch.

обе́дать ahBYEHdaht' - to
have lunch.

обезбо́ливание ahbeesBOH-
leevahneeyeh - anesthet-
ization.

обеща́ние ahbeeSHCHAH-
neeyeh - promise.

оби́да ahBEEdah - offence;
insult.

о́бласть OHblahst' - region;
area; field; domain.

обма́н ahbMAHN - fraud;
deception; deceit.

обме́н ahbMYEHN -
exchange.

обменя́ть ahbmeenYAHT' -
to exchange.

о́браз OHbrahs - image;
way; mode; manner.

образе́ц ahbrahzYEHTS -
sample; model; pattern.

образова́ние ahbrahzah-
VAHneeyeh - education.

обра́тный ahbRAHTnihy -
return; opposite (adj).

обстано́вка ahbstahNOHF-
kah - situation; setting.

о́бувь OHboovee - shoes.

обхо́д ahpKHOHT - detour.

общежи́тие ahpshchehZHEE
-teeyeh - dormitory.

о́бщество OHPshchehstvah
- society; company.

о́бщий OHPshcheey -
general; common (adj).

объявле́ние ahb"eevLYEH-
neeyeh - announcement.

объясне́ние ahb"eesNYEH-
neeyeh - explanation.

обы́чно ahBIHCHnah -
usually.

обяза́тельный ahbeeZAH-
teel'nihy - obligatory;
mandatory (adj).

овёс ahVYOHS - oats.

о́вощи OHvahshchee -
vegetables.

овся́нка ahfSYAHNkah -
oatmeal.

огурцы́ ahgoorTSIH -
cucumbers.

оде́жда ahdDYEHZHdah -
clothes.

одея́ло ahdeeYAHlah -
blanket.

одина́ковый ahdeeNAHkah-
vihy - identical (adj).

одна́жды ahdNAHZHdih -
once; one day.

одна́ко ahdNAHkah -
however; but.

одновреме́нный ahdnah-
VRYEHmeennihy -
simultaneous (adj).

ожере́лье ahzheeRYEHL'yeh
- necklace.

о́зеро OHzeerah - lake.

океа́н ahkeeAHN - ocean.

окно́ ahkNOH - window.

о́коло OHkahlah - around;
approximately; about.

оконча́ние ahkahnCHAH-
neeyeh - completion; end.

окра́ска ahKRAHSkah - dye;
hair coloring.

оле́нина ahLYEHneenah -
venison.

он ohn - he.

она́ ahNAH - she.

они́ ahNEE - they.

опазда́ть ahpahzDAHT' - to
be late.

опасный ahPAHSnihy - dangerous (adj).

опера OHpeerah - opera.

описание ahpeeSAHneeyeh - description.

опоздание ahpahzDAHneeyeh - delay; tardiness.

определённый ahpreedee-LYOHNnihy - definite; set; certain (adj).

оптик OPteek - optician.

опыт OHpiht - experience.

опять ahPYAHT' - again.

оранжевый ahRAHNzhehvihy - orange (adj).

орех ahRYEHKH - nut.

оркестр ahrKYEHSTR - orchestra.

оса ahSAH - wasp.

осень OHseen' - fall.

осложнение ahslahzh-NYEHneeyeh - complication.

осмотр ahsMOHTR - examination; checkup.

основа ahsNOHvah - basis.

особенно ahSOHbeennah - especially.

остановка ahstahnOHFkah - bus stop.

остаток ahsTAHtahk - remainder.

осторожно ahstahROHZHnah - beware; careful.

остров OHStrahf - island.

острый OHStrihy - sharp; pungent; keen (adj).

от aht - from.

ответ ahtVYEHT - answer.

отдел ahdDYEHL - section; department.

отдельно ahdDYEHL'nah - separately; individually.

отдых OHDdihkh - rest.

отец ahTYEHTS - father.

отечество ahTYEHCHehstvah - fatherland.

отказ ahtKAHS - refusal.

открытка ahtKRIHTkah - postcard.

открытый ahtKRIHtihy - open (adj).

отлёт ahtLYOHT - departure (airplane).

отношение ahtnahSHEHneeyeh - attitude; relationship; connection.

отопление ahttahpLYEHneeyeh - heating.

отпуск OHTpoosk - vacation from work.

отрава ahtRAHvah - poison.

отрицательный ahtreeTSAH-teel'nihy - negative (adj).

отрывок ahtRIHvahk - passage; excerpt; snatch.

отсутствие ahtSOOTSTveeyeh - absence.

отход ahtKHOHT - departure (train).

отчество OHTchehstvah - patronymic.

отчим OHTcheem - stepfather.

отъезд aht"YEHST - detour.

официант ahfeetseeAHNT - waiter.

официантка ahfeetsee-AHNTkah - waitress.

оформление ahfahrmLYEHneeyeh - processing (of documents).

охота ahKHOHtah - wish; desire.

очевидный ahchehVEEDnihy - obvious (adj).

о́чень OHcheen' - very.
о́чередь OHCHehreet' - line.
очки́ ahchKEE - glasses.
оши́бка ahshEEPkah -
mistake.
ощуще́нье ahshchoo-
SHCHEHneeyeh - feeling;
sensation.

П

паде́ж pahDYEHSH -
grammatical case.
паке́т pahKYEHT - packet;
package.
пала́тка pahLAHTkah -
tent.
па́лец PAHleets - finger.
пальто́ pahl'TOH - coat.
па́мятник PAHMeetneek -
monument.
па́мять PAHMeet' -
memory.
папиро́са pahpeeROHSah -
cigarette.
папиро́сница pahpeeROHS-
neetsah - cigarette case.
па́ра PAHrah - pair.
па́реный PAHreenihy -
steamed (adj).
парикма́хер pahreekMAH-
kheer - hairdresser;
barber.
пари́лья pahREEL'yah -
steam room.
парк pahrk - park.
паро́м pahROHM - ferry.
парохо́д pahrahKHOHT -
ship; steamship.
па́русная ло́дка PAHroos-
nahyah LOHTkah - sail
boat.
па́смурный PAHsmoornihy
- overcast (adj).

па́спорт PAHSpahrt -
passport.
пассажи́р pahssahZHEER -
passenger.
па́сха PAHSkhah - Easter;
Passover.
пау́к pahOOK - spider.
па́хнуть PAHKHnoot' - to
smell.
пацие́нт pahtseeEHNT -
patient.
па́чка PAHCHkah - pack;
bundle.
певе́ц peevYEHTS - singer.
педиа́тр peedeeAHTR -
pediatrician.
пеници́ллин peeneetseel-
LEEN - penicillin.
пе́пельница PYEHpeel'nee-
tsah - ashtray.
первонача́льный peervah-
nahCHAHL'nihy - original
(adj).
перевести́ peereeveesTEE -
to translate.
перево́д peereeVOHT -
translation.
перево́дчик peereeVOHT-
cheek - translator; interpreter.
перевя́зка peereeVYAHSkah
- bandaging; dressing.
переговоры peereegahVOH-
rihy - negotiations.
пе́ред PYEHreet - before; in
front of.
переда́ча peereeDAHchah -
broadcast; transmission.
пере́дний peeRYEHDneey -
front (adj).
перено́сный peereeNOHS-
nihy - portable (adj).
перепи́ска peereePEESkah -

161

correspondence.
перерыв peereeRIHF -
break; recess.
пересадка peereeSAHTkah -
change; transfer (on
planes, trains, buses etc).
переулок peereeOOLahk -
side street.
переход peereeKHOHT -
place to cross; crosswalk.
перец PYEHreets - pepper.
перманент peermahn-
YEHNT - permanent wave.
персик PYEHRseek - peach.
перцовка peerTSOHFkah -
pepper vodka.
перчатки peerCHAHTkee -
gloves.
песня PYEHSnyah - song.
песок peeSOHK - sand.
петрушка peeTROOSHkah -
parsley.
печальный peeCHAHL'nihy
- sad (adj).
печёнка peechOHNkah -
liver (the food).
печень PYEHchehn' - liver
(anatomy).
печенье peeCHEHN'yeh -
cookie; pastry.
печь pyehch - stove.
пешком peeshKOHM - on,
by foot.
пиво PEEvah - beer.
пиджак peedZHAHK -
man's suit jacket.
пижама peezhAHMah -
pyjamas.
пилав peeLAHF - pilaf.
пилюля peeLYOOlyah -
pill.
пинцет peenTSEHT -
tweezers.

пирог peeROHK - pie.
пирожное peeROHZH-
nahyeh - pastry.
писатель peeSAHteel' -
writer.
писать peeSAHT' - to write.
письменно PEES'meennah -
in writing.
письмо pees'MOH - letter.
пить peet' - to drink.
пишущая машинка PEESH-
ooshchahyah mahSHEEN-
kah - typewriter.
пища PEEshchah - food.
плавать PLAHvaht' - to
swim.
плакат plahKAHT - poster.
план plahn - city map.
пластырь – PLAHStihr' -
band-aide.
платить plahTEET' - to pay.
платок plahTOHK - ker-
chief.
платье PLAHT'yeh - dress.
плацкартный plahts-
KAHRTnihy - reserved (on
a train) (adj).
плащ plahshch - raincoat.
племянник pleemYAHN-
neek - nephew.
племянница pleemYAHNeet-
sah - niece.
плёнка PLYOHNkah - film.
плечо pleeCHOH -
shoulder.
плитка PLEETkah -
(chocolate) bar.
пломба PLOHMbah - (tooth)
filling.
плохо PLOHkhah - badly.
плохой plahKHOY - bad;
poor (adj).
площадь PLOHshchaht' -

162

пляж plyahsh - beach.
по pah - along; about; according to.
по крайне мере pah KRAYnyeh MYEHreh - at least.
победа pahBYEHdah - victory.
повар POHvahr - cook.
повторить pahftahREET' - to repeat.
погода pahGOHdah - weather.
под poht - under; beneath.
подарок pahDAHrahk - present; gift.
подгрузник pahdGROOZneek - diaper.
подмётка pahdMYOHTkah - sole (of a shoe).
подписать pahtpeeSAHT' - to sign.
подпись POHTpees' - signature.
подробность pahdROHPnahst' - detail.
подушка pahDOOSHkah - pillow.
поезд POHeest - train.
пожалуйста pahZHAHLstah - please.
пожар pahZHAHR - fire.
пожатие pahZHAHteeyeh - handshake.
пожилой pahzheeLOY - elderly (adj).
позавчера pahzahfcheeRAH - day before yesterday.
позвонить pahzvahNEET' - to call (on the phone).
поздний POHZDneey - late (adj).

поздравлять pahzdrahv-LYAHT' - to congratulate.
позже POHZHzheh - later.
познакомить pahznahKOHmeet' - to introduce.
пока pahKAH - meanwhile; goodbye (coll).
показать pahkahZAHT' - to show.
покупатель pahkooPAHteel' - customer.
покупка pahKOOPkah - purchase.
полдень POHLdeen' - noon.
поле POHLyeh - field; area.
полезный pahLYEHZnihy - useful; helpful (adj).
полёт pahLYOHT - flight.
поликлиника pahleeKLEEneekah - clinic.
политика pahLEEteekah - politics.
полка POHLkah - berth; shelf.
полночь POHLnahch - midnight.
полный POHLnihy - full; complete (adj).
половина pahlahVEEnah - half.
половые органы pahlah-VIHyeh OHRgahnih - genitals.
положение pahlahZHEHneeyeh - situation; condition.
положительный pahlah-ZHEEteel'nihy - positive; affirmative (adj).
полотенце pahlahTYEHNtseh - towel.
полтора pahltahRAH - one and a half.

163

полчаса́ pahlcheeSAH - half hour.

по́льза POHL'zah - use; benefit.

помидо́р pahmeeDOHR - tomato.

по́мощь POHmahshch - help.

понима́ть pahneeMAHT' - to understand.

поно́с pahNOHS - diarrhea.

по́нчик POHNcheek - doughnut.

поня́тный pahnYAHTnihy - understandable (adj).

попра́вка pahPRAHFkah - correction; adjustment.

пора́ pahRAH - it's time.

по́рох POHrahkh - powder.

по́рт pohrt - port.

портре́т pahrtRYEHT - portrait.

портфе́ль pahrtFYEHL' - briefcase.

поря́док pahRYAHdahk - order; sequence.

поса́дка pahSAHTkah - landing.

посла́ть pahsLAHT' - to send.

по́сле POHSlee - after.

по́сле обе́да POHSlee ahBYEHdah - afternoon.

после́дний pahsLYEHDneey - last; latest (adj).

послеза́втра pahslee-ZAHFtrah - day after tomorrow.

посло́вица pahsLOHveetsah - proverb.

посове́товать pahsahVYEH-tahvaht' - to recommend.

посо́льство pahSOHL'stvah - embassy.

посте́ль pahsTYEHL' - bed.

постепе́нно pahsteePYEHN-nah - gradually.

постоя́нный pahstahYAHN-nihy - constant; continuous (adj).

посу́да pahSOOdah - dishes.

посы́лка pahSIHLkah - package.

пот poht - sweat.

потвержде́ние pahdveerzh-DYEHneeyeh - confirmation.

потеря́ть pahteerYAHT' - to lose (sth.).

потоло́к pahtahLOHK - ceiling.

пото́м pahTOHM - then; next; afterwards.

потому́ что pahtahMOO shtah - because.

похо́жий pahKHOHzheey - similar; like (adj).

поцелу́й pahtseeLOOY - kiss.

почему́ pahcheeMOO - why.

почему́-то pahcheeMOO-tah - for some reason.

по́чка POHCHkah - kidney.

по́чта POHCHtah - mail; post office.

почта́мт POHCHTahmt - main postoffice.

почти́ pahchTEE - almost.

почто́вый я́щик pahchTOH-vihy YAHshcheek - mailbox.

по́шлина POHSHleenah - duty (customs).

поэ́зия pahEHzeeyah - poetry.

поэ́т pahEHT - poet.
поэ́тому pahEHtahmoo - therefore.
по́яс POHees - belt; waist.
пра́вда PRAHVdah - truth.
пра́вило PRAHveelah - rule.
пра́вильный PRAHVeel'-nihy - correct; right (adj).
прави́тельство prahVEEteel'stvah - government.
правосла́вный prahvah-SLAHVnihy - orthodox.
пра́вый PRAHvihy - right (direction).
пра́здник PRAHZneek - holiday.
пребыва́ние preebihVAHneeyeh - stay.
предложе́ние preedlah-ZHEHneeyeh - offer; proposal; suggestion.
предме́т preedMYEHT - subject.
предприя́тие preedpree-YAHteeyeh - undertaking; venture.
предупрежде́ние preedoo-preezhDYEHneeyeh - warning.
пре́жде PRYEHZHdyeh - before; formerly.
пре́жний PRYEHZHneey - former; previous (adj).
презервати́в preezeervah-TEEF - contraceptive.
прекра́сный preeKRAHS-nihy - beautfiful (adj).
преподава́тель preepah-dahVAHteel' - teacher.
преподава́тельница pree-pahdahVAHteelneetsah-teacher (f).
препя́тсвие preePYAHTS-veeyeh - hindrance.
преступле́ние preestoop-LYEHneeyeh - crime.
преувеличе́ние preeoovee-leeCHEHneeyeh - exaggeration.
при pree - before.
приве́т preeVYEHT - hi.
привы́чка preeVIHCHkah - habit.
приглаше́ние preeglah-SHEHneeyeh - invitation.
при́город PREEgahraht - suburb.
прие́зд preeYEHST - arrival.
прие́м preeYOHM - reception.
приле́т preeLYOHT - arrival (on a plane).
прили́чный preeLEESHnihy - proper; civilized (adj).
приме́р preeMYEHR - example.
принима́ть preeneeMAHT' - to accept.
приро́да preeROHdah - nature.
при́стань PREEstahn' - dock; pier; wharf.
причёска preeCHOHSkah - hair-do.
причи́на preeCHEEnah - reason.
прия́тный preeYAHTnihy - pleasant (adj).
про proh - about.
пробле́ма prahBLYEHmah - problem.
прогно́з prahgNOHS - prognosis; forecast.
продаве́ц prahdahVYEHTS - salesman.

продáжа prahDAHzhah - sale.

продáть prahDAHT' - to sell.

продолжéние prahdahlZHEHneeyeh - continuation.

произношéние praheeznahSHEHneeyeh - pronunciation.

происхождéние praheezkhahzhDYEHneeyeh - origin.

пролúв prahLEEF - strait; channel.

пропúска prahPEESkah - registration.

прóпуск PROHpoosk - admission; admittance.

простúте prahsTEEtyeh - sorry; excuse me.

прóсто PROHstah - simply.

простóй prahsTOY - simple; easy (adj).

простýда prahsTOOdah - head cold.

простынú prahstihnYAH - sheet.

прóсьба PROZ'bah - request.

протéз prahTYEHS - denture.

прóтив PROHteef - against.

профéссия prahFYEHSseeyah - profession.

профéссор prahFYEHSsahr - professor.

прохлáдный prahkhLAHDnihy - cool (adj).

прóшлый PROHSHlihy - past (adj).

прощáй prahSHCHAY - farewell.

проявлéние praheevLYEHneeyeh - (film) development.

пруд proot - pond.

прямóй preeMOY - straight (adj).

птúца PTEEtsah - bird.

пýговица POOgahveetsah - button.

пузырь poozIHR' - blister.

пулóвер poolOHveer - sweater.

пульс pool's - pulse.

пýнкт poonkt - point; station; center.

пустóй poosTOY - empty; vacant (adj).

путеводúтель pooteevahDEEteel' - guidebook.

путешéственник pooteeshEHSTveenneek - traveler.

путешéствие pooteeshEHSTveeyeh - travels; trip.

путь poot' - trip; way; path.

пчелá pcheeLAH - bee.

пшенúца pshehNEEtsah - wheat.

пьéса P'YEHsah - play; drama.

пьяный P'YAHnihy - drunk; intoxicated (adj).

пяница PYAHneetsah - drunkard.

пятнó peetNOH - spot; stain.

Р

рабóта rahBOHtah - work.

рабóтать rahBOHtaht' - to work.

рабóчий rahBOHcheey - worker.

равви́н rahvVEEN - rabbi.

равноду́шный rahvnah-DOOSHnihy - indifferent (adj).

ра́вный RAHVnihy - equal (adj)

рагу́ rahGOO - stew.

рад raht - glad; pleased.

ра́дио RAHdeeoh - radio.

радиоста́нция rahdeeah-STAHNtseeyah - radio station.

ра́достный RAHdahstnihy - joyful; joyous (adj).

раз rahs - time; once; one.

ра́зве RAHZveh - really?; is that so?

разви́тие rahzVEEteeyeh - development.

развлече́ние rahzvlee-CHEHneeyeh - amusement; entertainment.

разгово́р rahzgahVOHR - conversation.

разгово́рник rahzgahVOHRneek - phrasebook.

разгово́рный rahzgah-VOHRnihy - conversational; colloquial. (adj).

раздева́лка rahzdeeVAHLkah - cloakroom.

раздраже́ние rahzdrah-ZHEHneeyeh - irritation.

разду́тый rahzDOOtihy - swollen; puffed up (adj).

разме́р rahzMYEHR - size.

разни́ца rahzNEEtsah - difference; distinction.

ра́зный RAHZnihy - different (adj).

разреше́ние rahzreeSHEHneeyeh - permission; permit.

разу́мно rahzOOMnah - sensibly; rationally (adj).

рак rahk - crayfish.

ра́ковина RAHkahveenah - (bathroom) sink.

ра́на RAHnah - wound.

ра́неный RAHNeenihy - wounded, injured (adj).

ра́нний RAHNeey - early (adj).

ра́ньше RAHN'sheh - earlier; sooner.

расписа́ние rahspeeSAHneeyeh - schedule; timetable.

распро́дано rahsPROHdahnah - sold out.

рассве́т rahsSVYEHT - dawn; daybreak.

расска́з rahsSKAHS - story; tale; account.

рассо́льник rahsSOHL'neek - cucumber soup.

расстоя́ние rahsstahYAHneeyeh - distance.

расстро́йство желу́дка rahsSTROYstvah zheh-LOOTkah - indigestion.

расте́ние rahsTYEHneeyeh - plant.

растяже́ние rahsteeZHEHneeyeh - strain; sprain.

расхо́ды rahsKHOHdih - expenses.

рва́ный RVAHnihy - torn; ripped (adj).

ребёнок reeBYOHnahk - child.

ребро́ reebROH - rib.

ревмати́зм reevmahTEEZM - rheumatism.

реди́ска reeDEESkah - radish.

ре́дкий RYEHTkeey - rare; infrequent (adj).

ре́дько RYEHT'kah - rarely.

режиссёр reezheesSYOHR - (theater) director.

ре́заный RYEHZahnihy - cut; sliced (adj).

рези́новый reeZEEnahvihy - rubber (adj).

ре́йс reys - trip; flight.

река́ reeKAH - river.

рекла́ма reeKLAHmah - advertising; sign.

ре́льс ryehl's - rail; track.

ремо́нт reeMOHNT - repair.

ремо́нт о́буви reeMOHNT OHboovih - shoemaker.

рентге́н reentGYEHN - x-ray.

ре́па RYEHpah - turnip.

ресни́ца reesNEEtsah - eyelash.

респу́блика reesPOObleekah - republic.

рестора́н reestahRAHN - restaurant.

реце́пт reeTSEHPT - prescription.

ре́чь ryehch - speech.

реше́ние reeSHEHneeyeh - decision.

рис rees - rice.

рисова́ние reesahVAHneeyeh - drawing.

ри́фма REEFmah - ryhme.

ро́бкий ROHPkeey - timid; shy (adj).

ро́дина ROHdeenah - homeland.

роди́тели rahDEEteelee - parents.

родно́й rahdNOY - native (adj).

ро́дственник ROHSTveenneekee - relatives.

рожде́ние rahzhDYEHneeyeh - birth.

рождество́ rahzheestVOH - Christmas.

рожь rohsh - rye.

ро́за ROHzah - rose.

розе́тка rahzYEHTkah - electrical socket.

ро́ль rohl' - role; part.

рома́н rahMAHN - novel.

роса́ rahSAH - dew.

роско́шный rahsKOHSHnihy - luxurious (adj).

росси́йский rahsSEEYskeey - Russian (adj).

рост rohst - growth; height.

ро́стбиф ROHSTbeef - roast beef.

рот roht - mouth.

руба́шка rooBAHSHkah - shirt.

руби́н rooBEEN - ruby.

ру́бль roobl' - ruble.

рука́ rooKAH - hand; arm.

рука́в rooKAHF - sleeve.

рукави́ца rookahVEEtsah - mitten.

руково́дство rookahVOHTstvah - leadership.

ру́копись ROOkahpees' - manuscript.

рукоплеска́ние rookahpleesKAHneeyeh - applause.

руле́т rooLYEHT - meat loaf.

ру́сский ROOSskeey - Russian (noun & adj).

ру́сская ROOSskahyah - Russian (f).

ру́чка ROOCHkah - pen.

168

рыба RIHBah - fish.
рынок RIHNahk - market.
рюкзак ryookZAHK -
backpack.
рябчик RYAHPcheek - hazel
grouse.
ряд ryaht - row; file.
рядом RYAHdahm -
alongside; beside; next to.

С

с se - with; off; since.
сад saht - garden.
салат sahLAHT - salad.
салфетка sahlFYEHTkah -
napkin.
самовар sahmahVAHR -
samovar.
самолёт sahmahLYOHT -
airplane.
самообслуживание sah-
mahahpSLOOzheevahnee-
yeh - self-service (adj).
самостоятельный sahmah-
stahYAHteel'nihy - inde-
pendent (adj).
самоубийство sahmahoo-
BEEYSTvah - suicide.
самоуверенный sahmah-
ooVYEHreennihy - self
confident (adj).
сандалии sahnDAHleeee -
sandals.
санитарный день sahnee-
TAHRnihy dyehn' - one
day a month when stores
are closed for cleaning.
санки SAHNkee - sleigh;
sled.
сапоги sahpahGEE - boots.
сапфир sahpFEER -
saphire.
сарказм sahrKAHZM -

sarcasm.
сатира sahTEErah - satire.
сахар SAHkhahr - sugar.
сахарин sahkhahREEN -
saccharin.
сбор zbohr - collection;
gathering.
сборник ZBOHRneek -
anthology; collection.
свадьба SVAHT'bah -
wedding.
свежий SVYEHzheey -
fresh (adj).
свёкла SVYOHKlah - beets.
свекольник sveeKOHL'neek
- beet soup.
сверх svyehrkh - over and
above; in access of.
свет svyeht - light.
светло- SVYEHTlah- -
light-(color).
светлый SVYEHTlihy -
light; bright (adj).
светофор sveetahFOHR -
traffic light.
свеча sveeCHAH - candle.
свидание sveeDAHneeyeh -
appointment; meeting.
свинина sveeNEEnah -
pork.
свинья sveen'YAH - pig.
свобода svahBOHdah -
freedom.
свободный svahBOHDnihy -
free; vacant (adj).
святой sveeTOY - holy;
sacred (adj).
священник sveeshchEHN-
neek - priest; clergyman.
сдача ZDAHchah - change.
север SYEHveer - north.
северный SYEHveernihy -
northern (adj).

сего́дня seeVOHdnyah -
today.
сего́дняшний seeVOH-
dnyahshneey - today's
(adj).
сейча́с seeCHAHS - now.
секрета́рь seekreeTAHR' -
secretary.
секу́нда seekOONdah -
second (time measure).
се́кция SYEHKtseeyah -
section.
село́ seeLOH - village.
сельдь syehl't' - herring.
сёмга SYOHMgah - lox.
семья́ seem'YAH - family.
серви́з seerVEES - set (of
dishes or silverware).
серде́чный припа́док
seerDYEHCHnihy pree-
PAHdahk - heart attack.
серди́тый seerDEEtihy -
angry (adj).
се́рдце SYEHRtseh - heart.
серебро́ seereeBROH -
silver.
сере́бряный seerYEHB-
reenihy - silver (adj).
середи́на seereeDEEnah -
middle.
серёжки seerYOHSHkee-
earrings.
се́рьги SYEHR'gee -
earrings.
се́рый SYEHrihy - grey
(adj).
серьёзный seer'YOHZnihy -
serious (adj).
сестра́ seesTRAH - sister.
сига́ра seeGAHrah - cigar.
сигаре́та seegahRYEHtah -
cigarette.
си́ла SEElah - strength.

си́льный SEEL'nihy - strong
(adj).
синаго́га seenahGOHgah -
synagogue.
си́ний SEEneey - dark blue
(adj).
синя́к seenYAHK - bruise.
сире́нь seerYEHN' - lilac.
систе́ма seesTYEHmah -
system.
си́течко SEEteechkah -
strainer.
ска́зка SKAHSkah - tale.
скаме́йка skahMEYkah -
bench.
сквозь skvohs' - through.
ски́дка SKEETkah - sale.
сковорода́ skahvahrahDAH
- frying pan.
ско́льзкий SKOHL'skeey -
slippery (adj).
ско́лько SKOHL'kah - how
much.
ско́рая по́мощь SKOHrah-
yah POHmahshch - ambu-
lance.
скоре́е skahRYEHeh -
quickly!
скорлупа́ skahrlooPAH -
(egg) shell.
ско́рость SKOHrahst' -
speed.
ско́рый SKOHrihy -
quickly; rapidly (adj).
скро́мный SKROHMnihy -
modest (adj).
скры́тый SKRIHtihy -
hidden; secret (adj).
скульпту́ра skool'pTOOrah
- sculpture.
ску́чный SKOOCHnihy -
boring (adj).
слаби́тельное slahBEEteel'-

170

nahyeh - laxative.
слабый SLAHbihy - weak (adj).
слава SLAHvah - glory.
сладкий SLAHTkeey - sweet (adj).
сладкое (на) SLAHTkahyeh (nah) - (for) dessert.
следствие SLYEHTstveeyeh - result; consequence.
следующий SLYEHdooyooshcheey - next (adj).
слёзы SLYOHzih - tears.
слива SLEEvah - plum.
сливки SLEEFkee - cream.
слишком SLEESHkahm - too.
словарь slahVAHR' - dictionary.
слово SLOHvah - word.
сложный SLOHZHnihy - complex; difficult (adj).
сломать slahMAHT' - to break.
служба SLOOSHbah - church service.
случай SLOOchay - incident.
случайно slooCHAYnah - accidentally.
слышный SLIHSHnihy - audible (adj).
смелый SMYEHlihy - brave; courageous (adj).
смерть smyehrt' - death.
сметана smeeTAHnah - sour cream.
смех smyehkh - laughter.
смешной smeeshNOY - funny (adj).
смотреть smahTRYEHT' - to look.
смущение smooSHCHEHneeyeh - embarrassment.
сначала snahCHAHlah - at first; in the beginning.
снег snyehk - snow.
собака sahBAHkah - dog.
собор sahBOHR - cathedral.
собрание sahBRAHneeyeh - meeting.
событие sahBIHTeeyeh - event.
совет sahVYEHT - advice.
совпадение sahfpahDYEHneeyeh - coincidence.
современный sahvreemMYEHNnihy - contemporary (adj).
согласный sahGLAHSnihy - in agreement.
сок sohk - juice.
сокращение sahkrahSHCHEHneeyeh - abbreviation.
солдат sahlDAHT - soldier.
солёный sahlYOHnihy - salted (adj).
солнечный SOHLneechnihy - sunny (adj).
солнце SOHNtseh - sun.
соль sohl' - salt.
сомнение sahmNYEHneeyeh - doubt.
сон sohn - sleep; dream.
сообщать sahahpSHCHAHT' - to notify, inform.
соревнование sahreevnahVAHneeyeh - competition; sports match.
сорт sohrt - kind; sort.
сосед sahSYEHT - neighbor.
соска SOHSkah - pacifier.
состояние sahstahYAHneeyeh - condition.
сотный SOHTnihy - hundred.

171

со́ус sahOOS - sauce; gravy.
сочета́ние sahchehTAHneeyeh - combination.
сочу́вствие sahCHOOSTveeyeh - sympathy.
сою́з sahYOOS - union.
спа́льня SPAHL'nyah - bedroom.
спаси́бо spahSEEbah - thank you.
спать spaht' - to sleep.
спекта́кль speekTAHKL' - performance; play.
специа́льность speetseeAHL'nahst' - specialty.
спе́шный SPYEHSHnihy - hurried; rushed (adj).
спина́ speeNAH - back; spine.
спи́сок SPEEsahk - list.
спи́чка SPEECHkah - match.
споко́йный spahKOYnihy - calm; tranquil (adj).
спор spohr - argument.
спо́рный SPOHRnihy - controversial (adj).
спра́вка SPRAHFkah - reference; information.
сре́дний SRYEHDneey - middle; average (adj).
сре́дство от комаро́в SRYEHTstvah aht kahmahROHF - insect repellent.
срок srohk - (period of) time; date; deadline.
сро́чный SROHCHnihy - urgent; emergency (adj).
стадио́н stahdeeOHN - stadium.
стака́н stahKAHN - (drinking) glass.
ста́нция STAHNtseeyah - station.
ста́рший STAHRsheey - older; elder (adj).
ста́рый STAHrihy - old (adj).
стекло́ steekLOH - glass.
стена́ steeNAH - wall.
сте́пень STYEHpeen' - degree; extent.
сти́рка STEERkah - washing; laundry.
стол stohl - table.
столе́тие stahLYEHteeyeh - century.
столи́ца stahLEEtsah - capital (of a state).
столо́вая stahLOHvahyah - dining hall.
стоп stohp - stop.
сторона́ stahrahNAH - side.
стоя́нка stahYAHNkah - (bus) stop.
стоя́нка для маши́н stahYAHNkah dlyah mahSHEEN - parking lot.
страна́ strahNAH - country.
страни́ца strahNEEtsah - page.
стра́нный STRAHNnihy - strange; weird; odd (adj).
стра́стный STRAHSTnihy - passionate (adj).
страх strahkh - fear.
стра́шный STRAHSHnihy - horrible; terrifying (adj).
стри́жка STREESHkah - haircut; trim.
стро́гий STROHgeey - strict; harsh; severe (adj).
студе́нт stooDYEHNT - student.
студе́нь stooDYEHN' - aspic.

сту́к stook - knock.
сту́л stool - chair.
стыⷧ stiht - shame.
стюарде́сса styooahrDYEHS-
sah - stewardess.
сувени́р sooveeNEER -
souvenir.
судьба́ soot'BAH - fate.
сумасше́дший soomahsh-
EHTsheey - crazy; mad;
insane (adj).
су́п soop - soup.
супру́г soopROOK -
husband.
супру́га soopROOgah - wife.
су́тки SOOTkee - 24 hour
period; day.
сухо́й sooKHOY - dry (adj).
сце́на STSEHnah - stage.
счастли́вый shahstLEEvihy
- happy; lucky (adj).
счёт shchoht - check; bill.
съе́зд s"yehst - convention;
congress.
сы́н sihn - son.
сы́р sihr - cheese.
сыро́й sihROY - raw (adj).
сы́тый SIHTihy - full (of
food).

Т
таба́к tahBAHK - tobacco.
табле́тка tahbLYEHTkah -
pill; tablet.
та́к tahk - so; true.
та́кже TAHKzheh - as well.
такси́ tahkSEE - taxi.
та́лия TAHleeyah - waist.
тало́н tahLOHN - coupon.
тальк tahl'k - talcum
powder.
та́м tahm - there.
тамо́женник tahMOHZH-

ehnneek - customs
official.
тамо́жня tahMOHZHnyah -
customs.
тампо́н tahmPOHN -
tampon.
та́нец TAHneets - dance.
та́почки TAHPahchkee -
slippers.
тарака́н tahrahKAHN -
cockroach.
таре́лка tahRYEHLkah -
plate.
твёрдый TVYOHRdihy -
hard (adj).
творо́г tvahROHK - pot
cheese.
тво́рчество TVOHRchehst-
vah - creative work.
теа́тр teeAHTR - theater.
телеви́зор teeleeVEEzahr -
television.
телегра́мма teeleeGRAHM-
mah - telegram.
телегра́ф teeleeGRAHF -
telegraph office.
телефо́н teeleeFOHN -
telephone.
телефо́н-автома́т teelee-
FOHN-ahftahMAHT - pay
phone; phone booth.
телефони́стка teeleefahn-
EESTkah - operator.
те́ло TYEHlah - body.
теля́тина teelYAHteenah -
veal.
тёмно- TYOHMnah- - dark-
(color).
тёмные очки́ TYOHMnih-
yeh ahchKEE - sunglasses.
тёмный TYOHMnihy - dark
(adj).
температу́ра teempeerah-

TOOrah - temperature.
ténhис TYEHNnees - tennis.
тень tyehn' - shadow.
теперь teePYEHR' - now.
тёплый TYOHPlihy - warm (adj).
термос TYEHRmahs - thermos.
терпеливый teerpeeLEE- vihy - patient (adj).
тесный TYEHSnihy - crowded.
тетрадь teeTRAHT' - notebook.
тётя TYOHtyah - aunt.
тефтели TYEHFteelee - meatballs.
тихий TEEKHeey - quite (adj).
ткань tkahn' - fabric.
товар tahVAHR - merch- andise.
товарищ tahVAHReeshch - comrade.
тогда tahgDAH - then.
тоже TOHzheh - also.
толпа tahlPAH - crowd.
толстый TOHLstihy - fat (adj).
только TOHL'kah - only.
тонкий TOHNkeey - thin (adj).
топаз tahPAHS - topaz.
тормоза tahrmahZAH - brakes (car).
торт tohrt - cake.
тот toht - that (one).
точно TOHCHnah - exactly.
тошнота tashnahTAH - nausea.
трава trahVAH - grass.
трагедия trahGYEHdeeyah - tragedy.

трамвай trahmVAY - street car.
трасса TRAHSsah - high- way.
треска treesKAH - cod.
трогать TROHgaht' - to touch.
троллейбус trahlLEYboos - trolley bus.
тротуар trahtooAHR - side walk.
трубка TROOPkah - pipe.
трудный TROODnihy - difficult (adj).
трусы trooSIH - under- pants.
туалет tooahLYEHT - toilet.
туалетная бумага tooah- LYEHTnahyah booMAHgah - toiletpaper.
туда tooDAH - that way.
туда и обратно tooDAH ee ahbRAHTnah - roundtip (ticket).
туман tooMAHN - fog.
тунец tooNYEHTS - tuna.
турист tooREEST - tourist.
тут toot - here.
туфли TOOFlee - shoes.
тысяча TIHseechah - thousand.
тюрьма tyoor'MAH - prison.
тяжёлый teezhOHLihy - difficult (adj).

У

у oo - at.
убийство ooBEEYSTvah - murder.
убийца ooBEEYtsah - murderer.

убо́рная ооBOHRnahyah -
bathroom.
убо́рщик ооBOHRshcheek -
janitor; yardsman.
убо́рщица ооBOHRshchee-
tsah - cleaning woman.
уважа́емый оovahZHAH-
eemihy - respected (adj).
увеличе́ние ооveeleeCHEH-
neeyeh - increase.
уваре́ние ооveeRYEHneeyeh
- assurance.
увлечённый оovleeCHOHN-
nihy - enthusiastic (adj).
у́гол OOgahl - corner.
угро́за ооGROHzah - threat.
ударе́ние оodahRYEHnee-
yeh - grammatical stress .
уда́ча ооDAHchah -
success.
удиви́тельный оodeeVEE-
teel'nihy - surprising
(adj).
удо́бный ооDOHBnihy -
comfortable (adj).
удо́бство ооDOHBSTvah -
convenience.
удовлетворе́ние оodahvlee-
tvahRYEHneeyeh - satis-
faction.
удово́льствие оodahVOHL'-
stveeyeh - pleasure.
удостовере́ние оodahstah-
veeRYEHneeyeh - identi-
fication.
у́дочка OODahchkah -
fishing pole.
ужа́сный оozhAHSnihy -
horrible (adj).
уже́ оozhEH - already.
у́жин OOZHeen - supper.
у́зкий OOSkeey - narrow
(adj).

укло́н оokLOHN - bias;
incline.
уко́л оoKOHL - injection.
украше́ние оokrahSHEH-
neeyeh - decoration;
embellishment.
у́лица OOLeetsah - street.
улы́бка ооLIHPkah - smile.
уменьше́ние оomeen'SHEH-
neeyeh - decrease.
у́мный OOMnihy - smart;
intelligent (adj).
универма́г ооneeveerMAHK
- department store.
университе́т ооneeveersee-
TYEHT - university.
упо́рный ооPOHRnihy -
stubborn (adj).
упражне́ние ооprahzh-
NYEHneeyeh - exersise.
упрёк ооpRYOHK - rebuke.
у́ровень OOrahveen' - level.
уро́к ооROHK - lesson.
усло́вие ооsLOHveeyeh -
condition.
успе́х ооsPYEHKH -
success.
успокои́тельное сре́дство
оospahKOHeeteel'nahyeh
SRYEHTstvah - sedative.
уста́л(а) оosTAHL(ah) -
tired(f) (adj).
у́стный OOSTnihy - oral;
verbal (adj).
усы́ оosIH - mustache.
утомле́ние оotahmLYEH-
neeyeh - exhaustion.
у́тренний OOTreeneey -
morning (adj).
у́тро OOTrah - morning.
утю́г ооTYOOK - iron.
уха́ ооKHAH - fish soup.
у́хо OOKHah - ear.

участие ooCHAHSTeeyeh - participation.
учебник ooCHEHBneek - textbook.
учёный ooCHOHnihy - scholar; scientist.
учитель oocheeTYEHL' - teacher.
учительница oochee- TYEHL'neetsah - teacher (f).
учиться ooCHEET'sah - to study.
учреждение oochreezh- DYEHneeyeh - institution.

Ф

фальшивый fahl'SHEEvihy - fake; falsified (adj).
фамилия fahMEEleeyah - last name; sir name.
фары FAHrih - headlights.
фарфор fahrFOHR - china.
фарцовщик fahrTSOHF- shcheek - blackmarketeer.
фаршированный fahrshee- ROHvahnnihy - stuffed (food) (adj).
фасоль fahSOHL' - beans.
фен fyehn - hairdryer.
ферма FYEHRmah - farm.
фильм feel'm - movie.
флот floht - navy.
фойе fayYEH - lobby.
фонтан fahnTAHN - fountain.
форель fahRYEHL' - trout.
фотоаппарат fahtahahp- pahRAHT - camera.
фотография fahtahGRAH- feeyah - photograph.
фраза FRAHzah - phrase; sentence.

фрукт frookt - fruit.
фунт foont - pound.
фут foot - foot (measure).
футбол footBOHL - soccer.

Х

халат khahLAHT - robe.
харчо kharCHOH - mutton soup.
химчистка kheemCHEEST- kah - dry cleaning.
хирург kheerOORK - surgeon.
хлеб khlyehp - bread.
хлебосольный khleebah- SOHL'nihy - hospitable (adj).
хлопчатобумажный khlah- pchahtahbooMAHZHnihy - cotten (adj).
хозяйка khazYAYkah - housewife.
хоккей kahkKEY - hockey.
холодец khalahDYEHTS - aspic.
холодильник khahlah- DEEL'neek - refrigerator.
холодный khahLOHDnihy - cold (adj).
хор khohr - choir.
хороший khahROHsheey - good (adj).
хотеть khahTYEHT' - to want.
хотя khahtYAH - although.
храм khrahm - cathedral; temple.
хрен khryehn - horse- radish.
хромой khrahMOY - lame (adj).
художник khooDOHZHneek - artist.

худо́й khooDOY - thin (adj).
ху́же KHOOzheh - worse.
хулига́ны khooleeGAHnih - hooligans.

Ц

царь tsahr' - tsar.
цве́т tsvyeht - color.
цвето́к tsveeTOHK - flower.
це́лый TSEHlihy - whole; entire (adj).
це́ль tsehl' - goal; aim.
цена́ tseeNAH - price.
це́нный TSEHNnihy - valuable.
це́нтр tsehntr - center.
це́пь tsehp' - chain.
це́рковь TSEHRkahf' - church.
цирк tseerk - circus.
цита́та tseeTAHtah - quote.
ци́фра TSEEfrah - number; numeral.
цыга́н tsihGAHN - gypsy.

Ч

чаевы́е chahehVIHyeh - tip.
ча́й chay - tea.
ча́йник CHAYneek - tea kettle.
ча́йница CHAYneetsah - tea caddy.
час chahs - time; hour.
ча́сто CHAHStah - often.
частота́ chahstahTAH - frequency.
ча́сть chahst' - part.
часы́ cheesih - watch.
ча́шка CHAHSHkah - cup.
че́к chehk - check.
челове́к chehlahVYEHK - person.
чем chehm - than.

чемода́н chehmahDAHN - suitcase.
чепуха́ chehpooKHAH - nonsense.
че́рез CHEHrees - through; within.
чере́шня chehRYEHSHnyah - sweet cherries.
черни́ка chehrNEEkah - blueberries.
черни́ла chehrNEElah - ink.
чёрно-бе́лый CHOHRnah-BYEHlihy - black-and-white (adj).
чёрный CHOHRnihy - black; dark (adj).
чёрный ры́нок CHOHRnihy RIHNahk - black market.
чёрт chohrt - devil.
черта́ chehrTAH - feature; trait; characteristic.
чесно́к chehsNOHK - garlic.
че́стный CHEHSTnihy - honest (adj).
че́тверть CHEHTveert' - quarter.
чёткий CHOHTkeey - clear; distinct (adj).
чино́вник cheeNOHVneek - clerk.
число́ cheesLOH - number.
чи́стый CHEEStihy - clean (adj).
чита́тель cheeTAHteel' - reader.
чита́ть cheeTAHT' - to read.
чиха́нье cheeKHAHN'yeh - sneezing.
член chlyehn - member.
что shtoh - what.
что́бы SHTOHbih - in order to.
что́-нибудь SHTOHneeboot'

177

\- anything; something.

чувствительный choofst-VEEteel'nihy - sensitive (adj).

чувство CHOOFSTvah - feeling; sensitivity.

чувствовать себя CHOOFSTvahvaht' seeBYAH - to feel.

чудесный chooDYEHSnihy - wonderful; miraculous (adj).

чужой chooZHOY - not one's own; foreign (adj).

чулки choolKEE - stockings.

чуть choot' - hardly; scarsely; barely.

чучело CHOOchehlah - stuffed animal.

Ш

шаг shahk - step.

шампанское shahmPAHNskahyeh - champagne.

шампунь shahmPOON' - shampoo.

шапка SHAHPkah - hat.

шарф shahrf - scarf.

шахматы SHAHKHmahtih - chess.

шашлык shahshLIHK - shish kebob.

швейцар shveyTSAHR - doorman.

шёпот SHOHpaht - whisper.

шерстяной shehrsteeNOY - woolen (adj).

шея SHEHyah - neck.

ширина sheereeNAH - width.

широкий sheeROHkeey - wide; broad (adj).

шкаф shkahf - closet; cabinet.

школа SHKOHlah - school.

шкура SHKOOrah - skin; hide.

шнуры SHNOOrih - shoe laces.

шоколад shahkahLAHT - chocolate.

шорты SHOHRtihy - shorts.

шоссе shahsSYEH - highway.

штат shtaht - state.

штатский SHTAHTskeey - civilian (adj).

штопор SHTOHpahr - corkscrew.

штраф shtrahf - fine.

шуба SHOObah - fur coat.

шум shoom - noise.

шумный SHOOMnihy - noisy (adj).

шутка SHOOTkah - joke.

Щ

щедрый SHCHEHDrihy - generous (adj).

щека shchehKAH - cheek.

щётка SHCHOHTkah - brush.

щи shchee - cabbage soup.

щука SHCHOOkah - pike.

Э

экземпляр egzeemPLYAHR - copy; edition.

экран ehkRAHN - screen.

экскурсия ehksKOORseeyah - tour; excursion.

экскурсовод ehkskoorsahVOHT - tour guide.

экспресс ehksPRYEHSS - express.

электри́ческий ehleek-TREEchehskeey - electrical (adj).

электри́чество ehleekTREEchehstvah - electricity.

эскала́тор ehskahLAHtahr - escalator.

эта́ж ehTAHSH - floor; story.

э́тот EHtaht - that (one).

Ю

юбиле́й yoobeeLEY - anniversary.

ю́бка YOOPkah - skirt.

ювели́рный yooveeLEERnihy - jewelry (adj).

юг yook - south.

ю́жный YOOZHnihy - southern (adj).

ю́мор YOOmahr - humor.

ю́ность YOOnahst' - youth.

Я

я yah - I.

я́блоко YAHBlahkah - apple.

я́годы YAHgahdih - berries.

яд yaht - poison.

я́зва YAHZvah - ulcer.

язы́к yeezIHK - language; tonuge.

яи́чница yahEECHneetsah - fried eggs.

яйцо́ yayTSOH - egg.

я́ркий YAHRkeey - bright (adj).

я́рмарка YAHRmahrkah - fair.

я́сно YAHSnah - clearly.

я́щик YAHshcheek - box.

179

A

abbreviation - сокращéние sahkrahSHCHEHneeyeh.

about - о/про oh/proh.

above - наверху́/нáд nahveerKHOO/naht.

abscess - нары́в nahRIHF.

absence - отсу́тствие ahtSOOTSTveeyeh.

absorbent cotton - вáта VAHtah.

accent - акцéнт ahkTSEHNT.

accept (to) - принимáть preeneeMAHT'.

access - дóступ DOHstoop.

accident - несчáстный слу́чай neeSHCHAHSTnihy SLOOchay.

accidentally - случáйно slooCHAYnah.

acquaintance - знакóмство znahKOHMstvah.

acquainted; familiar (adj) - знакóмый znahKOHmihy.

act - акт ahkt.

act, take action (to) - дéйствовать DEYSTvahvaht'.

action - дéйствие DEYSTveeyeh.

actor - актёр ahkTYOHR.

actress - актри́са ahkTREEsah.

address - áдрес AHdrees.

admission pass - прóпуск PROHpoosk.

admission; admittance - впу́ск fpoosk.

admit, let in (to) - впускáть fpoosKAHT'.

adult - взрóслый VZROHslihy.

advertising; sign - реклáма reeKLAHmah.

advice - совéт sahVYEHT.

after - пóсле POHSlee.

afternoon - пóсле обéда POHSlee ahBYEHdah.

afterwards - потóм pahTOHM.

again - опя́ть/ещё раз ahpYAHT'/yeeSHCHOH rahs.

against - прóтив PROHteef.

age - вóзраст VOHZrahst.

agreement (in) - соглáсный sahGLAHSnihy.

agreement; contract - договóр dahgahVOHR.

air - вóздух VOHZdookh.

air conditioning - кондиционéр kahndeetseeahNYEHR.

airmail - авиапóчта ahveeahPOHCHtah.

airplane - самолёт sahmahLYOHT.

airport - аэропóрт ahehrahPOHRT.

alarm clock - буди́льник booDEEL'neek.

alcohol - алкогóль ahlkahGOHL'.

all; the whole - весь vyehs'.

allergy аллéргия ahlLYEHRgeeyah.

almost - почти́ pahchTEE.

along; about; according to - по pah.

alongside; beside; next to - ря́дом RYAHdahm.

aloud - **вслух** fslookh.

alphabet - **а́збука** AHS-bookah.

already - **уже́** oozhEH.

also; as well - **то́же** TOH-zheh.

although - **хотя́** khahtYAH.

always - **всегда́** fseegDAH.

ambulance - **ско́рая по́мощь** SKOHrahyah POHmahshch.

American (adj) - **америка́н-ский** ahmeereeKAHN-skeey.

American/(f) - **америка́нец** /(-**ка́нка**) ahmeereeKAH-neets/(-KAHNkah).

amusement; entertainment - **развлече́ние** rahzvlee-CHEHneeyeh.

ancient (adj) - **дре́вний** DRYEHVneey.

and; also - **и** ee.

anesthesia - **нарко́з** nahr-KOHS.

anesthetization -**обезбо́ли-вание** ahbeesBOHleevah-neeyeh.

anger - **гнев** gnyehf.

angry (adj) - **серди́тый** seerDEEtihy.

animal - **живо́тное** zheeVOHTnahyeh.

ankle - **лоды́жка** lahDIHSHkah.

anniversary - **юбиле́й** yoobeeLEY.

announcement - **объявле́ние** ahb"eevLYEHneeyeh.

answer - **отве́т** ahtVYEHT.

anthology; collection - **сбо́рник** ZBOHRneek.

antibiotic - **антибио́тик** ahnteebeeOHteek.

any - **любо́й** lyooBOY.

anyone - **кто́-нибудь** KTOHneeboot'.

anything - **что́-нибудь** SHTOHneeboot'.

apartment - **кварти́ра** kvahrTEERah.

apparently; evidently - **ви́димо** VEEdeemah.

appearance - **вид** veet.

appendicitis - **аппендици́т** appeendeeTSEET.

appendix - **аппе́ндикс** ahPYEHNdeeks.

appetite (hearty appetite!) - **аппети́т (прия́тного аппети́та!)** ahpeeTEET (preeYAHTnahvah ahpee-TEEtah!).

appetizer - **заку́ска** zah-KOOSkah.

applause - **рукоплеска́ние** rookahpleesKAHneeyeh.

apple - **я́блоко** YAHBlah-kah.

appointment; date; meeting - **свида́ние** sveeDAHneeyeh.

approximately; about - **о́коло** OHkahlah.

architecht - **архите́ктор** ahrkheeTYEHKtahr.

architechture - **архитек-ту́ра** ahrkheeteekTOORah.

area; square - **пло́щадь** PLOHshchaht'.

argument - **спор** spohr.

arm; hand - **рука́** rooKAH.

arm chair - **кре́сло** KRYEHS-lah.

around (location) - **вокру́г** vahkROOK.

arrival (on a plane) -

прилёт preeLYOHT.
arrival (on a train) - приезд preeYEHST.
art - искусство eesKOOST-vah.
artery - артерия ahrTYEH-reeyah.
arthritis - артрит ahrt-REET.
artificial (adj) -искусственный eesKOOSTveen-nihy.
artist - художник khoo-DOHZHneek.
as well; also - также TAHKzheh.
ashtray - пепельница PYEHpeel'neetsah.
aspic - студень/холодец stooDYEHN'/ khalah-DYEHTS.
aspirin - аспирин ahspee-REEN.
assurance - уверение ooveeRYEHneeyeh.
asthma - астма AHSTmah.
at - у oo.
at first; in the beginning - сначала snahCHAHlah.
atheism - безбожие bees-BOHzheeyeh.
atheist - безбожник bees-BOHZHneek.
athletic (adj) - атлетический ahtLYEHTeechskeey.
athletics - атлетика aht-LYEHTeekah.
at least - по крайне мере pah KRAYnyeh MYEHreh.
attention - внимание vnee-MAHneeyeh.
attitude; relationship - отношение ahtnahSHEH-

neeyeh.
attentively - внимательно vneeMAHteel'nah.
audible (adj) - слышный SLIHSHnihy.
aunt - тётя TYOHtyah.
author - автор AHFtahr.
autumn - осень OHseen'.
avenue - авеню/проспект ahveenYOO/prahsPYEHKT.
awkward; clumsy (adj) - неловкий neeLOHFkeey.

В

baby; infant - младенец mlahDYEHneets.
back; backwards - назад nahzAHT.
back; spine - спина spee-NAH.
backpack - рюкзак ryook-ZAHK.
bacon - бекон beeKOHN.
bad; poor (adj) - плохой plahKHOY.
badge - значок znahCHOHK.
badly - плохо PLOHkhah.
bag; sack - мешок mee-SHOHK.
baggage - багаж bahgAHSH.
baggage room - камера хранения KAHmeerah khrahNYEHneeyah.
bakery - булочная BOO-lahchnahyah.
balalaika - балалайка bahlahLAYkah.
balcony - балкон bahl-KOHN.
ball - мяч myahch.
ballet - балет bahLYEHT.
banana - банан bahNAHN.
bandage - бинт beent.

bandaging; dressing - перевязка peereeVYAHSkah.
band-aide - пластырь PLAHStihr'.
bank - банк bahnk.
banquet - банкет bahnKYEHT.
bar of chocolate - плитка шоколада PLEETkah shahkahLAHdah.
barber; hairdresser - парикмахер pahreekMAHKHeer.
basket - корзина kahrZEEnah.
bathing cap - купальная шапочка kooPAHL'nahyah SHAHPahchkah.
bathing suit - купальник koopAHL'neek.
bathroom - уборная/ванная ooBOHRnahyah/VAHNnahyah.
bathtub - ванна VAHNnah.
battery - батарея bahtahREEyah.
bay; gulf - залив zahLEEF.
bazaar - базар bahZAHR.
beach - пляж plyahsh.
beads - бусы BOOsih.
beans - фасоль fahSOHL'.
beard - борода bahrahDAH.
beat, strike (to) - бить beet'.
beautiful (adj) - красивый KRAHSeevihy.
beauty - красота krahsahTAH.
because - потому что pahtahMOOshtah.
because of - из-за eezzah.
bed - кровать/постель krahVAHT'/pahsTYEHL'.

bedbug - клоп klohp.
bedroom - спальня SPAHL'nyah.
bee - пчела pchehLAH.
beef - говядина gahvYAHDeenah.
beer - пиво PEEvah.
beet soup - свекольник sveeKOHL'neek.
beets - свёкла SVYOHKlah.
before; formerly - прежде PRYEHZHdyeh.
before; in front of - перед/до PYEHreet/dah.
begin, start (to) - начинать nahcheeNAHT'.
beginning - начало nahCHAHlah.
behind; beyond; past; for; in; after - за zah.
belief; faith - вера VYEHrah.
believe, have faith (to) - верить VYEHreet'.
bell - колокол KOHlahkahl.
belt; waist - пояс POHees.
bench - скамейка skahMEYkah.
berries - ягоды YAHgahdih.
berth; shelf - полка POHLkah.
better - лучше LOOCHsheh.
better; the best - лучший LOOCHsheey.
between - между MYEHZHdoo.
beware - осторожно ahstahROHZHnah.
bias; incline; slant - уклон ookLOHN.
Bible - библия BEEbleeyah.
bicycle - велосипед veelahseePYEHT.

183

big; large; great (adj) -
больш́о́й bahl'SHOY.
bill - счёт shchoht.
billion - миллиа́рд meel-
leeAHRT.
binoculars; opera glasses -
бино́кль beeNOHKL'.
birch - берёза beerYOHzah.
bird - пти́ца PTEEtsah.
birth - рожде́ние rahzh-
DYEHneeyeh.
birthday - де́нь рожде́ния
dyehn' rahzhDYEHneeyah.
bitter (adj) - го́рький
GOHR'keey.
black-and-white (adj) -
чёрно-бе́лый CHOHRnah-
BYEHlihy.
black; dark (adj) - чёрный
CHOHRnihy.
blackberries - ежеви́ка
yeezhehVEEkah.
black market - чёрный
ры́нок CHOHRnihy RIHN-
ahk.
blackmarketeer - фарцо́в-
щик fahrTSOHFshcheek.
bladder - мочево́й пузы́рь
mahcheeVOY poozIHR'.
blanket - оде́яло ahdee-
YAHlah.
bleed (to) - кровоточи́ть
krahvahtahCHEET'.
blessing - благослове́ние
blahgahslahVYEHneeyeh.
blister - пузы́рь poozIHR'.
block (in a city) - кварта́л
kvahrTAHL.
blonde/(f) - блонди́н/(-ка)
blahnDEEN/(-kah).
blood - кро́вь krohf'.
blood pressure - давле́ние
dahvLYEHneeyeh.

blood type - гру́ппа кро́ви
GROOPpah KROHvee.
blouse - блу́зка BLOOSkah.
blue (adj) - си́ний SEE-
neey.
blue (light) (adj) - голубо́й
gahlooBOY.
blueberries - черни́ка
chehrNEEkah.
boat - ло́дка LOHTkah.
body - те́ло TYEHlah.
boiled (adj) - варёный
vahRYOHnihy.
bone - ко́сть kohst'.
book - кни́га KNEEgah.
book store - кни́жный
магази́н KNEEZHnihy
mahgahZEEN.
booth; cubicle - каби́на
kahBEEnah.
boots - сапоги́ sahpahGEE.
border - грани́ца grahNEE-
tsah.
boring (adj) - ску́чный
SKOOCHnihy.
borsch; beet soup - бо́рщ
bohrshch.
botanical garden - ботан-
и́ческий сад bahtahn-
EECHehskeey saht.
both - о́ба OHbah.
bottle - буты́лка booTIHL-
kah.
bouillon - бульо́н bool'-
OHN.
boulevard бульва́р bool'-
VAHR.
bowl - ми́ска MEESkah.
box - коро́бка/я́щик kahr-
OHPkah/YAHshcheek.
boy - ма́льчик MAHL'cheek.
bra - бюстга́льтер byooz-
KHAHL'teer.

brain - мозг mohsk.

brakes (car) - тормоза tahrmahZAH.

brave; courageous (adj) - смелый SMYEHlihy.

bread - хлеб khlyehp.

break (to) - сломать slahMAHT'.

break; recess - перерыв peereeRIHF.

breakdown (car) - авария ahVAHreeyah.

breakfast - завтрак ZAHFtrahk.

breakfast (to eat) - завтракать ZAHFtrahkaht'.

breathe (to) - дышать dihshAHT'.

breathing; respiration - дыхание dihKHAHneeyeh.

bribe - взятка VZYAHTkah.

bride - невеста neeVYEHStah.

bridge - мост mohst.

brief; not long - недолго neeDOHLgah.

briefcase - портфель pahrtFYEHL'.

bright (adj) - яркий YAHRkeey.

British (adj) - английский ahngLEEYskeey.

broadcast; transmission - передача peereeDAHchah.

brooch - брошь brohsh'.

brother - брат braht.

brother-in-law - зять zyaht'.

brown (adj) - коричневый kahREECHneevihy.

bruise - синяк seenYAHK.

brunette/(f) - брюнет/(-ка) bryooNYEHT/(-kah).

brush - щётка SHCHOHTkah.

bucket - ведро veedROH.

building - здание ZDAHneeyeh.

burn (to) - жечь zhehch.

bus - автобус ahfTOHboos.

bus stop - остановка ahstahnOHFkah.

business (adj) - деловой deelahVOY.

business trip - командировка kahmahndeeROHFkah.

businessman/(f) - бизнесмен/(-ка) beezneesMYEHN/(-kah).

busy; occupied (adj) - занятый zahnYAHtihy.

but - но noh.

butter - масло MAHSlah.

button - пуговица POOgahveetsah.

buy (to) - купить kooPEET'.

by heart - наизусть naheezOOST'.

by; near - близко BLEESkah.

C

cabbage - капуста kahPOOstah.

cabbage soup - щи shchee.

cafe - кафе kahFYEH.

cake - торт tohrt.

calendar - календарь kahleenDAHR'.

call (to) - позвонить pahzvahNEET'.

called, named (to be) - называть nahzihVAHT'.

calm; tranquil (adj) - спо-
кóйный spahKOYnihy.

calorie - калóрия kahLOH-
reeyah.

camel - верблюд veer-
BLYOOT.

camera - фотоаппарáт
fahtahahppahRAHT.

camp - лáгерь LAHgeer'.

campfire - костёр kahs-
TYOHR.

camping - кéмпинг KYEHM-
peeng.

Canadian (adj) - канáдский
kahNAHTskeey.

Canadian/(f) - канáдец
(-нáдка) kahNAHdeets/
(-NAHTkah).

canal - канáл kahNAHL.

candle - свечá sveeCHAH.

candy - конфéты kahn-
FYEHtih.

canned goods - консéрвы
kahnSYEHRvih.

can opener - консéрвный
нóж kahnSYEHRVnihy
nohsh.

capital (of a state) - столúца
stahLEEtsah.

car - автомобúль/машúна
ahftahmahBEEL'/mah-
SHEEnah.

carat - карáт kahRAHT.

care; concern - забóта
zahBOHtah.

careful - осторóжно ahs-
tahROHZHnah.

careless; negligent; sloppy;
slipshod (adj) - небрéж-
ный neeBRYEHZHnihy.

carnation - гвоздúка gvahz-
DEEkah.

carnival - карнавáл kahr-

nahVAHL.

carrots - моркóвь mahr-
KOHF'.

cartoon (film) - мýльт-
фúльм MOOL'Tfeel'm.

cashier - кассúр kahsSEER.

cassette - кассéта kahs-
SYEHtah.

cast - гúпс geeps.

cat - кóшка KOHSHkah.

cathedral - собóр/хрáм
sahBOHR/khrahm.

caution - берегúсь beeree-
GEES'.

caviar - икрá eekRAH.

cavity - дуплó doopLOH.

ceiling - потолóк pahtah-
LOHK.

cemetary - клáдбище
KLAHTbeeshcheh.

center - цéнтр tsehntr.

century - столéтие stah-
LYEHteeyeh.

century; age - вéк vyehk.

certainly; absolutely -
безуслóвно beez-
oosLOHVnah.

chain - цéпь tsehp'.

chair- стýл stool.

champagne - шампáнское
shahmPAHNskahyeh.

change (coins) - сдáча
ZDAHchah.

change; transfer (on planes,
trains, buses etc). -
пересáдка peereeSAHT-
kah.

check - счёт/чéк shchoht/
chehk.

check mate - мáт maht.

cheek щекá shchehKAH.

cheerful (adj) - бóдрый
BOHdrihy.

cheese - **сы́р** sihr.

cherries (sour) - **ви́шня** VEESHnyah.

cherries (sweet) - **чере́шня** chehRYEHSHnyah.

chess - **ша́хматы** SHAHKHmahtih.

chest; breast - **гру́дь** groot'.

chicken - **ку́рица** KOOreetsah.

chief; boss - **нача́льник** nahCHAHL'neek.

child - **ребёнок** reeBYOHnahk.

children - **де́ти** DYEHtee.

children's (adj) - **де́тский** DYEHTskeey.

china - **фарфо́р** fahrFOHR.

chocolate - **шокола́д** shahkahLAHT.

choice; assortment; selection - **вы́бор** VIHbahr.

choir - **хор** khohr.

Christmas - **рождество́** rahzheestVOH.

church - **це́рковь** TSEHRkahf'.

church service - **слу́жба** SLOOSHbah.

cigar - **сига́ра** seeGAHrah.

cigarette - **сигаре́та/ папиро́са** seegahRYEHtah/pahpeeROHSah.

cigarette case - **папиро́сница** pahpeeROHSneetsah.

cigarette lighter - **зажига́лка** zahzheeGAHLkah.

cinnamon - **кори́ца** kahREEtsah.

circle - **круг** krook.

circus - **цирк** tseerk.

ciruclar; round (adj) - **кру́глый** KROOGlihy.

citizen/(f) - **граждани́н/ (-да́нка)** grahzhdahNEEN/(-DAHNkah).

citizenship - **гражда́нство** grahzhDAHNSTvah.

city - **го́род** GOHraht.

civil; civilian (adj) - **гражда́нский** grahzhDAHNskeey.

classical (adj) - **класси́ческий** klahsSEECHehskeey.

clay - **гли́на** GLEEnah.

clean (adj) - **чи́стый** CHEEStihy.

cleaning woman - **убо́рщица** ooBOHRshcheetsah.

clear; distinct (adj) - **чёткий** CHOHTkeey.

clearly - **я́сно** YAHSnah.

clerk - **чино́вник** cheeNOHVneek.

climate - **кли́мат** KLEEmaht.

clinic - **поликли́ника** pahleeKLEEneekah.

clip-on earrings - **кли́пс** kleeps.

cloakroom - **гардеро́б/раздева́лка** gahrdeeROHP/rahzdeeVAHLkah.

cloakroom attendant/(f) - **гардеро́бщик/(-щица)** gahrdeeROHPsheek/(-shcheetsah).

close by; not far - **недалеко́** needahleeKOH.

closed (adj) - **закры́тый** zahKRIHtihy.

closet; cabinet - **шкаф** shkahf.

clothes - **оде́жда** ahDYEHZHdah.

club - **клуб** kloop.

coast; bank; shore - **берег** BYEHreek.

coat - **пальто** pahl'TOH.

coat-check ticket - **номерок** nahmeeROHK.

cockroach - **таракан** tahrahKAHN.

cocoa - **какао** kahKAHoh.

cod - **треска** treesKAH.

coffee - **кофе** KOHfyeh.

cognac; brandy - **коньяк** kahn'YAHK.

coin - **монета** mahNYEHtah.

coincidence - **совпадение** sahfpahDYEHneeyeh.

cold (adj) - **холодный** khahLOHDnihy.

cold (head) - **простуда** prahsTOOdah.

collection; gathering - **сбор** zbohr.

collective farm - **колхоз** kahlKHOHS.

color - **цвет** tsvyeht.

colorless; dull (adj) - **бесцветный** beesTSVEHTnihy.

comb - **гребёнка** greebYOHNkah.

combination - **сочетание** sahchehTAHneeyeh.

comedy - **комедия** kahMYEHdeeyah.

comfortable (adj) - **удобный** ooDOHBnihy.

communal (adj) - **коммунальный** kahmmoonAHL'nihy.

competition; contest; sports match - **конкурс/соревнование** KOHNkoors/sahreevnahVAHneeyeh.

complaint - **жалоба** ZHAHlahbah.

completion; end - **окончание** ahkahnCHAHneeyeh.

completly; absolutely - **совершенно** sahveerSHEHNnah.

complex; difficult (adj) - **сложный** SLOHZHnihy.

complication - **осложнение** ahslahzhNYEHneeyeh.

composer - **композитор** kahmpahZEEtahr.

computer - **компьютер** kahmP'YOOteer.

comrade - **товарищ** tahVAHReeshch.

concert - **концерт** kahnTSEHRT.

conclusion - **заключение** zahklyooCHEHneeyeh.

condition; state - **состояние** sahstahYAHneeyeh.

conditions - **условия** oosLOHveeyah.

conductor (musical) - **дирижёр** deereezhOHR.

confectionery shop -**кондитерская** kahnDEEteerskahyah.

confirmation - **потвержде-ние** pahdveerzhDYEHneeyeh.

congratulate (to) - **поздравлять** pahzdrahvLYAHT'.

consequently - **следовательно** SLYEHdahvahteel'nah.

considerable; significant (adj) - **значительный** znahCHEEteel'nihy.

constant; continuous (adj) - **постоянный** pahstah-

YAHNnihy.
constipation - запо́р
zahPOHR.
consulate - ко́нсульство
KOHNsool'stvah.
contact lens - конта́ктная
ли́нза kahnTAHKTnahyah
LEENzah.
contemporary (adj) - совре-
ме́нный sahvreeMYEHN-
nihy.
continuation - продолже́н-
ие prahdahlZHEHneeyeh.
contraceptive - презерва-
ти́в preezeervahTEEF.
controversial (adj) - спо́р-
ный SPOHRnihy.
convenience - удо́бство
ooDOHBSTvah.
convention; congress - съе́зд
s"yehst.
conversation - разгово́р/
бесе́да rahzgahVOHR/
beeSYEHdah.
conversational; colloquial.
(adj) - разгово́рный
rahzgahVOHRnihy.
cook - по́вар POHvahr.
cook, boil (to) - вари́ть
vahrEET'.
cookie; pastry - пече́нье
peeCHEHN'yeh.
cool (adj) - прохла́дный
prahkhLAHDnihy.
cooperative store - коо-
перати́в kahahpeerah-
TEEF.
copy; edition - экземпля́р
egzeemPLYAHR.
corkscrew - што́пор
SHTOHpahr.
corner - у́гол OOgahl.
correct (adj) - пра́вильный

PRAHVeel'nihy.
correction; adjustment -
попра́вка pahPRAHFkah.
correspondence - перепи́ска
peereePEESkah.
cottage - да́ча DAHchah.
cotton (adj) - хлопчато-
бума́жный khlahpchah-
tahbooMAHZHnihy.
cough - ка́шель KAHSHehl'.
country - страна́ strahNAH.
countryside - дере́вня dee-
RYEHVnyah.
coupon - тало́н tahLOHN.
courage - му́жество
MOOZHehstvah.
cousin (f) - двою́родная
сестра́ dvahYOOrahd-
nahyah seesTRAH.
cousin (m) - двою́родный
бра́т dvahYOOrahdnihy
braht.
cranberries - клю́ква
KLYOOKvah.
crayfish - рак rahk.
crazy; mad; insane (adj) -
сумасше́дший soomahsh-
EHTsheey.
cream (dairy) - сли́вки
SLEEFkee.
cream; lotion - кре́м
kryehm.
creative work - тво́рчество
TVOHRchehstvah.
credit card - креди́тная
ка́рточка kreeDEETnah-
yah KAHRtahchkah.
crime - преступле́ние
preestoopLYEHneeyeh.
crisis - кри́зис KREEzees.
crooked (adj) - криво́й
kreeVOY.
cross - кре́ст kryehst.

crosswalk - переход pee-reeKHONT.

crowd - толпа tahlPAH.

crowded (adj) - тесный TYEHSnihy.

cruel; brutal (adj) - жестокий zhehsTOHkeey.

cruise - круиз krooEEZ.

cucumber soup - рассольник rahsSOHL'neek.

cucumbers - огурцы ahgoorTSIH.

culture - культура kool'-TOOrah.

cup - чашка CHAHSHkah.

curious (adj) - любопытный lyoobahPIHTnihy.

currants - коринка kahr-EENkah.

current (adj) - актуальный ahktooAHL'nihy.

curtain - занавес ZAHnah-vees.

customer - покупатель pahkooPAHteel'.

customs; habits - нравы NRAHvih.

customs - таможня tah-MOHZHnyah.

customs official - таможенник tahMOHZHehnneek.

customs charge; duty - пошлина POHSHleenah.

cut; sliced (adj) - резаный RYEHZahnihy.

cute; sweet; dear - миленький MEEleen'keey.

cutlet - котлета kaht-LYEHtah.

D

daily (adj) - ежедневный yeezhehdNYEHVnihy.

dairy - молочная mah-LOHCHnahyah.

dance - танец TAHneets.

dangerous (adj) - опасный ahPAHSnihy.

dark (adj) - тёмный TYOHMnihy.

dark-(color) - тёмно-TYOHMnah.

daughter - дочь dohch.

daughter-in-law - невестка neeVYEHSTkah.

dawn; daybreak - рассвет rahsSVYEHT.

day - день dyehn'.

day after tomorrow - послезавтра pahsleeZAHFtrah.

day before yesterday - позавчера pahzahfcheh-RAH.

day off - выходной день vihkhahdNOY dyehn'.

daytime (adj) - дневной dneevNOY.

dead (adj) - мёртвый MYOHRTvihy.

deaf (adj) - глухой gloo-KHOY.

death - смерть smyehrt'.

deception; deceit; fraud - обман ahbMAHN.

decision - решение reeSHEHneeyeh.

decoration; embellishment - украшение ookrahSHEH-neeyeh.

decrease - уменьшение oomeen'SHEHneeyeh.

deep; in depth (adj) - глубокий glooBOHkeey.

deficit - дефицит deefee-TSEET.

definite; set; certain (adj) -

определённый ahpree-deeLYOHNnihy.

degree; extent - сте́пень STYEHpeen'.

delay; tardiness - опозда́ние ahpahzDAHneeyeh.

deliberately; on purpose - наро́чно nahROHCHnah.

demon - бес byehs.

dentist - зубно́й врач zoobNOY vrahch.

denture - проте́з prah-TYEHS.

deoderant - дезодара́тор deezahdahRAHtahr.

department - отде́л/ ка́федра ahdDYEHL/ KAHfeedrah.

department store - универма́г ooneeveerMAHK.

departure (airplane) - отлёт ahtLYOHT.

departure (train) - отхо́д ahtKHOHT.

description - описа́ние ahpeeSAHneeyeh.

dessert - десе́рт/на сла́дкое deeSYEHRT/nah SLAHTkahyeh.

detail - подро́бность pahdROHBnahst'.

detour - обхо́д/отъе́зд ahpKHOHT/aht"YEHST.

development (film) - проявле́ние praheevLYEH-neeyeh.

development; growth - разви́тие rahzVEEteeyeh.

devil - чёрт chohrt.

diabetes - диабе́т deeah-BYEHT.

diagnosis - диа́гноз dee-AHGnahs.

diamond - брилли́нт bree-leeAHNT.

diaper - подгру́зник pahd-GROOZneek.

diarrhea - поно́с pahNOHS.

dictionary - слова́рь slah-VAHR'.

diet - дие́та deeYEHtah.

difference; distinction - разни́ца rahzNEEtsah.

different (adj) - ра́зный RAHZnihy.

differently; otherwise - ина́че eeNAHcheh.

difficult (adj) - тру́дный TROODnihy.

dining hall - столо́вая stahLOHvahyah.

director (theater) - режиссёр reezhehsSYOHR.

dirt; filth - грязь gryahs'.

dirty; filthy (adj) - гря́зный GRYAHZnihy.

disability - инвали́дность eenvahLEEDnahst'.

disabled person - инвали́д eenvahLEET.

dish; food; course - блю́до BLYOOdah.

dishes - посу́да pahSOO-dah.

dishonest (adj) - нече́стный neeCHEHSTnihy.

disinfect (to) - дезинфици́ровать deezeenfeets-EERahvaht'.

dissatisfied (adj) - недово́льный needahVOHL'-nihy.

distance - расстоя́ние rahsstahYAHneeyeh.

diverse (adj) - многообра́зный mnahgahahbRAHZ-

nihy.
do (to) - де́лать DYEHlaht'.
dock; pier; wharf - при́-
стань PREEstahn'.
doctor - вра́ч vrahch.
dog - соба́ка sahBAHkah.
doll; puppet - ку́кла KOOK-
lah.
dollar - до́ллар DOHLlahr.
door - две́рь dvyehr'.
doorman - швейца́р shvey-
TSAHR.
dormitory - общежи́тие
ahpshchehZHEEteeyeh.
dosage - дозиро́вка dahzee-
ROHFkah.
double occupency (adj) -
двуспа́льный dvoo-
SPAHL'nihy.
doubt - сомне́ние sahm-
NYEHneeyeh.
doughnut - по́нчик POHN-
cheek.
down; below (location) -
внизу́ vneeZOO.
down; downward (destin-
ation) - вни́з vnees.
dozen - дю́жина DYOO-
zheenah.
drawing - рисова́ние
reesahVAHneeyeh.
dress - пла́тье PLAHT'yeh.
drink (to) - пить peet'.
drink - напи́ток nahPEE-
tahk.
drive (to) - е́здить/е́хать
YEHZdeet'/YEHkhaht'.
driver - води́тель vahDEE-
teel'.
driver's license - води́тель-
ские права́ vahDEEteel'-
skeeyeh prahVAH.
drop - ка́пля KAHPlyah.

drugstore - апте́ка ahp-
TYEHkah.
drunk (adj) - пья́ный
P'YAHnihy.
drunkard - пя́ница PYAH-
neetsah.
dry (adj) - сухо́й sooKHOY.
dry cleaning - химчи́стка
kheemCHEESTkah.
duty (customs) - по́шлина
POHSHleenah.
duty-free - беспо́шлинный
beesPOHSHleennihy.
dye; hair coloring - окра́ска
ahKRAHSkah.

E

ear - у́хо OOKHah.
earlier; sooner - ра́ньше
RAHN'sheh.
early (adj) - ра́нний RAHN-
eey.
earmuff; headphone - нау́ш-
ник nahOOSHneek.
earrings - се́рьги/серёжки
SYEHR'gee/seerYOHSHkee.
easily - легко́ leekhKOH.
east - восто́к vahsTOHK.
eastern (adj) - восто́чный
vahsTOHCHnihy.
Easter; Passover - па́сха
PAHSkhah.
easy (adj) - лёгкий
LYOHKHkeey.
eat (to) - есть yehst'.
edge; rim - кра́й kray.
education - образова́ние
ahbrahzahVAHneeyeh.
egg - яйцо́ yayTSOH.
egg shell - скорлупа́
skahrlooPAH.
eggplant - баклажа́н bahklahzhAHN.

elbow - ло́коть LOHkaht'.

elderly (adj) - пожило́й pahzheeLOY.

elections - вы́боры VIHbahrih.

electrical (adj) - электри́ческий ehleekTREEchehskeey.

electrical socket - розе́тка rahzYEHTkah.

electricity - электри́чество ehleekTREEchehstvah.

elevator - лифт leeft.

embarrassment - смуще́ние smooSHCHEHneeyeh.

embassy - посо́льство pahSOHL'stvah.

embroidered (adj) - вы́шитый VIHsheetihy.

emerald - изумру́д eezoomROOT.

empty; vacant (adj) - пусто́й poosTOY.

end - коне́ц kahnYEHTS.

enemy - враг vrahk.

engineer - инжене́р eenzheeNYEHR.

English, British (adj) -англи́йский ahngLEEYskeey.

Englishman/(f) - англича́нин(-ча́нка) ahngleeCHAHneen (-CHAHNkah).

enjoy (to) - нра́виться NRAHveetsah.

enjoy oneself (to); have fun - весели́ться veeseeLEEtsah.

enough; sufficiently -доста́точно dahsTAHtahchnah.

enter (to) - входи́ть fkhahDEET'.

enthusiastic (adj) - увлечённый oovleeCHOHNnihy.

entrance - вход fkhoht.

envelope - конве́рт kahnVYEHRT.

equal (adj) - ра́вный RAHVnihy.

escalator - эскала́тор ehskahLAHtahr.

especially - осо́бенно ahSOHbeennah.

eternally - ве́чно VYEHCHnah.

European (adj) - европе́йский yeevrahPEYskeey.

European/(f) - европе́ец/ (-пе́йка) yeevrahPYEHeets/(-PEYkah).

evening (adj) - вече́рний veeCHEHRneey.

evening - ве́чер VYEHchehr.

event - собы́тие sahBIHTeeyeh.

every (adj) - ка́ждый KAHZHdihy.

everything - всё fsyoh.

everywhere - везде́ veezDYEH.

evil; mean; malicious (adj) - злой zloy.

exactly - то́чно/и́менно TOHCHnah/EEMeennah.

exaggeration - преувеличе́ние preeooveeleeCHEHneeyeh.

examination; checkup - осмо́тр ahsMOHTR.

example - приме́р preeMYEHR.

except for; but; besides - кро́ме KROHmyeh.

excessive; superfluous (adj) - изли́шний eezLEESHneey.

exchange - обме́н ahb-MYEHN.

exchange (to) - обменя́ть ahbmeenYAHT'.

excited (adj) - возбуждён-ный vahzboozhDYOHN-nihy.

excursion - экску́рсия ehksKOORseeyah.

excuse, pardon (to) -извиня́ть eezveenYAHT'.

exersise - упражне́ние ooprahzhNYEHneeyeh.

exhaustion - утомле́ние ootahmLYEHneeyeh.

exhibtion; display - вы́-ставка VIHstahfkah.

exit - вы́ход VIHkhaht.

expenses - расхо́ды rahs-KHOHdih.

expensive; valuable; dear (adj) - дорого́й dahrah-GOY.

experience - о́пыт OHpiht.

explanation - объясне́ние ahb"eesNYEHneeyeh.

express - экспре́сс ehks-PRYEHSS.

eye - гла́з glahs.

eyebrow - бро́вь brohf'.

eyelash - ресни́ца reesNEE-tsah.

eyesight - зре́ние ZRYEH-neeyeh.

F

fabric - тка́нь tkahn'.

face - лицо́ leeTSOH.

factory - заво́д zahVOHT.

fair - я́рмарка YAHRmahr-kah.

fake; falsified (adj) - фаль-ши́вый fahl'SHEEvihy.

fall; autumn - о́сень OHseen'.

false (adj) - ло́жный LOHZHnihy.

family - семья́ seem'YAH.

famous (adj) - знамени́тый znahmeeNEEtihy.

fan - ве́ер VYEHeer.

far away - далеко́ dahlee-KOH.

farewell - проща́й prah-SHCHAY.

farm - фе́рма FYEHRmah.

farther; continue - да́льше DAHL'sheh.

fashion; style - мо́да MOH-dah.

fashionable; stylish (adj) - мо́дный MOHDnihy.

fast; quickly; rapidly - бы́стро BIHStrah.

fat (adj) - то́лстый TOHL-stihy.

fat; grease - жи́р zheer.

fate - судьба́ soot'BAH.

father - оте́ц ahTYEHTS.

fatherland - оте́чество ahtYEHCHehstvah

faucet - кра́н krahn.

fear, be afraid (to) - боя́ться bahYAHTsah.

fear - стра́х strahkh.

feature; trait; characteristic - черта́ chehrTAH.

feel (to) - чу́вствовать себя́ CHOOFSTvahvaht' see-BYAH.

feel sorry for, pity (to) - жале́ть zhahLYEHT'.

feeling; sensation - ощущ-е́ние ahshchooSHCHEH-neeyeh.

feeling; sensitivity - чу́вст-

во CHOOFSTvah.
feminine; woman's (adj) -
женский ZHEHNskeey.
ferry - паром pahROHM.
fever - жар zhahr.
few; some; several - не-
сколько neeSKOHL'kah.
field; area - поле POHLyeh.
fight (to) - биться BEETsah.
fight, struggle - борьба
bahr'BAH.
filled dumpling - вареник
vahRYEHneek.
filling (tooth) - пломба
PLOHMbah.
film - плёнка PLYOHNkah.
finally; at last - наконец
nahkahnYEHTS.
find (to) - найти nayTEE.
fine - штраф shtrahf.
finger - палец PAHleets.
fire - пожар pahZHAHR.
first-aid kit - аптечка
ahpTYEHCHkah.
fish - рыба RIHBah.
fish soup - уха ooKHAH.
fishing pole - удочка
OODahchkah.
flashlight - карманный
фонарь kahrMAHNnihy
fahNAHR'.
flexible (adj) - гибкий
GEEPkeey.
flight - полёт pahLYOHT.
flood - наводнение
nahvahdNYEHneeyeh.
floor; story - этаж eh-
TAHSH.
flounder; sole - камбала
KAHMbahlah.
flour - мука mooKAH.
flower - цветок tsveeTOHK.
flu - грипп greep.

fly - муха MOOkhah.
fog - туман tooMAHN.
food - еда/пища yeeDAH/
PEEshchah.
fool (f) - дура DOOrah.
fool (m) - дурак dooRAHK.
foot (by, on) - пешком
peeshKOHM.
foot (measure) - фут foot.
foot; leg - нога nahGAH.
for - для dlyah.
for example - например
nahpreeMYEHR.
for some reason - почему-
то pahcheeMOOtah.
for the first time; first -
впервые fpeerVIHyeh.
forbid (to) - запрещать
zahpreeshchAHT'.
forbidden (to be) - воспре-
щаться vahspree-
SHCHAHTsah.
forehead - лоб lohp.
foreign (adj) - иностранный
eenahsTRAHNnihy.
foreign; not one's own (adj)
- чужой chooZHOY.
foreigner/(f) - иностра-
нец/(-транка) eenahs-
TRAHNeets/(-TRAHNkah).
forest - лес lyehs.
forever - навсегда nahf-
seegDAH.
forget (to) - забывать
zahbihVAHT'.
forgotten (adj) - забытый
zahBIHTihy.
fork - вилка VEELkah.
form, blank, survey -
анкета ahnKYEHtah.
former; previous (adj) -
прежний/бывший
PRYEHZHneey/BIHFsheey.

195

forward; ahead - **вперёд** fpeeRYOHT.

found, located (to be) - **находиться** nahkhah-DEETsah.

fountain - **фонтан** fahn-TAHN.

fragile (adj) - **крупкий** KROOPkeey.

fragrant (adj) - **ароматный** ahrahMAHTnihy.

free of charge (adj) - **бесплатный** beesPLAHTnihy.

free; vacant (adj) - **свободный** svahBOHDnihy.

freedom - **свобода/воля** svahBOHdah/VOHLyah.

freely; voluntarily - **вольно** VOHL'nah.

frequency - **частота** chahs-tahTAH.

fresh (adj) - **свежий** SVYEHzheey.

fried eggs - **яичница** yahEECHneetsah.

• friend - **друг** drook.

friendly; amicable (adj) - **дружный** DROOZHnihy.

friendship - **дружба** DROOSHbah.

from - **от** aht.

front (adj) - **передний** peeRYEHDneey.

frost - **мороз** mahROHS.

frozen (adj) - **мороженный** mahROHZHehnnihy.

fruit - **фрукт** frookt.

fry, roast, broil - **жарить** ZHAHReet'.

frying pan - **сковорода** skahvahrahDAH.

full (of food); satiated (adj) - **сытый** SIHTihy.

full; complete (adj) - **полный** POHLnihy.

fully; completely; quite - **вполне** fpahlNYEH.

funny (adj) - **смешной** smeeshNOY.

fur (adj) - **меховой** meekhahVOY.

fur - **мех** myehkh.

fur coat - **шуба** SHOObah.

fur hat - **меховая шапка** meekhahVAHyah SHAHPkah.

furniture - **мебель** MYEHbeel'.

further; farther - **далее** DAHleeyeh.

future - **будущий** BOOdooshcheey.

G

game - **игра** eegRAH.

garage - **гараж** gahRAHSH.

garden - **сад** saht.

garlic - **чеснок** chehsNOHK.

garnet - **гранат** grahNAHT.

gas - **бензин** beenZEEN.

gas meter - **газомер** gahzahMYEHR.

gas station - **бензозаправочная станция** beenzahzahPRAHvahchnahyah STAHNtseeyah.

gas tank - **бензобак** beenzahBAHK.

gastritis - **гастрит** gahsTREET.

gate - **ворота** vahROHtah.

general; common; total (adj) - **общий** OHPshcheey.

generous (adj) - **щедрый** SHCHEHDrihy.

genitals - **половые органы**

pahlahVIHyeh OHRgahnih.

geriatric (adj) - **гериатри́-
ческий** geereeahtREE-
cheeskeey.

German (adj) - **герма́нский**
geerMAHNskeey.

German/(f) - **герма́нец/
(-ка́нка)** geerMAHNeets/
(-MAHNkah).

get, stand up (to) - **встава́ть**
fstahVAHT'.

gift; souvenir - **пода́рок**
pahDAHrahk.

gilded (adj) - **вы́золочен-
ный** VIHzahlahchehn-
nihy.

girl - **де́вочка** DYEH-
vahchkah.

give (to) - **дава́ть** dah-
VAHT'.

give as a gift (to) - **дари́ть**
dahREET'.

glad; pleased - **рад** raht.

gland - **железа́** zhehlee-
ZAH.

glass (drinking) - **стака́н**
stahKAHN.

glass - **стекло́** steekLOH.

glasses - **очки́** ahchKEE.

glory - **сла́ва** SLAHvah.

gloves - **перча́тки** peer-
CHAHTkee.

glue - **клей** kley.

go by, past - **ми́мо** MEEmah.

go, walk (to) - **ходи́ть/идти́**
khahDEET'/EETtee.

goal; aim - **цель** tsehl'.

God - **бог** bohkh.

gold (adj) - **золото́й** zahlahTOY.

gold - **зо́лото** ZOHlahtah.

good (adj) - **хоро́ший** khah-
ROHsheey.

goodbye - **до свида́ния**
dahsveeDAHneeyah.

goodbye (coll) - **пока́**
pahKAH.

goose - **гусь** goos'.

goulash - **гуля́ш** gool-
YAHSH.

government - **прави́тельство**
prahVEEteel'stvah.

gradually - **постепе́нно**
pahsteePYEHNnah.

graduate student/(f) -
аспира́нт/(-ка) ahspee-
RAHNT/(-kah).

grain - **зерно́** zeerNOH.

gram - **грамм** grahm.

grammar - **грамма́тика**
grahmMAHteekah.

grammatical case - **паде́ж**
pahDYEHSH.

granddaughter - **вну́чка**
VNOOCHkah.

grandfather - **де́душка**
DYEHdooshkah.

grandmother - **ба́бушка**
BAHbooshkah.

grandson - **внук** vnook.

grapes - **виногра́д** veenahg-
RAHT.

grapefruit - **гре́йпфрут**
GREYPfroot.

grass - **трава́** trahVAH.

grave - **моги́ла** mahGEElah.

greasy; oily; fatty (adj) -
жи́рный ZHEERnihy.

great (adj) - **вели́кий**
veeLEEkeey.

greedy (adj) - **жа́дный**
ZHAHDnihy.

green (adj) - **зелёный** zee-
LYOHnihy.

greengrocer - **зеленщи́к**
zeeleenSHCHEEK.

grey (adj) - **cépыs** SYEH-rihy.
grief - **rópe** GOHRyeh.
grocery store - **гастроном** gahstrahNOHM.
ground; dirt; earth - **земля** zeemLYAH.
group - **группа** GROOPpah.
growth; height - **рост** rohst.
growth; tumor - **нарост** nahROHST.
guard; sentry - **караул** kahrahOOL.
guest - **гость** gohst'.
guide - **гид** geet.
guidebook - **путеводитель** pooteevahDEEteel'.
guilt - **вина** veeNAH.
guilty (adj) - **виноватый** veenahVAHtihy.
guitar - **гитара** geeTAHrah.
gynecologist - **гинеколог** geeneeKOHlahk.
gypsy - **цыган** tsihGAHN.

Н

habit - **привычка** pree-VIHCHkah.
hair - **волосы** VOHlahsih.
haircut; trim - **стрижка** STREESHkah.
hair-do - **причёска** pree-CHOHSkah.
hairdresser; barber - **парикмахер** pahreek-MAHKHeer.
hairdryer - **фён** fyehn.
half - **половина** pahlah-VEEnah.
half hour - **полчаса** pahlcheeSAH.
hall; room - **зал** zahl.
hall monitor - **дежурная**

deezhOORnahyah.
ham - **ветчина** veetchee-NAH.
hand; arm - **рука** rooKAH.
handshake - **пожатие** pah-ZHAHteeyeh.
hanger - **вешалка** VYEH-shahlkah.
happy; lucky (adj) - **счастливый** shahstLEEvihy.
hard (adj) - **твёрдый** TVYOHRdihy.
hard currency - **валюта** vahLYOOtah.
hard-currency store - **Берёзка** beerYOHSkah.
hardly; scarsely; barely - **едва** yeedVAH.
hare - **заяц** ZAHeets.
harmful (adj) - **вредный** VRYEHDnihy.
hat - **шапка** SHAHPkah.
hazel grouse - **рябчик** RYAHPcheek.
he - **он** ohn.
head - **голова** gahlahVAH.
headache - **головная боль** gahlahvNAHyah bohl'.
head cold - **насморк** NAH-smahrk.
headlights - **фары** FAHrih.
headphone; earmuff - **наушник** nahOOSHneek.
health - **здоровье** zdah-ROHV'yeh.
healthy (adj) - **здоровый** zdahROHvihy.
heart - **сердце** SYEHRtseh.
heart attack - **сердечный припадок** seerDYEHCH-nihy preePAHdahk.
heavy (adj) - **тяжёлый** teezhOHLihy.

hedgehog - ёж yohsh.
heel - каблук kahbLOOK.
height; altitude - высота
vihsahTAH.
hello - здравствуйте
ZDRAHSTvooytyeh.
hello (on the telephone) -
алло ahlLOH.
help - помощь POH-
mahshch.
hemophilia - гемофилия
geemahfeeLEEyah.
hemorrhage - кровоизли-
яние krahvaheezlee-
YAHneeyeh.
hemorrhoids - геморрой
geemahrROY.
hepatitis - гепатит gee-
pahTEET.
her; its - её yeeYOH.
here (is) - вот voht.
here - тут/здесь toot/
zdyehs'.
hernia - грыжа GRIHzhah.
hero - герой geeROY.
herring - сельдь syehl't'.
hi - привет preeVYEHT.
hidden; secret (adj) - скры-
тый SKRIHtihy.
high blood pressure - гин-
пертония geepeertahNEE-
yah.
high; tall; lofty (adj) -
высокий vihSOHkeey.
highway - трасса/шоссе
TRAHSsah/shahsSYEH.
hindrance - препятсвие
preePYAHTSveeyeh.
hip; thigh - бедро beedROH.
his; its - его yeeVOH.
history; story - история
eesTOHreeyah.
hockey - хоккей kahkKEY.

hold, keep, support (to) -
держать deerZHAHT'.
hole - дыра dihRAH.
holiday - праздник PRAHZ-
neek.
holy; sacred (adj) - святой
sveeTOY.
homeland - родина ROH-
deenah.
homosexuality - гомосекс-
уализм gahmahseeks-
ooahlEEZM.
honest (adj) - честный
CHEHSTnihy.
honey - мёд myoht.
hooligan - хулиган khoo-
leeGAHN.
hope - надежда nah-
DYEHZHdah.
horn; whistle - гудок goo-
DOHK.
horrible (adj) - ужасный
oozhAHSnihy.
horrible; terrifying (adj) -
страшный STRAHSHnihy.
horse - лошадь LOHSHaht'.
horseradish - хрен
khryehn.
hospitable (adj) - хлебо-
сольный khleebahSOHL'-
nihy.
hospital - больница bahl'-
NEEtsah.
hot; intense (adj) - горячий
gahrYAHcheey.
hot (weather) (adj) - жар-
кий ZHAHRkeey.
hotel - гостиница gahsTEE-
neetsah.
hotel room; issue - номер
NOHmeer.
hour - час chahs.
house; home - дом dohm.

199

housewife - **хозяйка** khaz-YAYkah.
‹ how - **как** kahk.
‹ how far - **как далеко** kahk dahleeKOH.
‹ how long - **как долго** kahk DOHLgah.
how much - **сколько** SKOHL'kah.
however; but - **однако** ahdNAHkah.
humid (adj) - **влажный** VLAHZHnihy.
humidity - **влажность** VLAHZHnahst'.
humor - **юмор** YOOmahr.
hundred - **сотный** SOHTnihy.
. hunger - **голод** GOHlaht.
hungry (adj) - **голодный** gahLOHDnihy.
hurried; rushed (adj) - **спешный** SPYEHSHnihy.
ↅ husband - **муж/супруг** moosh/soopROOK.

I
ↅ I - **я** yah.
ice - **лёд** lyoht.
ↅ ice cream - **мороженое** mahROHZHehnahyeh.
icon - **икона** eekOHnah.
iconostasis - **иконостас** eekahnahSTAHS.
idea - **идея** eedYEHyah.
identical (adj) - **одинаковый** ahdeeNAHkahvihy.
identification - **удостоверение** oodahstahveeRYEHneeyeh.
if; when - **если** YEHSlee.
if; whether **ли** lee.
ill (to be) - **болеть** bahl-YEHT'.
ill (to fall) - **заболеть** zahbahLYEHT'.
illegal (adj) - **незаконный** neezahKOHNnihy.
illness; disease - **болезнь** bahLYEHZN'.
image; way; mode; manner - **образ** OHbrahs.
imagination - **воображение** vahahbrahZHEHneeyeh.
impatience - **нетерпение** neeteerPYEHneeyeh.
importance - **важность** VAHZHnahst'.
important (adj) - **важный** VAHZHnihy.
ↅ impossible; one can not - **нельзя** neel'ZYAH.
impression - **впечатление** fpeechahtLYEHneeyeh.
improper; indecent (adj) - **неприличный** neepreeLEECHnihy.
in advance - **заранее** zahRAHnehyeh.
in front; ahead - **впереди** fpeereeDEE.
in general - **вообще** vahahpSHCHEH.
in order to - **чтобы** SHTOHbih.
in the distance - **вдали** vdahLEE.
in vain; for nothing - **напрасно** nahPRAHSnah.
in, at, for, to - **в** v.
inaudible (adj) - **неслышный** neeSLIHSHnihy.
inch - **дюйм** dyooym.
incident - **случай** SLOOchay.
incidentally; by the way -

кстати KSTAHtee.
income - доход dahKHOHT.
incomprehensible (adj) -
непонятный neepahn-
YAHTnihy.
increase - увеличение
ooveeleeCHEHneeyeh.
incredible; unbelievable -
невероятный neeveerah-
YAHTnihy.
independence - независи-
мость neezahVEEsee-
mahst'.
independent (adj) - само-
стоятельный sahmahstah-
YAHteel'nihy.
indifferent (adj) - равно-
душный rahvnahDOOSH-
nihy.
indigestion - расстройство
желудка rahsSTROYstvah
zhehLOOTkah.
inexpensive; cheap -
дешёвый deeSHOHvihy.
inexperienced (adj) - нео-
пытный neeOHpihtnihy.
infection - заражение zah-
rahZHEHneeyeh.
inflamation - воспаление
vahspahLYEHneeyeh.
influence - влияние vlee-
YAHneeyeh.
influential (adj) - влия-
тельный vleeYAHteel'-
nihy.
injection - укол ooKOHL.
ink - чернила chehrNEElah.
innocent (adj) - безвинный
beezVEENnihy.
inscription - надпись
nahtPEES'.
insect - насекомое nahsee-
KOHmahyeh.

insect repellent - средство
от комаров SRYEHTstvah
aht kahmahROHF.
inside - внутри vnooTREE.
insomnia - бессонница bees-
SOHneetsah.
instead of - вместо VMYEH-
stah.
institution - заведение/
учреждение zahvee-
DYEHneeyeh/oochreezh-
DYEHneeyeh.
instructions - инструкция
eenSTROOKtseeyah.
insufficient - недостаточно
needahsTAHtahchnah.
intention - намерение
nahMYEHreeneeyeh.
interesting (adj) - интерес-
ный eenteeRYEHSnihy.
intermission - антракт
ahnTRAHKT.
internal (adj) inner - вну-
тренний VNOOtreenneey.
international (adj) - международный meezhdoo-
nahROHDnihy.
interpreter - переводчик
peereeVOHTcheek.
intestine - кишка keesh-
KAH.
Intourist office - бюро
Интуриста byooROH
eentooREESTah.
introduction - введение
vveeDYEHneeyeh.
invitation - приглашение
preeglahSHEHneeyeh.
iodine - йод yoht.
iron (to) - гладить GLAH-
deet'.
iron - утюг ooTYOOK.
irritation - раздражение

rahzdrahZHEHneeyeh.

island - **о́стров** OHStrahf.

issue; edition; output - **вы́пуск** VIHpoosk.

issue; number - **но́мер** NOHmeer.

J

jam - **варе́нье** vah-RYEHN'yeh.

janitor; yardsman - **убо́р- щик** ooBOHRshcheek.

jar; can - **ба́нка** BAHNkah.

jeans - **джи́нсы** DZHEENsih.

Jew/(f) - **евре́й/(-ка)** yeevREY/(-kah).

jewel - **драгоце́нность** drahgahTSEHNnahst'.

jewelry (adj) - **ювели́рный** yooveeLEERnihy.

Jewish; Hebrew (adj) - **евре́йский** yeevREYskeey.

joke - **шу́тка** SHOOTkah.

journalist - **журнали́ст** zhoornahLEEST.

joyful; joyous (adj) - **ра́- достный** RAHdahstnihy.

juice - **сок** sohk.

K

kerchief - **плато́к** plahTOHK.

key - **ключ** klyooch.

kidney - **по́чка** POHCHkah.

kilogram - **килогра́мм** kee-lahgRAHM.

kilometer - **киломе́тр** kee-lahMYEHTR.

kind; good (adj) - **до́брый** DOHbrihy.

kind; sort - **сорт** sohrt.

kindness - **доброта́** dah-brahTAH.

kiosk - **кио́ск** keeOHSK.

kiss - **поцелу́й** pahtsee-LOOY.

kitchen - **ку́хня** KOOKH-nyah.

knee - **коле́но** kahLYEHnah.

knife **нож** nohsh.

knock - **стук** stook.

know (to) - **знать** znaht'.

knowledge - **зна́ние** ZNAH-neeyeh.

known (well) (adj) - **изве́ст- ный** eezVYEHSTnihy.

kopeck - **копе́йка** kahPEY-kah.

kosher (adj) - **коше́рный** kahshEHRnihy.

kvass (fermented drink) - **квас** kvahs.

L

ladies (adj) - **да́мский** DAHMskeey.

lake - **о́зеро** OHzeerah.

lame (adj) - **хромо́й** khrah-MOY.

lamp - **ла́мпа** LAHMpah.

landing - **поса́дка** pah-SAHTkah.

language; tonuge - **язы́к** yeezIHK.

larger; bigger; greater - **бо́льше** BOHL'sheh.

last; latest (adj) - **после́д- ний** pahsLYEHDneey.

last (to) - **дли́ться** DLEE-tsah.

last name; sir name - **фами́- лия** fahMEEleeyah.

late (adj) - **по́здний** POHZDneey.

late (to be) - **опазда́ть** ahp-ahzDAHT'.

later - по́зже POHZHzheh.
laughter - сме́х smyehkh.
laundry; linen - бельё
beel'YOH.
law - зако́н zahKOHN.
lawyer - адвока́т ahdvah-
KAHT.
laxitive - слаби́тельное
slahBEEteel'nahyeh.
leadership - руково́дство
rookahVOHTstvah.
leaf; sheet (of paper) листо́к
leesTOHK.
leather (adj) - ко́жаный
KOHzhahnihy.
leave, go out, exit (to) -
выходи́ть vihkhahDEET'.
lecture - ле́кция LYEHK-
tseeyah.
left (direction) - ле́вый
LYEHvihy.
leg - нога́ nahGAH.
legal; legitimate (adj) - за-
ко́нный zahKOHNnihy.
lemon - лимо́н leeMOHN.
lemonade - лимона́д leem-
ahnAHT.
length - длина́ dleeNAH.
less - ме́ньше MYEHN'sheh.
lesson - уро́к ooROHK.
let's; go ahead! - дава́й
dahVAY.
letter - письмо́ pees'MOH.
letter of the alphabet - бу́к-
ва BOOKvah.
level - у́ровень OOrahveen'.
library - библиоте́ка beeb-
leeahTYEHkah.
lid; cover - кры́шка KRIH-
shkah.
lie, tell lies (to) - врать
vraht'.

life - жизнь zheezn'.
light - свет svyeht.
light bulb - ла́мпочка
LAHMpahchkah.
light-(color) - све́тло-
SVYEHTlah-.
light; bright (adj) - све́тлый
SVYEHTlihy.
lightning - мо́лния
MOHLneeyah.
lilac - сире́нь seeRYEHN'.
line - о́чередь OHCHehreet'.
lip - губа́ gooBAH.
list - спи́сок SPEEsahk.
liter - литр leetr.
literature - литерату́ра
leeteerahTOOrah.
little; not enough - ма́ло
MAHlah.
little; not much - немно́го
neemNOHgah.
live (to) - жить zheet'.
liver (anatomy) - пе́чень
PYEHchehn'.
liver (the food) - печёнка
peechOHNkah.
loaf of bread - буха́нка
bookhAHNkah.
lobby - фойе́ fayYEN.
local (adj) - ме́стный
MYEHSTnihy.
lock - замо́к zahMOHK.
long (measure) (adj) -
дли́нный DLEENnihy.
long (time) (adj) - до́лгий
DOHLgeey.
long ago - давно́ dahvNOH.
long time (for a) - до́лго
DOHLgah.
long underwear - кальсо́ны
kahl'SOHnih.
look (to) - смотре́ть smah-
TRYEHT'.

203

look; glance - **взгляд**
vzglyaht.
lose (to) - **потерять** pahteerYAHT'.
loud (adj) - **громкий**
GROHMkeey.
love (to) - **любить** lyoo-
BEET'.
love - **любовь** lyooBOHF'.
lower (adj) - **нижний**
NEEZHnihy.
lox - **сёмга** SYOHMgah.
luggage - **багаж** bahGAHSH.
lunch - **обéд** ahBYEHT.
lunch (to eat) **обéдать** ah-
BYEHdaht'.
lungs - **лёгкие** LYOHKH-
keeyeh.
luxurious (adj) - **роскош-
ный** rahsKOHSHnihy.

M
magazine - **журнáл** zhoor-
NAHL.
maid - **горничная** GOHR-
neechnahyah.
mail; postoffice - **пóчта**
POHCHtah.
mailbox - **почтóвый ящик**
pahchTOHvihy YAH-
shcheek.
main; principle (adj) -
глáвный GLAHVnihy.
majority - **большинствó**
bahl'sheenstVOH.
make-up - **космéтика** kahs-
MYEHteekah.
malachite - **малахит** mahlahKHEET.
malicious; spiteful (adj) -
злóбный ZLOHBnihy.
man - **мужчина** moosh-
CHEEnah.

manager - **администрáтор/
дирéктор** ahdmeenees-
TRAHtahr/deeRYEHKtahr.
manager - **завéдующий**
zahVYEHdooyooshcheey.
manuscript - **рýкопись**
ROOkahpees'.
map (of the city) - **плáн**
plahn.
map - **кáрта** KAHRtah.
marinated (adj) - **маринó-
ванный** mahreeNOHvahn-
nihy.
market - **рынок** RIHNahk.
marriage - **брáк** brahk.
married (for women) - **зá-
мужем** ZAHmoozhehm.
married (for men) - **женáт**
zhehNAHT.
match - **спичка** SPEECHkah.
matroshka dolls (wooden,
nested dolls) - **матрёшка**
mahtRYOHSHkah.
matter; affair; business -
дéло DYEHlah.
mausoleum - **мавзолéй**
mahvzahLEY.
may; can - **мóжно** MOHZH-
nah.
mean (to) - **знáчить** ZNAH-
cheet'.
meaning; sense - **значéние**
znahCHEHneeyeh.
meanwhile - **покá** pahKAN.
measure; extent; degree -
мéра MYEHrah.
meat - **мясо** MYAHsah.
meat loaf - **рулéт** roo-
LYEHT.
meatballs - **тéфтели**
TYEHFteelee.
mechanism - **механизм**
meekhahnEEZM.

medical treatment - печé-
нне leeCHEHneeyeh.
medicine - лекáрство
leeKAHRstvah.
meet (to) - встречáть
fstreechAHT'.
meeting - собрáнне sah-
BRAHneeyeh.
meeting; encounter -
встрéча FSTRYEHchah.
melon - дыня DIHNyah.
member - член chlyehn.
memory - пáмять PAHM-
eet'.
memory; recollection - вос-
помннáнне vahspahmee-
NAHneeyeh.
men's (adj) - мужскóй
mooshSKOY.
menstruation - менстру-
áцня meenstrooAHtsee-
yah.
mental; emotional (adj) -
душéвный dooshEHV-
nihy.
menu - менм meenYOO.
merchandise - товáр tah-
VAHR.
meter - мéтр myehtr.
middle - середнна
seereeDEEnah.
middle; average (adj) -
срéднвй SRYEHDneey.
midnight - пóлночь POHL-
nahch.
military (adj) - воéнный
vahYEHNnihy.
milk - молокó mahlahKOH.
million - мнллнóн meellee-
OHN.
minute - мннýта meenOOT-
ah.
mirror - зéркало ZYEHR-

kahlah.
misfortune - бедá beeDAH.
mistake - ошнбка ahshEEP-
kah.
misunderstanding - непо-
разумéнне needah-
rahzooMYEHneeyeh.
mitten - рукавнца rookah-
VEEtsah.
modest (adj) - скрóмный
SKROHMnihy.
monastary - монастырь/
лáвра mahnahsTIHR'/
LAHVrah.
money - дéньгн DYEHN'gee.
money order - дéнежный
перевóд DYEHneezhnihy
peereeVOHT.
month - мéсяц MYEHSeets.
monthly (adj) -ежемéсяч-
ный yeezhehMYEHseech-
nihy.
monument - пáмятннк
PAHMeetneek.
mood - настроéнне nahs-
trahYEHneeyeh.
moon - лунá looNAH.
more - бóлее BOHleeyeh.
morning (adj) - ýтреннй
OOTreeneey.
morning - ýтро OOTrah.
Moscow (adj) - москóвскнй
mahsKOHFskeey.
mosquito - комáр kah-
MAHR.
mother - мáть maht'.
motor - мотóр mahTOHR.
motorcycle - мотоцнкл
mahtahTSEEKL.
motorist - автомабнлнст
ahftahmahbeeLEEST.
mountain - горá gahRAH.
mouse - мышь mihsh.

205

mouth - рот roht.

movement; traffic - движе́ние dveeZHEHneeyeh.

movie - фильм feel'm.

movie theater - кинотеа́тр keenahteeAHTR.

movie; the cinema - кино́ keeNOH.

Mr. (pre-revolutionary) - господи́н gahspahDEEN.

Mrs. (pre-revolutionary) - госпожа́ gahspahZHAH.

much; a lot - мно́го MNOHgah.

much, far - гора́здо gahRAHZdah.

multicolored (adj) - многоцве́тный mnahgahTSVYEHTnihy.

murder - уби́йство ooBEEYSTvah.

murderer - уби́йца ooBEEYtsah.

muscle - му́скул MOOSkool.

museum - музе́й mooZEY.

mushrooms - грибы́ greeBIH.

music - му́зыка MOOZihkah.

must - на́до/ну́жно NAHdah/NOOZHnah.

mustache - усы́ oosIH.

mustard - горчи́ца gahrCHEEtsah.

mutton; lamb - бара́нина bahRAHneenah.

mutton soup - харчо́ kharCHOH.

mutual understanding - взаимопонима́ние vzaheemahpahneeMAHneeyeh.

mystery (story/movie) - детекти́в deeteekTEEF.

N

nail, tack - гвоздь gvohst'.

naked (adj) - го́лый GOHlihy.

name (first) - и́мя EEMyah.

name (last); sir name - фами́лия fahMEEleeyah.

name; title - назва́ние nahzVAHneeyeh.

napkin - салфе́тка sahlFYEHTkah.

narrow (adj) - у́зкий OOSkeey.

nasty; foul; vile (adj) - га́дкий GAHTkeey.

nation - на́ция NAHtseeyah.

national; folk (adj) - наро́дный nahROHDnihy.

nationality - национа́льность nahtseeahNAHL'nahst'.

native (adj) - родно́й rahdNOY.

naturally - есте́ственно yeestYEHSTveennah.

nature - приро́да preeROHdah.

nausea - тошнота́ tashnahTAH.

navy - флот floht.

near; nearby - бли́зко BLEESkah.

nearby; not far off (adj) - недалёкий needahLYOHkeey.

nearest; next (adj) - ближа́йший bleeZHAYsheey.

neat, punctual (adj) – аккура́тный ahkooRAHTnihy.

necessary; essential (adj) - необходи́мый neeahpkhahDEEmihy.

neck - шея SHEHyah.

necklace - ожерелье ahzheeRYEHL'yeh.

need - нужда noozhDAH.

needle - иголка eeGOHLkah.

negative (adj) - отрицательный ahtreeTSAHteel'nihy.

negotiations - переговоры peereegahVOHrihy.

neighbor - сосед sahSYEHT.

nephew - племянник pleem-YAHNneek.

nerve - нерв nyehrf.

nervous; irritable (adj) - нервный NYEHRVnihy.

neutral (adj) - нейтральный neytRAHL'nihy.

never - никогда neekahg-DAH.

new (adj) - новый NOHvihy.

New Year - Новый год NOHvihy goht.

news - известие eez-VYEHSTeeyeh.

newspaper - газета gah-ZYEHtah.

next (adj) - следующий SLYEHdooyooshcheey.

nice; sweet; dear; darling (adj) - милый MEElihy.

niece - племянница pleem-YAHNeetsah.

night - ночь nohch.

no - нет nyeht.

no one - никто neekTOH.

no way - никак neeKAHK.

noise - шум shoom.

noisy (adj) - шумный SHOOMnihy.

nonalcoholic - безалкогольный beezahlkah-GOHL'nihy.

nonsense - чепуха/вздор chehpooKHAH/vzdohr.

nonstop (of a flight) (adj) - беспосадочный beespah-SAHdahchnihy.

noon - полдень POHLdeen'.

normal (adj) - нормальный nahrMAHL'nihy.

north - север SYEHveer.

northern (adj) - северный SYEHveernihy.

nose - нос nohs.

not - не nee.

not long ago; recently - недавно neeDAHVnah.

notebook - тетрадь teetRAHT'.

nothing - ничего neechee-VOH.

noticably; visibly - заметно zahMYEHTnah.

notify (to) - сообщать sah-ahpSHCHAHT'.

novel - роман rahMAHN.

now - сейчас/теперь seeCHAHS/teePYEHR'.

number - число cheesLOH.

numeral - цифра tseefRAH.

nurse - медсестра meedseesTRAH.

nut - орех ahrYEHKH.

O

oatmeal - овсянка ahf-SYAHNkah.

oats - овёс ahVYOHS.

objection - возражение vahzrahZHEHneeyeh.

obligatory; mandatory (adj) - обязательный ahbee-ZAHteel'nihy.

obstetrician - акушёр

ahkooSHOHR.
obvious (adj) - очевидный
ahchehVEEDnihy.
occupation; work; studies -
занятие zahnYAHteeyeh.
ocean - океан ahkeeAHN.
of course - конечно kahn-
YEHSHnah.
offence; insult - обида
ahBEEdah.
offer; proposal; suggestion -
предложение preedlah-
ZHEHNneeyeh.
office - контора kahnTOH-
rah.
office; bureau - бюро
byooROH.
often - часто CHAHStah.
ok - ладно LAHDnah.
old (adj) - старый STAH-
rihy.
older; elder (adj) - старший
STAHRsheey.
olives - маслина mahsLEE-
nah.
on; in - на nah.
on the contrary; the other
way around - наоборот
nahahbahROHT.
on the left - налево nah-
LYEHvah.
on the right - направо
nahPRAHvah.
on time - вовремя VOH-
vreemyah.
once; one day - однажды
ahdNAHZHdih.
one and a half - полтора
pahltahRAH.
one-way (ticket) - в один
конец vahdEEN kahn-
YEHTS.
onion - лук look.

only - только TOHL'kah.
open (adj) - открытый aht-
KRIHtihy.
opera - опера OHpeerah.
opera glasses - бинокль
beeNOHKL'.
operator - телефонистка
TYEHleefahneestkah.
opinion - мнение MNYEH-
neeyeh.
opportunity - возможность
vahzMOHZHnahst'.
opposite; facing - напротив
nahPROHteef.
optician - оптик OPteek.
or - или/либо EElee/
LEEbah.
oral; verbal (adj) - устный
OOSTnihy.
orange (adj) - оранжевый
ahRAHNzhehvihy.
orange (fruit) - апельсин
ahpeel'SEEN.
orchestra - оркестр ahr-
KYEHSTR.
order; sequence - порядок
pahRYAHdahk.
order (to) - заказать zahkahzAHT'.
origin - происхождение
praheeskhahzhDYEH-
neeyeh.
original (adj) - первона-
чальный peervahnah-
CHAHL'nihy.
orthodox (adj) - православ-
ный prahvahSLAHVnihy.
other; another; the other -
другой drooGOY.
out-raged (adj) - возмущ-
ённый vahzmooshch-
OHNnihy.
outpatient clinic - амбула-

тория ahmboolahTOH-
reeyah.
outside; out of - вне vnyeh.
outward; external (adj) -
внешний VNYEHSHneey.
over and above; in access of
- сверх svyehrkh.
overcast (adj) - пасмурный
PAHsmoornihy.
oxygen - кислород
keeslahROHT.

P
pacifier - соска SOHSkah.
pack; bundle - пачка
PAHCHkah.
package - посылка
pahSIHLkah.
packet; package -
пакет pahKYEHT.
page - страница
strahNEEtsah.
pain - боль bohl'.
painkiller - болеутоляющее
средство bahleeootahl-
YAHyooshchehyeh
SRYEHTstvah.
painting - живопись ZHEE-
vahpees'.
pair - пара PAHrah.
palace - дворец dvahr-
YEHTS.
pale (adj) - бледный
BLYEHDnihy.
palm (anatomy) - ладонь
lahDOHN'.
pancake - блин bleen.
pants - брюки BRYOOkee.
paper - бумага booMAHgah.
parents - родители rah-
DEEteelee.
park - парк pahrk.
parking lot - стоянка для

машин stahYAHNkah
dlyah mahshEEN.
parsley - петрушка pee-
TROOSHkah.
part - часть chahst'.
participation - участие
ooCHAHSTeeyeh.
passage; excerpt; snatch -
отрывок ahtRIHvahk.
passenger - пассажир
pahssahZHEER.
passionate (adj) - страст-
ный STRAHSTnihy.
passport - паспорт PAHS-
pahrt.
past (adj) - прошлый
PROHSHlihy.
pastry - пирожное pee-
ROHZHnahyeh.
patient (adj) - терпеливый
teerpeeLEEvihy.
patient - пациент pahtsee-
EHNT.
patronymic - отчество
OHTchehstvah.
pay (to) - платить plah-
TEET'.
pay phone - телефон-
автомат teeleeFOHN-
ahftahMAHT.
peace - мир meer.
peach - персик PYEHRseek.
pear - груша GROOshah.
pearl - жемчуг ZHEHM-
chook.
peas - горох gahROHKH.
peasant's hut; cabin - изба
eesBAH.
pediatrician - педиатр
peedeeAHTR.
pen - ручка ROOCHkah.
pencil - карандаш kah-
rahnDAHSH.

penicillin - **пенициллин** peeneetseelLEEN.

people (a) - **народ** nahROHT.

people - **люди** LYOOdee.

pepper - **перец** PYEHreets.

pepper vodka - **перцовка** peerTSOHFkah.

performance; play - **спектакль** speekTAHKL'.

performer - **артист** ahrTEEST.

perfume - **духи** dooKHEE.

perhaps - **может быть** MOHZHeht biht'.

period of twenty-four hours; day - **сутки** SOOTkee.

permanent wave - **перманент** peermahnYEHNT.

permission; permit - **разрешение** rahzreeSHEHneeyeh.

person - **человек** chehlahVYEHK.

personal; private (adj) - **личный** LEECHnihy.

photograph - **фотография** fahtahGRAHfeeyah.

phrasebook - **разговорник** rahzgahVOHRneek.

phrase; sentence - **фраза** FRAHzah.

picture; drawing - **картина** kahrTEEnah.

pie - **пирог** peeROHK.

piece - **кусок** kooSOHK.

pig - **свинья** sveen'YAH.

pigeon; dove - **голубь** GOHloop'.

pike - **щука** SHCHOOkah.

pilaf - **пилав** peeLAHF.

pill - **пилюля** peeLYOOlyah.

pill; tablet - **таблетка** tahbLYEHTkah.

pillow - **подушка** pahDOOSHkah.

pillowcase - **наволочка** NAHvahlahchkah.

pin - **булавка** booLAHFkah.

pineapple - **ананас** ahnahNAHS.

pipe - **трубка** TROOPkah.

pity - **жаль** zhahl'.

place; seat; site - **место** MYEHStah.

plant - **растение** rahsTYEHneeyeh.

plate - **тарелка** tahRYEHLkah.

play (to) - **играть** eegRAHT'.

play; drama - **пьеса** P'YEHsah.

playwright - **драматург** drahmahTOORK.

pleasant (adj) - **приятный** preeYAHTnihy.

please - **пожалуйста** pahZHAHLstah.

pleasure - **удовольствие** oodahVOHL'stveeyeh.

plum - **слива** SLEEvah.

plumber - **водопроводчик** vahdahprahVOHTcheek.

pneumonia - **воспаление легких** vahspahLYEHneeyeh LYOHKHkeekh.

pocket - **карман** kahrMAHN.

poet - **поэт** pahEHT.

poetry - **поэзия** pahEHzeeyah.

point; station; center - **пункт** poonkt.

poison - **отра́ва/яд**
ahtRAHvah/yaht.

police - **мили́ция** meeLEE-
tseeyah.

policeman - **милиционе́р**
meeleetseeahNYEHR.

polish; lacquer - **лак** lahk.

polite; courteous (adj) -
ве́жливый VYEHZH-
leevihy.

politics - **поли́тика** pah-
LEEteekah.

pond - **пруд** proot.

pool - **бассе́йн** bahsSEYN.

poor (adj) - **бе́дный** BYEHD-
nihy.

poor-quality (adj) - **недо-
брока́чественный** nee-
dahbrahKAHCHehstveen-
nihy.

poppy - **мак** mahk.

population - **населе́ние**
nahseeLYEHneeyeh.

pork - **свини́на** sveeNEE-
nah.

port - **порт** pohrt.

portable (adj) - **перено́сный**
peereeNOHSnihy.

porter - **носи́льщик** nah-
SEEL'shcheek.

portrait - **портре́т**
pahrtRYEHT.

positive; affirmative (adj) -
положи́тельный pahlah-
ZHEEteel'nihy.

postcard - **откры́тка** aht-
KRIHTkah.

poster - **плака́т** plahKAHT.

poster; play bill - **афи́ша**
ahFEEshah.

post office (main branch) -
по́чтамт POHCHTahmt.

post office - **по́чта** POHCH-

tah.

pot; saucepan - **кастрю́ля**
kahstRYOOLyah.

pot cheese - **творо́г** tvah-
ROHK.

potato - **карто́фель** kahr-
TOHfeel'.

pound - **фунт** foont.

powder - **по́рох** POHrahkh.

powerful (adj) - **мо́щный/
могу́чий** MOHSHCHnihy/
mahGOOcheey.

prayer book - **моли́тва**
mahLEETvah.

pregnant (adj) - **бере́менная**
beeRYEHmeennahyah.

prepare (to) - **гото́вить**
gahTOHveet'.

prescription - **реце́пт**
reetsEHPT.

present - **пода́рок** pahDAH-
rahk.

present; real; true (adj) -
настоя́щий nahstahYAH-
shcheey.

pressure - **давле́ние** dahv-
LYEHneeyeh.

pressure (physical) - **напо́р**
nahPOHR.

pretty (adj) - **краси́вый**
krahsEEVihy.

price - **цена́** tseeNAH.

priest; clergyman - **свящ-
е́нник** sveeshchEHNneek.

prison - **тюрьма́** tyoor'-
MAH.

probably - **наве́рно/веро-
я́тно** nahVYEHRnah/
veerahYAHTnah.

problem - **пробле́ма** prah-
BLYEHmah.

processing - **оформле́ние**
ahfahrmLYEHneeyeh.

profession - **профе́ссия**
prahFYEHSseeyah.

professor - **профе́ссор**
prahFYEHSsahr.

profitable; favorable (adj) -
вы́годный VIHgahdnihy.

prognosis; forecast - **прог-
но́з** prahgNOHS.

promise - **обеща́ние**
ahbeeSHCHAHneeyeh.

pronunciation - **произ-
наше́ние** praheeznah-
SHEHneeyeh.

proper (adj) - **прили́чный**
preeLEESHnihy.

property - **иму́щество**
eemOOSHCHehstvah.

proud (adj) - **го́рдый** GOHR-
dihy.

proverb - **посло́вица**
pahsLOHveetsah.

public bath - **ба́ня** BAHN-
yah.

puddle - **лу́жа** LOOZHah.

pulse - **пульс** pool's.

punishment - **наказа́ние**
nahkahZAHneeyeh.

purchase - **поку́пка** pah-
KOOPkah.

push button; snap - **кно́пка**
KNOHPkah.

pyjamas - **пижа́ма** peezh-
AHMah.

Q

quality - **ка́чество** KAH-
chehstvah.

quantity - **коли́чество**
kahlEECHehstvah.

quarter - **че́тверть** CHEHT-
veert'.

question - **вопро́с** vahp-
ROHS.

quickly! - **скоре́е!** skah-
RYEHeh.

quickly; rapidly (adj) -
ско́рый SKOHRihy.

quiet (adj) - **ти́хий**
TEEKHeey.

quote - **цита́та** tseeTAHtah.

R

rabbi - **равви́н** rahvVEEN.

rabbit - **кро́лик** KROHleek.

radio - **ра́дио** RAHdeeoh.

radio station - **радиоста́н-
ция** rahdeeahSTAHNtsee-
yah.

radish - **реди́ска** reeDEES-
kah.

rail; track - **рельс** ryehl's.

railroad car - **ваго́н** vah-
GOHN.

rain - **до́ждь** dohsht'.

raincoat - **плащ** plahshch.

raisins - **изю́м** eezYOOM.

rare; infrequent (adj) -
ре́дкий RYEHTkeey.

rarely - **ре́дька** RYEHT'kah.

raspberries - **мали́на**
mahLEEnah.

rate of exchange - **валю́т-
ный курс** vahLYOOtnihy
koors.

rather; fairly - **дово́льно**
dahVOHL'nah.

raw (adj) - **сыро́й** sihROY.

razor - **бри́тва** BREETvah.

razor blades - **ле́звия**
LYEHZveeyah.

read (to) - **чита́ть** chee-
TAHT'.

reader - **чита́тель** chee-
TAHteel'.

ready (adj) - **гото́вый**
gahTOHvihy.

real; actual; effective - (adj) действительный deyst-VEEteel'nihy.

really; truly - действительно deystVEEteel'nah.

really?; is that so? - разве? RAHZveh.

rear; back; hind (adj) - задний ZAHDneey.

reason - причина preeCHEEnah.

reception - приём preeYOHM.

recommend (to) - посоветовать pahsahVYEHtahvaht'.

record - грампластинка grahmplahsTEENkah.

recording (record/tape) - запись ZAHpees'.

red (adj) - красный KRAHSnihy.

reference; information - справка SPRAHFkah.

refrigerator - холодильник khahlahDEEL'neek.

refusal - отказ ahtKAHS.

region; area; field; domain - область OHblahst'.

registration - регистрация reegeesTRAHtseeyah.

relationship; connection - отношение ahtnahSHEHneeyeh.

relatives - родственник ROHTSTveenneekee.

reluctantly - неохотно neeahKHOHTnah.

remainder - остаток ahsTAHtahk.

rent (to) - взять напрокат vzyaht' nahprahKAHT.

repair - ремонт reeMOHNT.

repeat (to) - повторить pahftahREET'.

republic - республика reesPOObleekah.

request - просьба PROZ'bah.

research - исследование eesSLYEHdahvahneeyeh.

reserved (on a train) (adj) - плацкартный plahtsKAHRTnihy.

resident - житель ZHEEteel'.

resort - курорт koorOHRT.

respected (adj) - уважаемый oovahZHAHeemihy.

rest - отдых OHDdihkh.

restaurant - ресторан reestahRAHN.

return (to) - возвращать vahzvrahSHCHAHT'.

return; reverse; opposite (adj) - обратный ahbRAHTnihy.

reward - награда nahGRAHdah.

rheumatism - ревматизм reevmahTEEZM.

rib - ребро reebROH.

rice - рис rees.

rich (adj) - богатый bahGAHtihy.

ride; drive - езда yeezDAH.

right; correct (adj) - правильный PRAHveel'nihy.

right (direction) - правый PRAHvihy.

ripe; mature (adj) - зрелый ZRYEHlihy.

river - река reeKAH.

road - дорога dahROHgah.

roast beef - ростбиф ROHSTbeef.

robe - **халát** khahLAHT.
rock - **кáмень** KAHmeen'.
role; part - **роль** rohl'.
roll; bun - **бýлка** BOOLkah.
roof - **крýша** KRIHshah.
room - **кóмната** KOHM-
nahtah.
rope; string; cord - **верёвка**
veeRYOHFkah.
rose - **рóза** ROHzah.
roundtrip (ticket) - **тудá и
обрáтно** tooDAH ee ahb-
RAHTnah.
row - **ряд** ryaht.
rubber (adj) - **резúновый**
reeZEEnahvihy.
rubbers; galoshes - **галóши**
gahLOHshee.
ruble - **рубль** roobl'.
ruby - **рубúн** rooBEEN.
rude; course (adj) - **грýбый**
GROObihy.
rug - **ковёр** kahVYOHR.
rule - **прáвило** PRAHveelah.
run (to) - **бéгать** BYEHgaht'.
run; race - **бег** byehk.
Russian (adj) - **россúйский**
rahsSEEYskeey.
Russian/(f) - **рýсский /
(рýсская)** ROOSskeey/
(ROOSskahyah).
rye - **рожь** rohsh.
ryhme - **рúфма** REEFmah.

S

saccharin - **сахарúн**
sahkhahREEN.
sad; melancholy (adj) -
грýстный/печáльный
GROOSTnihy/peeCHAHL'-
nihy.
safe - **несгорáемый шкаф**
neezgahRAHeemihy

shkahf.
safe (adj) - **безопáсный**
beezahPAHSnihy.
safely; without mishap -
благополýчно blah-
gahpahLOOCHnah.
safety pin - **англúйская
булáвка** ahngLEEYskah-
yah booLAHFkah.
sail boat - **пáрусная лóдка**
PAHroosnahyah LOHTkah.
salad - **салáт** sahLAHT.
sale - **продáжа/скúдка**
prahDAHzhah/SKEETkah.
salesman - **продавéц** prahdahVYEHTS.
salmon - **лососúна** lahsah-
SEEnah.
salt - **соль** sohl'.
salty (adj) - **солёный** sahl-
YOHnihy.
samovar - **самовáр** sahmah-
VAHR.
sample; model; pattern -
образéц ahbrahzYEHTS.
sand - **песóк** peeSOHK.
sandals - **сандáлии** sahn-
DAHleeee.
sandwich - **бутербрóд**
booteerBROHT.
sanitary day (one day a
month when stores/
museums are closed for
cleaning) - **санитáрный
день** sahneeTAHRnihy
dyehn'.
saphire - **сапфúр** sahp-
FEER.
sarcasm - **саркáзм** sahr-
KAHZM.
satire - **сатúра** sahTEErah.
satisfaction - **удовлетво-
рéние** oodahvleetvah-

214

RYEHneeyeh.

sauce; gravy - соус sahOOS.

sausage - колбаса kahlbah-SAH.

save, keep (to); to guard - беречь beeRYEHCH.

scarf - шарф shahrf.

schedule; timetable - расписание rahspeeSAHneeyeh.

scholar; scientist - учёный ooCHOHnihy.

school - школа SHKOHlah.

school vacation - каникулы kahNEEkoolih.

scissors - ножницы NOHZHneetsih.

screen - экран ehkRAHN.

sculpture - скульптура skool'pTOOrah.

sea - море MOHRyeh.

sea food - дары моря DAHrih MOHRyah.

seat - место MYEHStah.

second (time measure) - секунда seekOONdah.

secondhand book dealer - букинист bookeenEEST.

secretary - секретарь seekreeTAHR'.

section - секция SYEHKtseeyah.

sedative - успокоительное средство oospahKOHeeteel'nahyeh SRYEHTstvah.

see (to) - видеть VEEdeet'.

self confident (adj) - самоуверенный sahmahoo-VYEHreennihy.

self-service - самообслуживание sahmahahpSLOOzheevahneeyeh.

sell (to) - продать prah-DAHT'.

send (to) - послать pahs-LAHT'.

sensibly; rationally (adj) - разумно rahzOOMnah.

sensitive (adj) чувствительный choofstVEEteel'nihy.

separately; individually - отдельно ahdDYEHL'nah.

serious (adj) - серьёзный seer'YOHZnihy.

service station - автозаправочная станция ahftahzahPRAHvahchnahyah STAHNtseeyah.

set (of dishes or silverware) - сервиз seerVEES.

set - комплект kahm-PLYEHKT.

shadow - тень tyehn'.

shame - стыд stiht.

shampoo - шампунь shahm-POON'.

share, divide (to) - делить deelEET'.

share; lot - доля DOHLyah.

sharp; pungent; keen (adj) - острый OHStrihy.

shave (to); get a shave - бриться BREETsah.

she - она ahNAH.

sheet - простыня prahstihnYAH.

ship - корабль kahRAHBL'.

ship; steamship - пароход pahrahKHOHT.

shirt - рубашка rooBAHSHkah.

shish kebob - шашлык shahshLIHK.

shoe laces - шнуры SHNOOrih.

215

shoemaker - ремо́нт о́буви reeMOHNT OHboovee.

shoes - о́бувь/ту́фли OHboovee/TOOFlee.

short (adj) - коро́ткий kahROHTkeey.

shortage; scarcity; defect; deficiency - недоста́ток needahsTAHtahk.

shorts - шо́рты SHOHRtihy.

should; must; ought to - до́лжен DOHLzhehn.

shoulder - плечо́ plehCHOH.

shout; cry - крик kreek.

show (to) - показа́ть pahkahZAHT'.

shower - душ doosh.

• sick (adj) - больно́й bahl'NOY.

side - сторона́/бок stahrahNAH/bohk.

side street - переу́лок peereeOOLahk.

side walk - тротуа́р trahtooAHR.

sideways - бо́ком BOHkahm.

sight; vision - ви́дение VEEdeeneeyeh.

sign (to) - подписа́ть pahtpeeSAHT'.

sign; signal - знак znahk.

sign up (to) - записа́ться zahpeeSAHTsah.

signature - по́дпись POHTpees'.

silence - молча́ние mahlCHAHneeyeh.

silver (adj) - сере́бряный seeRYEHBreenihy.

silver - серебро́ seereeBROH.

similar; like (adj) - похо́жий pahKHOHzheey.

simple; easy (adj) - просто́й prahsTOY.

simply - про́сто PROHstah.

simultaneous (adj) - одновре́менный ahdnahVRYEHmeennihy.

sin - грех gryehkh.

since - с seh.

sincere (adj) - и́скренний EESkreenneey.

singer - певе́ц peevYEHTS.

sink (bathroom) - ра́ковина RAHkahveenah.

sister - сестра́ seesTRAH.

sister-in-law - неве́стка neeVYEHSTkah.

situation; condition - положе́ние pahlahZHEHneeyeh.

situation; setting - обстано́вка ahpstahNOHFkah.

size - разме́р rahzMYEHR.

skates - коньки́ kahn'KEE.

skating rink - като́к kahTOHK.

skis - лы́жи LIHzhee.

skin; hide - шку́ра SHKOOrah.

skin; leather - ко́жа KOHzhah.

skirt - ю́бка YOOPkah.

skullcap - ермо́лка yeerMOHLkah.

sky; heaven - не́бо NYEHbah.

skyscraper - небоскрёб neebahsKRYOHP.

sleep; dream - сон sohn.

sleep (to) - спать spaht'.

sleeve - рука́в rooKAHF.

sleigh; sled - са́нки SAHN-

kee.
slip - комбина́ция kahm-
beenAHTseeyah.
slippers - та́почки TAHP-
ahchkee.
slippery (adj) - ско́льзкий
SKOHL'skeey.
slow (adj) - ме́дленный
MYEHDleennihy.
small (adj) - ма́ленький
MAHLeen'keey.
small change - ме́лочь
MYEHlahch.
smart; intelligent (adj) -
у́мный OOMnihy.
smell (to) - па́хнуть
PAHKHnoot'.
smell - за́пах ZAHpahkh.
smile - улы́бка ooLIHPkah.
smoke (to) - кури́ть koo-
REET'.
smoke - дым dihm.
smokey (adj) - ды́мный
DIHMnihy.
smooth (adj) - гла́дкий
GLAHTkeey.
snack bar - буфе́т boof-
YEHT.
snack; appetizer - заку́ска
zahKOOSkah.
snackbar - заку́сочная
zahKOOsahchnahyah.
sneakers - ке́ды KYEHdih.
sneezing - чиха́нье chee-
KHAHN'yeh.
snow - снег snyehk.
so; true - так tahk.
soap - мы́ло MIHlah.
soccer - футбо́л footBOHL.
society; company - о́бщест-
во OHPshchehstvah.
socks - носки́ nahsKEE.
sofa - дива́н deeVAHN.

soft (adj) - мя́гкий
MYAHKHkeey.
sold out - распро́дано rahs-
PROHdahnah.
soldier - солда́т sahlDAHT.
sole (of a shoe) - подме́тка
pahdMYOHTkah.
somehow - ка́к-то KAHK-
tah.
someone - кто́-нибудь
KTOHneeboot'.
something - что́-нибудь
SHTOHneeboot'.
sometimes - иногда́ eenahg-
DAH.
somewhere - где́-нибудь
GDYEHneeboot'.
son - сын sihn.
son-in-law - зять zyaht'.
song - пе́сня PYEHSnyah.
sorry - прости́те/извини́те
prahsTEEtyeh/eezveeNEE-
tyeh.
sort; kind; type - род roht.
soul - душа́ dooSHAH.
sound; noise - звук zvook.
soup - суп soop.
soup noodle - лапша́ lahp-
SHAH.
sour (adj) - ки́слый KEES-
lihy.
sour cream - смета́на
smeeTAHnah.
south - юг yook.
southern (adj) - ю́жный
YOOZHnihy.
souvenir - сувени́р soovee-
NEER.
spare; extra - ли́шний
LEESHneey.
speak (to); talk (about) -
говори́ть gahvahrEET'.
specialty - специа́льность

speetseeAHL'nahst'.
spectator - зри́тель
ZREEteel'.
speech - ре́чь ryehch.
speed - ско́рость SKOH-
rahst'.
spider - пау́к pahOOK.
spoiled; rotten; tainted (adj)
- испо́рченный eesPOHR-
chehnnihy.
spoon - ло́жка LOHSHkah.
sports fan - боле́льщик
bahlYEHL'shcheek.
sports match - ма́тч
mahtch.
sports team - кома́нда
kahMAHNdah.
spot; stain - пятно́ peet-
NOH.
spring - весна́ veesNAH.
spring (adj) - весе́нний
veesYEHNneey.
spruce; Christmas tree -
ёлка YOHLkah.
square (adj) - квадра́тный
kvahDRAHTnihy.
stadium - стадио́н stahdee-
OHN.
stage - сце́на STSEHnah.
stairs - ле́стница LYEHST-
neetsah.
stamp - ма́рка MAHRkah.
star - звезда́ zvyehzDAH.
starch - крахма́л krahkh-
MAHL.
State - госуда́рство gahsoo-
DAHRstvah.
state - штат shtaht.
state; government (adj) -
госуда́рственный gahsoo-
DAHRSTveennihy.
station - ста́нция STAHN-
tseeyah.

station (train) - вокза́л
vahkZAHL.
stay - пребыва́ние pree-
bihVAHneeyeh.
steak - бифште́кс beef-
SHTYEHKS.
steal (to) - накра́сть
nahkRAHST'.
steam room - пари́лья
pahREEL'yah.
steamed (adj) - па́реный
PAHreenihy.
step - шаг shahk.
step-mother - ма́чеха
MAHchehkhah.
stepfather - о́тчим OHT-
cheem.
stew - рагу́ rahGOO.
stewardess - стюарде́сса
styooahrDYEHSsah.
sticky (adj) - ли́пкий
LEEPkeey.
still; all the same - всё-
таки VSYOHtahkee.
still; yet; else; more;
another - ещё yee-
SHCHOH.
stockings - чулки́ chool-
KEE.
stomach - живо́т zhee-
VOHT.
stop - сто́п stohp.
store - магази́н mahgah-
ZEEN.
storm - бу́ря BOORyah.
stormy; violent (adj) -
бу́рный BOORnihy.
story; floor - эта́ж
ehTAHSH.
story; tale; account -
расска́з rahsSKAHS.
stove - пе́чь pyehch.
straight (adj) - прямо́й

218

preeMOY.
strain; sprain - растяжéние
rahsteeZHEHneeyeh.
strainer - сúтечко SEE-
teechkah.
strait; channel - пролúв
prahLEEF.
strange; weird; odd (adj) -
стрáнный STRAHNnihy.
stranger - незнакóмец
neeznahKOHMeets.
strawberries - земляникка
zeemleeNEEkah.
street - úлица OOLeetsah.
street car - трамвáй trahm-
VAY.
strength - сúла SEElah.
stress (grammatical) -
ударéние oodahRYEH-
neeyeh.
stretcher - носúлки nah-
SEELkee.
strict; harsh; severe (adj) -
стрóгий STROHgeey.
stroke - инсýльт
eenSOOL'T.
stroll, walk (to) - гулять
goolYAHT'.
strong (adj) - сúльный
SEEL'nihy.
strong; durable - крéпкий
KRYEHPkeey.
stubborn (adj) - упóрный
ooPOHRnihy.
student/(f) - студéнт/(-ка)
stooDYEHNT/(-kah).
study (to) - учúться
ooCHEETsah.
stuffed (food) (adj) -
фаршúрóванный fahr-
sheeROHvahnnihy.
stuffed animal - чýчело
CHOOchehlah.

stuffed cabbage - голубцы́
gahloopTSIH.
stuffy - дýшно DOOSHnah.
stupid; silly (adj) - глýпый
GLOOpihy.
subject - предмéт preed-
MYEHT.
substitution - замéна
zahMYEHnah.
suburb - прúгород PREE-
gahraht.
subway - метрó meeTROH.
success - удáча/успéх
ooDAHchah/oosPYEHKH.
suddenly - вдрýг vdrook.
suede - зáмша ZAHMshah.
sugar - сáхар SAHkhahr.
suicide - самоубúйство
sahmahooBEEYSTvah.
suit - костюм kahsTYOOM.
suit jacket (man's) -
пиджáк peedZHAHK.
suitcase - чемодáн cheh-
mahDAHN.
summer - лéто LYEHtah.
summer (adj) - лéтний
LYEHTneey.
sun - сóлнце SOHNtseh.
sunburn; sun tan - загáр
zahGAHR.
sunglasses - тёмные очки
TYOMnihyeh ahchKEE.
sunny (adj) - сóлнечный
SOHLneechnihy.
sunrise - восхóд vahs-
KHOHT.
supper - ýжин OOZHeen.
supper (to eat) - ужинáть
oozheenAHT'.
surgeon - хирýрг kheer-
OORK.
surprising (adj) - удивú-
тельный oodeeVEEteel'-

nihy.

swallow (to) - глота́ть glah-TAHT'.

sweat - пот poht.

sweater - пуло́вер poolOH-veer.

sweet (adj) - сла́дкий SLAHTkeey.

swim (to) - пла́вать PLAH-vaht'.

swollen; puffed up (adj) - разду́тый rahzDOOtihy.

sympathy - сочу́вствие sahCHOOSTveeyeh.

synagogue - синаго́га see-nahGOHgah.

system - систе́ма sees-TYEHmah.

T

t-shirt - ма́йка MAYkah.

table - стол stohl.

take, seize (to) - брать/взять braht'/vzyaht'.

takeoff (airplane) - взлёт vzlyoht.

talcum powder - тальк tahl'k.

tale - ска́зка SKAHSkah.

talk, chat (to) - бесе́довать beeSYEHdahvaht'.

talkative (adj) - болтли́вый bahltLEEvihy.

tampon - тампо́н tahm-POHN.

tangerine - мандари́н mahndahREEN.

tape recorder - магнитофо́н mahgneetahFOHN.

tasteless (adj) - безвку́сный beezVKOOSnihy.

tasty - вку́сный VKOOSnihy.

tax - нало́г nahLOHK.

taxi - такси́ tahkSEE.

taxi stop - стоя́нка stah-YAHNkah.

tea - чай chay.

tea caddy - ча́йница CHAYneetsah.

tea kettle - ча́йник CHAY-neek.

teacher (f) - преподава́-тель/(-ница)//учи́тель/(-ница) preepahdahVAH-teel'/(-neetsah) oochee-TYEHL'/(-neetsah).

tears - слёзы SLYOHzih.

teddy bear - ми́шка MEESHkah.

telegram - телегра́мма teeleeGRAHMmah.

telegraph office - телегра́ф teeleeGRAHF.

telephone - телефо́н teelee-FOHN.

telephone booth - телефо́н-автома́т teeleeFOHN-ahftahMAHT.

television - телеви́зор teeleeVEEzahr.

temperature - гра́дус GRAHdoos.

temporarily - вре́менно VRYEHmeennah.

tender; gentle; delicate (adj) - не́жный NYEHZH-nihy.

tennis - те́ннис TYEHN-nees.

tension; stress; strain - напряже́ние nahpree-ZHEHeeyeh.

tent - пала́тка pahLAHT-kah.

textbook - уче́бник

ooCHEHBneek.

than - **чем** chehm.

thank (to) - **благодарить** blahgahdahREET'.

thank you - **спасибо** spahSEEbah.

thankful; grateful (adj) - **благодарный** blahgahDAHRnihy.

thanks a lot - **большое спасибо** bahl'SHOHyeh spahSEEbah

that (one) - **этот** EHtaht.

that way - **туда** tooDAH.

theater - **театр** teeAHTR.

theater box - **ложа** LOHZHah.

then - **тогда** tahgDAH.

then; next; afterwards - **потом** pahTOHM.

there - **там** tahm.

therefore - **поэтому** pahEHtahmoo.

thermometer - **градусник** GRAHdoosneek.

thermos - **термос** TYEHRmahs.

they - **они** ahNEE.

thick, dense (adj) - **густой** goosTOY.

thief - **вор** vohr.

thin (adj) - **тонкий/худой** TOHNkeey/khooDOY.

thirst - **жажда** ZHAHZHdah.

thought; idea - **мысль** mihsl'.

thousand - **тысяча** TIHseechah.

thread - **нитка** NEETkah.

threat - **угроза** ooGROHzah.

threatening (adj) - **грозный** GROHZnihy.

throat - **горло** GOHRlah.

through - **сквозь** skvohs'.

through; within - **через** CHEHrees.

thumb - **большой палец** bahl'SHOY PAHleets.

thunder - **гром** grohm.

thunderstorm - **гроза** grahZAH.

ticket - **билет** beeLYEHT.

ticket office - (**билетная**) **касса** beeLYEHTnahyah KAHSsah.

tie - **галстук** GAHLstook.

tie; connection - **связь** svyahs'.

tightly packed (adj) - **набитый** nahBEEtihy.

time (it's) - **пора** pahRAH.

time (period of); date; deadline - **срок** srohk.

• time - **время** VRYEHmyah.

time; hour - **час** chahs.

timetable - **расписание** rahspeeSAHneeyeh.

time; once; one - **раз** rahs.

timid; shy (adj) - **робкий** ROHPkeey.

tip - **чаевые** chahehVIHyeh.

tired (f) (adj) - **устал(а)** oosTAHL(ah).

to; toward - **к** k.

to; up to; before **до** dah.

tobacco - **табак** tahBAHK.

today - **сегодня** seeVOHdnyah.

today's (adj) - **сегодняшний** seeVOHdnyahshneey.

together - **вместе** VMYEHstyeh.

toilet - **туалет** tooahLYEHT.

toilet paper - **туалетная бумага** tooahLYEHT-

221

nahyah booMAHgah.
tomato - помидóр
pahmeeDOHR.
tombstone - надгрóбный
кáмень nahdGROHBnihy
KAHmeen'.
¶ tomorrow - зáвтра
ZAHFtrah.
tomorrow's (adj) - зáв-
трашний ZAHFtrahsh-
neey.
tongue; language- язы́к
yeezIHK.
tonsil - миндáлина
meenDAHleenah.
tonsils - глáнды GLAHN-
dih.
too (much) - слúшком
SLEESHkahm.
tooth - зуб zoop.
toothache - зубнáя боль
zoobNAHyah bohl'.
toothbrush - зубнáя щётка
zoobNAHyah SHCHOHT-
kah.
toothpaste - зубнáя пáста
zoobNAHyah PAHStah.
top - верх vyehrkh.
topaz - топáз tahPAHS.
torch - фонáрь fahNAHR'.
torn; ripped (adj) - рвáный
RVAHnihy.
touch (to) - трóгать TROH-
gaht'.
tour - экскýрсия ehksKOOR-
seeyah.
tour guide - экскурсовóд
ehkskoorsahVOHT.
tourist - турúст tooREEST.
towel - полотéнце pahlah-
TYEHNtseh.
tower - бáшня BAHSHnyah.
toy - игрýшка eegROOSH-

kah.
¶ traffic light - светофóр
sveetahFOHR.
tragedy - трагéдия
trahGYEHdeeyah.
¶ train - пóезд POHeest.
train compartment - купé
koopYEH.
transfer; change (planes,
trains, buses etc) - пересáдка peereeSAHTkah.
translate (to) - перевестú
peereeveesTEE.
translation - перевóд
peereeVOHT.
¶ translator - перевóдчик
peereeVOHTcheek.
trash- мýсор MOOsahr.
traveler - путешéственник
pooteeshEHSTveenneek.
travels; trip - путешéствие
pooteeshEHSTveeyeh.
treatment - лечéние
leeCHEHneeyeh.
¶ tree - дéрево DYEHreevah.
trip; flight - рéйс reys.
trip; way; path. - путь
poot'.
trolley bus - троллéйбус
trahlLEYboos.
trout - форéль fahRYEHL'.
truck - грузовúк groozah-
VEEK.
true; faithful (adj) - вéрный
VYEHRnihy.
¶ truth - прáвда PRAHVdah.
tsar - царь tsahr'.
tuna - тунéц tooNYEHTS.
turkey - индéйка eenDEY-
kah.
turn on, switch on (to) -
включáть vklyooCHAHT'.
turn out, switch off (to) -

222

выключа́ть vihklyoo-
CHAHT'.
turnip - ре́па RYEHpah.
tweezers - пинце́т peen-
TSEHT.
typewriter - пи́шущая
маши́нка PEESHooshch-
ahyah mahSHEENkah.

U

ugly (adj) - некраси́вый
neekrahsEEVihy.
ulcer - я́зва YAHZvah.
umbrella - зо́нтик ZOHN-
teek.
unattainable (adj) - недо-
стижи́мый needahstee-
ZHEEmihy.
uncle - дя́дя DYAHdyah.
unclean; dirty (adj) - не-
чи́стый neeCHEEStihy.
unclear (adj) - нея́сный
neeYAHSnihy.
uncomfortable (adj) - неу-
до́бный neeooDOHBnihy.
unconscious (adj) - бессоз-
на́тельный beessahzNAH-
teel'nihy.
under; beneath - под poht.
underpants - трусы́ troo-
SIH.
undershirt - ма́йка MAY-
kah.
understand (to) - понима́ть
pahneeMAHT'.
understandable (adj) - пон-
я́тный pahnYAHTnihy.
undertaking; venture - пре-
дприя́тие preetpreeYAH-
teeyeh.
underwear - ни́жнее бельё
NEEZHneeyeh beel'YOH.
unfair; injust (adj) - нес-

праведли́вый neesprah-
veedLEEvihy.
unfamiliar (adj) - незна-
ко́мый neeznahKOHMihy.
unfortunate; unhappy (adj)
неблагополу́чный nee-
blahgahpahLOOCHnihy.
unhappy; unfortunate (adj)
несча́стный neeSHAHST-
nihy.
unimportant (adj) - нева́ж-
ный neeVAHZHnihy.
unintentional; involuntary
(adj) - нево́льный nee-
VOHL'nihy.
union - сою́з sahYOOS.
universal; general (adj) -
всео́бщий fseeOHP-
shcheey.
university - университе́т
ooneeveerseeTYEHT.
unknown (adj) - неизве́ст-
ный neeeezVYEHSTnihy.
unnatural (adj) - неесте́ст-
венный neeyehstEHST-
veennihy.
unnoticable (adj) - неза-
ме́тно neezahMYEHTnah.
unpleasant; disagreeable
(adj) - неприя́тный
neepreeYAHTnihy.
unprofitable; unfavorable
(adj) - невы́годный
neeVIHgahdnihy.
unripe; not mature (adj) -
незре́лый neezRYEHlihy.
unsuccessful (adj) - неус-
пе́шный neeoosPYEHSH-
nihy.
until - до dah.
untruth; falsehood; lie -
непра́вда neePRAHVdah.
unusual; uncommon (adj) -

необыкновённый neeah-bihknahVYEHNnihy.
up, upwards - (destination) вверх vvyehrkh.
up; upwards (location) - наверх nahVYEHRKH.
upper; top (adj) - верхний VYEHRKHneey.
uprising; revolt - восстание vahsSTAHneeyeh.
urgent; emergency (adj) - срочный SROHCHnihy.
urine - моча mahCHAH.
use; benefit - польза POHL'zah.
useful; helpful (adj) - полезный pahLYEHZnihy.
useless (adj) - бесполезный beespahlYEHZnihy.
usually - обычно ahBIHCHnah.

V

vacation (from work) - отпуск OHTpoosk.
vagina - влагалище vlahGAHleeshcheh.
vaginal infection - воспаление влагалища vahspahLYEHneeyeh vlahGAHleeshchah.
vague; indefinite; uncertain (adj) - неопределённый neeahpreedeeLYOHNnihy.
valley - поляна dahLEEnah.
valuable (adj) - ценный TSEHNnihy.
value; worth - достоинство dahsTOHeenstvah.
vanilla - ваниль vahNEEL'.
vaseline - вазелин vahzeeLEEN.
veal - телятина teelYAH-

teenah.
vegetable salad - винегрет veeneegRYEHT.
vegetables - овощи OHvahshchee.
vegetarian - вегетарианец veegeetahreeAHNeets.
vein - жила ZHEElah.
vein - вена VYEHnah.
vending machine - автомат ahftahMAHT.
venison - оленина ahLYEHneenah.
verb - глагол glahGOHL.
very - очень OHcheen'.
vest - жилет zheeLYEHT.
victory - победа pahBYEHdah.
village - село seeLOH.
violence - насилие nahSEEleeyeh.
virus - вирус VEEroos.
visa - виза VEEzah.
visible; clear; obvious - видно VEEDnah.
vitamins - витамины veetahMEEnih.
vodka - водка VOHTkah.
voice - голос GOHlahs.
voltage - вольтаж vahl'TAHSH.
vote (to) - голосовать gahlahsahVAHT'.

W

waist - талия TAHleeyah.
wait (to) - ждать zhdaht'.
waiter - официант ahfeetseeAHNT.
waitress - официантка ahfeetseeAHNTkah.
wall - стена steeNAH.
wallet; billfold - бумажник

booMAHZHneek.

want (to) - хоте́ть khah-
TYEHT'.

war - война́ voyNAH.

warm (adj) - тёплый
TYOHPlihy.

warning - предупрежде́ние
preedoopreezhDYEH-
neeyeh.

washing; laundry - сти́рка
STEERkah.

wasp - оса́ ahSAH.

watch - часы́ cheesih.

water - вода́ vahDAH.

waterfall - водопа́д
vahdahPAHT.

watermelon - арбу́з ahr-
BOOZ.

wave - волна́ vahlNAH.

we - мы́ mih.

weak (adj) - сла́бый SLAH-
bihy.

weather - пого́да pahGOH-
dah.

wedding - сва́дьба SVAHT'-
bah.

week - неде́ля needYEH-
lyah.

weekday - бу́дний день
BOODneey dyehn'.

weight - вес vyehs.

well; healthy (adj) - здоро́в-
ый zdahROHVihy.

well; well then - ну́ noo.

west - за́пад ZAHpaht.

western (adj) - за́падный
ZAHpahdnihy.

wet (adj) - мо́крый MOHK-
rihy.

what - что́ shtoh.

wheat - пшени́ца psheh-
NEEtsah.

wheel - колесо́ kahleeSOH.

when - когда́ kahgDAH.

where - где́ gdyeh.

where to - куда́ kooDAH.

which - како́й kahKOY.

whisper - шёпот SHOHpaht.

white (adj) - бе́лый BYEH-
lihy.

who - кто ktoh.

whole; entire (adj) - це́лый
TSEHlihy.

why - почему́ pahcheeMOO.

wide; broad (adj) - широ́кий
sheeROHkeey.

widow - вдова́ vdahVAH.

widower - вдове́ц vdahv-
YEHTS.

width - ширина́ sheeree-
NAH.

wife - жена́/супру́га
zhehNAH/soopROOgah.

wild (adj) - ди́кий
DEEkeey.

wild game - дичь deech.

wind - ве́тер VYEHteer.

window - окно́ ahkNOH.

windshield - ветрово́е
стекло́ veetrahVOHyeh
steekLOH.

windy (adj) - ве́треный
VYEHTreenihy.

wine - вино́ veeNOH.

winter - зима́ zeeMAH.

winter (adj) - зи́мний
ZEEMneey.

wish; desire - охо́та
ahKHOHtah.

with; off; since - с se.

without - без byehs.

without transfer - беспере-
са́дочный beespeeree-
SAHdahchnihy.

woman - же́нщина ZHEHN-
shcheenah.

225

wonderful; miraculous (adj) - **чудéсный** chooDYEHSnihy.

woodcock - **вáльдшнеп** VAHL'Tshneep.

wooden (adj) - **деревя́нный** deereevYAHNnihy.

woolen (adj) - **шерстянóй** shehrsteeNOY.

word - **слóво** SLOHvah.

work - **рабóта** rahBOHtah.

work (to) - **рабóтать** rah-BOHtaht'

worker - **рабóчий** rah-BOHcheey.

workers' cooperative - **артéль** ahrTYEHL'.

world - **мир** meer.

worried, agitated (to be) - **волновáться** vahlnah-VAHtsah.

worried; troubled (adj) - **беспокóйный** bees-pahKOYnihy.

worry, trouble, bother, disturb (to) - **беспокóить** beespahKOHeet'.

worse - **хýже** KHOOzheh.

worship service - **бого-служéние** bahgahsloo-ZHEHneeyeh.

wound - **рáна** RAHnah.

wounded (adj) - **рáненый** RAHNeenihy.

wrapping for mailing printed matter - **бандерóль** bahndeeROHL'.

write (to) - **писáть** pee-SAHT'.

writer - **писáтель** peeSAH-teel'.

writing (in) - **письменно** PEES'meennah.

wrong; incorrect (adj) - **непрáвильный** nee-PRAHveel'nihy.

X

x-ray - **рентгéн** reentGYEHN.

Y

year - **год** goht.

years - **лет** lyeht.

yearly; annual (adj) - **ежегóдный** yeezheh-GOHDnihy.

yellow (adj) - **жёлтый** ZHOHLtihy.

yes - **да** dah.

yesterday - **вчерá** fcheh-RAH.

yesterday's (adj) - **вчерáш-ний** fcheeRAHSHneey.

yogurt-like drink - **кефир** keeFEER.

young (adj) - **молодóй** mahlahDOY.

young lady; waitress - **дéв-ушка** DYEHvooshkah.

young people - **молодёжь** mahlahDYOHSH.

younger (adj) - **млáдший** MLAHTsheey.

youth - **юность** YOOnahst'.

Z

zero - **ноль** nohl'.

zipper - **мóлния** MOHLneeyah.

zoo - **зоопáрк** zahahPAHRK.

The Moscow Subway System

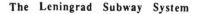

воквал = station
Ж.Д. СТАНЦИИ = train station

The Leningrad Subway System

228

More Dictionaries from Hippocrene Books:

CZECH-ENGLISH/ENGLISH-CZECH CONCISE DICTIONARY
Nina Trnka
0276　ISBN 0-87052-586-7　$6.95 paper

DANISH-ENGLISH/ENGLISH-DANISH PRACTICAL DICTIONARY
0198　ISBN 0-87052-823-8　$9.95 paper

DUTCH-ENGLISH/ENGLISH-DUTCH CONCISE DICTIONARY:
With a Brief Introduction to Dutch Grammar
0606　ISBN 0-87052-910-2　$7.95 paper

FINNISH-ENGLISH/ENGLISH-FINNISH CONCISE DICTIONARY
0142　ISBN 0-87052-813-0　$8.95 paper

HUNGARIAN-ENGLISH/ENGLISH-HUNGARIAN DICTIONARY
Magay Tamas, et al.
2039　ISBN 0-88254-986-3　$7.95 cloth

INDONESIAN-ENGLISH/ENGLISH-INDONESIAN PRACTICAL DICTIONARY
Helen and Rossall Johnson
0127　ISBN 0-87052-810-6　$8.95 paper

NORWEGIAN-ENGLISH/ENGLISH-NORWEGIAN DICTIONARY
E.D. Gabrielsen
0202　ISBN 0-88254-584-1　$7.95 paper

DATE DUE

OCT 0 4 2001

**POLISH-ENGLISH/ENGLISH-POLISH STANDARD
DICTIONARY (Revised)**
Iwo Cyprian Pogonowski
0207   ISBN 0-87052-882-3 $12.95 paper
0665   ISBN 0-87052-908-0 $22.50 cloth

**PORTUGUESE-ENGLISH/ENGLISH-PORTUGUESE
PRACTICAL DICTIONARY**
Antonio Houaiss and I. Cardim
0477   ISBN 0-87052-574-3 $9.95 paper

**RUSSIAN-ENGLISH/ENGLISH-RUSSIAN
PRACTICAL DICTIONARY:
With Complete Phonetics**
O.P. Benyuch and G.V. Chernov
0164   ISBN 0-87052-336-8 $10.95 paper

**SWEDISH-ENGLISH/ENGLISH-SWEDISH
STANDARD DICTIONARY**
Vincent and Kerstin Petti
0755   ISBN 0-87052-870-X $11.95 paper
0761   ISBN 0-87052-871-8 $19.95 cloth

**TURKISH-ENGLISH/ENGLISH-TURKISH CONCISE
DICTIONARY**
0569   ISBN 0-87052-241-8 $5.95 paper